CRICUT BIBLE

Effortlessly Dominate Design Space, Machines & Tools, Unlocking a World of Boundless Creativity. Are You Ready to Reign Supreme over Your Cricut?

———————————————

Ylenia Dowson

BUNDLE BOOKS

1

Cricut for Beginners

Pag.6

2

Cricut Design Space

Pag.56

3

Cricut Accessories

Pag.96

4

Cricut Materials

Pag.116

5

Cricut Maker 3

Pag.138

6

Cricut Explore Air 3

Pag.154

7

Cricut Joy

Pag.174

8

Cricut Press

Pag.194

9

Business Opportunities With Cricut

Pag.214

10

Cricut Projects Ideas

Pag.238

BUNDLE BOOKS

11

FAQ

Pag. 257

12

Cricut Projects
Step - by - step

Pag. 260

13

Cricut Projects for
Special Events:
S. Valentine - 4 July
- Christmas
Pag. 275

14

Take Your Gift

Pag.288

15

Conclusion

Pag.290

JOIN THE FACEBOOK COMMUNITY

Hello Creative Trailblazers!

The voyage from a Cricut novice to a seasoned maestro is an exhilarating one, filled with boundless creativity and the joy of crafting. Yet, every journey is smoother and more enjoyable with a tribe of like-minded explorers by your side. That's exactly what inspired me to craft not just a guidebook to navigate the enchanting waters of Cricut crafting, but also to cultivate a vibrant community where the voyage of discovery thrives beyond the pages.

With immense joy, I present to you an exclusive hub of passionate crafters – our newly minted Facebook Support Group! This isn't just a group; it's your go-to sanctuary for every Cricut query, your gallery to flaunt those awe-inspiring projects, and your resource library that's ever-evolving with fresh ideas and insights. The doors to this exclusive community are wide open, awaiting your unique creative flair. All it takes is a click to step into a world where every day is a new learning adventure. Scan this QR code to join our Facebook group now!

Your crafting journey, dotted with questions, ideas, and the thrill of creation, is yearning for a space to flourish. And what better place than a community that echoes your passion and curiosity? Let's nurture the seeds of creativity together in a garden of supportive, enthusiastic, and imaginative souls. Come, be a part of something magical. Your tribe awaits!

See you in the community

HOW CAN YOU HELP ME AND THIS BOOK?

Creating this book, nurturing a vibrant Facebook community, and consistently delivering fresh content have been journeys filled with challenges and creative leaps. Battling through writer's block, investing hours of dedication, and infusing passion into every word – that's what it took to bring this book to life. You see, possessing knowledge is one thing, but translating it into a compelling, insightful narrative is an entirely different adventure.

Your perspective matters immensely, and it holds the potential to guide other readers toward this captivating narrative. We often tend to write a review only if our experience was negative, whereas if we enjoyed what we purchased, we are less likely to leave feedback. That's why I'd be over the moon if you'd consider leaving a review on Amazon. Your few minutes can have a monumental impact on my journey and, importantly, assist other readers in their purchasing decision.

Please, take a moment to scan the QR code below and share your thoughts through an Amazon review. Your words serve as a beacon guiding fellow readers to this treasure trove of knowledge.

If you're up for it, creating a brief video where you discuss your book experience would be fantastic! But if that feels like a Herculean task, fret not. Even a review accompanied by a picture of the book would be an invaluable gift. There's no pressure, but your support in this endeavor would mean the world to me.

I genuinely hope that your reading experience has been as exhilarating as my writing journey.

INTRODUCTION

We are at the onset of our journey together through the marvelous world of Cricut. Starting today, a new adventure unfolds in your life, one that will allow you to mold your creativity and imagination. This book aspires to be your beacon in the boundless ocean of Cricut, guiding you step by step through the various chapters until you morph into an autonomous user capable of crafting fantastic objects, while saving ample time and money. When I embarked on my initial journey into this realm, I lacked a guide like the one I've created here, and trust me, it would have been immensely beneficial. I can still recall the early days of attempting to decipher how Design Space functioned and the purposes of all the buttons and menus that comprised it.

It appeared to be software tailored for nerds and geeks, whereas with this book in hand, you'll encounter no such hurdles. Instead, you'll learn effort-lessly and enjoyably, evolving into a pro in no time. This book delineates all the available Cricut machines in detail, discussing their pros and cons, and assisting you in selecting the right machine for your needs. We will explore the tools and accessories that will empower you to elevate your work and craft incredible objects. We'll delve into all the usable materials and also introduce the brand-new "smart materials." To facilitate your le-arning, you'll find some step-by-step explained projects to experiment with, enabling you to promptly familiarize yourself with the Cricut machi-ne and the Design Space workspace. Without further ado, let's commence this journey now, as I am as eager as you are.

TABLE OF CONTENTS

Chapter 1
What Is the Cricut Machine and What Does It Do?

9

11

Chapter 2
The Different Types of Cricut Machines and Their Differences

Chapter 3
Which Machine Is Best for You? Let's Find Out Together

19

23

Chapter 4
Cricut Design Space, the Cricut Software

Chapter 5
Cricut Accessories and Tools

25

33

Chapter 6
Materials That Can Be Used with Cricut

Chapter 7
Cricut Cheat Sheet

41

53

Chapter 8
Tips and Tricks (and Maintenance)

BOOK 1 - CRICUT FOR BEGINNERS

CHA PTER 1

WHAT IS THE CRICUT MACHINE AND WHAT DOES IT DO?

Welcome aboard!!! If you have arrived here, it is because you are probably interested in knowing in detail what the Cricut machines are all about, either because you want to start a business or because this is the equipment that has come to give answers to the projects you have in mind. This chapter will explain important aspects of this incredible machine.

For those who do not know, the **"Cricut,"** as they are usually known, are machines whose main function is based on cutting and not printing, as many tend to think. These devices are frequently considered tools composed of blades; this is because it is their main feature.

Any creative person interested in the world of crafts has surely come across the Cricut at some point, an art for which a special cutting device is required.

It has a variety of special blades that facilitate different types of cuts of different materials, such as paper, fabric, vinyl, cardboard, and others, that you will see below.

Certainly, the invention of this equipment is ideal for all who wish to elaborate on any **DIY** and **crafts**. These machines are in great demand by graphic designers and entrepreneurs who see them as a good business opportunity. The truth is that they are not wrong at all.

Cricut machines, also known as cutting plotters, are quite unknown devices for some people. However, **if you are passionate about the sewing world**, you will likely not live without one after we explain its usefulness.

You should know that when we refer to cutting plotters, we are talking about machines that resemble a printer whose main function is to cut designs that will be fixed to another surface.

It is common to see it on T-shirts, walls, and glass. In addition, they are widely used in sewing for pieces such as patchwork and quilting. As mentioned above, the main function of the plotter is to scan the image you want and cut it on a piece of fabric.

Cricut Has Specialized Machines for Each Type of Project

As with all brands, Cricut has set itself the task of perfecting its equipment occasionally and has launched different models on the market so that users can choose the one that best suits their needs. Whoever is interested in one of these machines should know that each model has different characteristics, offers a greater or lesser number of features, and has a different price depending on what it provides.

In addition to offering multiple functions, these machines have the particularity of working with the software. Indeed, what Cricut machines have in common is that they use the Cricut Design Space.

This own application of the brand, in addition to the fact that it can be installed on any device, whether computer, smartphone, or Tablet, allows the users of the cutting plotter to begin the cutting process when they have finished creating their patterns.

Another point in its favor is that it allows you to work without an internet connection and gives access to an incredible library with thousands of patterns, images, and fonts to use in your designs, so it is highly recommended.

Want a reason before we get into the details? All Cricut cutting plotters have total precision and speed when designing your projects. In any of its versions, you will find an excellent professional result regardless of the model of your Cricut machine.

This company has undoubtedly succeeded in producing a large selection of tools that work only with the Cricut Maker, such as the Knife Blade, with which you will cut the thickest materials, the Scoring Wheel, which allows you to make a much more precise marking, the engraving blade, the wave blade, the perforating blade, and the debossing blade.

In conclusion, if your projects are based on vinyl or thin cardboard, the Cricut Explore Air 2 is the best solution, but if you want to go further, buy the Cricut Maker. And if your projects are small or long runs, vinyl or cardboard, we recommend the Cricut Joy.

CHA PTER 2

THE DIFFERENT TYPES OF CRICUT MACHINES AND THEIR DIFFERENCES

This chapter details a little more about the Cricut machines and their functions because, as you know, as a new one comes out on the market, the functions usually vary a little, and your purchase decision may depend on this. I invite you to learn more about each model.

Cricut Joy

The Cricut Joy, the latest launch of this brand, is presented as the smallest cutting machine in history, and precisely this feature is what attracts more attention from consumers who want to move their work equipment comfortably. With this machine, you can do just that.

You can transport it anywhere because it is intended and designed to be a complementary or travel plotter.

It has a maximum cutting area of 11 cm (4.33 in) wide.

Its basic features include drawing and cutting up to 50 materials, including vinyl, cardboard, paper, and infusible ink. It also has a single head where you can put both the blade and the marker.

A detail that differentiates it from other machines is that, with certain materials, the user doesn't need to place the cutting mat, and it can cut very long runs of up to 1.2 meters and repeat it six times.

The blade and the markers are placed in the same place; you only have to change the accessory depending on whether you want to cut or draw.

What Other Functions Does the Cricut Joy Perform?

Another of the great novelties of this machine is that it incorporates a new special mat for card making in its small space. You can cut folded cards, the machine will cut only the top layer, and you can put cardboard with effects underneath.

Certainly, this machine has come to give answers to what everyone wished for, to be able to cut without a mat. You can cut 10 cm (3.93 in) wide and 1 meter-long (3.28 ft), but it can repeat vinyl cuts up to 6 meters (19.7 ft) long.

These are the materials that the Cricut Joy can cut.

With this machine, you can use the most common materials, which are not extremely thick, such as adhesive vinyl, cardboard, textile vinyl, paper, and adhesive paper. A detail to consider is that if you try to cut much thicker materials, you could risk breaking the machine as it is not made for it.

Another curiosity about the Cricut Joy is that it has no buttons. You must connect via Bluetooth to use it perfectly from your mobile or tablet through the Design Space app.

If you want to work with the PC, it must have Bluetooth; otherwise, it will not work.

It is the easiest cutting plotter, perfect for small and last-minute projects.

Here's what the Cricut Joy machine includes:

- The Cricut Joy machine.
- One regular adhesion mat 11.4 x 16.5 cm (4.4-6.49 in).
- A book that welcomes you with some information.
- A power adapter.
- One blade + blade holder.
- A 0.4 mm black felt-tip pen.
- A free trial for Cricut Access (this only applies to new subscribers).
- A pack of 50 free projects.
- Sample materials for a first test run.

Why Buy the Cricut Joy?

Many people have already worked with a larger cutting plotter and are looking for a different, smaller option. It happens because it is simply the most practical proposition on the market.
It has the great advantage of helping you save time, it makes no noise, and you can take it anywhere with you and work quietly.

Finally, it is the perfect cutting plotter for those creators who do not have any of these devices or for those who want a machine as a complement to the big ones.

As for its physical characteristics, its small size is the main reason to tip the balance towards buying it. The Cricut Joy machine manages a compact design, so you can easily carry it from one place to another.

Secondly, this is the most economical model of the Cricut cutting plotters. It shouldn't be your first reason to buy, but it's something to consider. If you are on a limited budget and want a cutting plotter at home to customize many items, this is what you are looking for.

Finally, its incredible ease of use is the feature that ends up making it especially attractive.

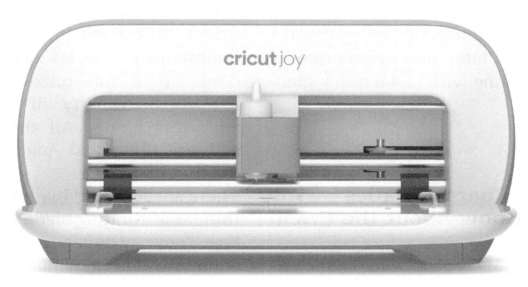

You will be impressed to know that this great machine, in terms of dimensions, does not even weigh 2 kg (4.4 lb.), so it is the perfect ally if you want to go to workshops or usually move around for work. Suppose you want to take it on vacation or do not want it to take up much space at home because you do not have room for everything.

It is a machine designed to do everything you want in just a few minutes.

This machine has been created for you who have the ability and desire to customize countless products in a short time and enjoy the speed and efficiency of a Cricut every time you use it. It is simply one of the best options for your day-to-day life.

Cricut Maker

The Cricut Maker machine can draw, mark, engrave, and cut various materials to produce unique and original personalized goods. It has been available on the market for some time and can be easily purchased both in physical stores and online. The machine ensures quality, ease of use, and high performance for its users. One of its notable features is its well-constructed design, which is evident in the choice of materials and accessories. Anyone can easily recognize the attention to detail and overall quality of the machine with just a quick glance.

Some Characteristics You Should Know About the Cricut Maker

The Cricut Maker machine has a cutting area that can accommodate materials with a maximum width of 30.5 cm and a maximum length of 61 cm (1-2 ft). It's important to note that cutting is done using a drag blanket, so you cannot directly cut rolls or materials.

When it comes to the different adhesion drag blankets, they are distinguished by color. These blankets are of high quality and cost-effective. The machine comes with two blankets: a low tack blue one and a pink one specifically designed for fabrics.

The Cricut Maker is capable of cutting materials up to 2.4 mm thick. It utilizes self-adjusting blades made of metal, which are characteristic of cutting plotters. The machine exerts a force of 4 kg (8.8 lb.), enabling it to cut anything from thin vinyl to tougher and thicker materials like balsa wood.

One of the standout features of the Cricut Maker cutting plotter is undoubtedly its blades and blade holders. Cricut has once again excelled in the quality of construction with this model. All the blades are self-adjusting and made of metal.

There are standard blades that feature the classic rotating blade found in plotters. They can be easily replaced by pushing up and removing the blade from the inside. Various models are available, ranging in quality, such as the standard fine tip or the deep-cutting blade.

The rotating blade holders have a built-in metal-toothed wheel that fits into the B carriage of the Maker. This mechanism is genuine and allows for the use of specialized tools, like the rotary craft blade for denser materials or scoring.

It's worth noting that when purchasing or owning the Cricut Maker, the fabric blade is included. Additionally, you can insert markers or a marking tool into the carriage. Another added benefit is receiving a black fine-tip marker with the Maker.

These features make it clear that those who choose the Cricut Maker are seeking a versatile machine. This model goes beyond being just a cutting plotter, as its multiple functionalities enable effortless cutting of various materials, resulting in impeccable outcomes.

you are not only acquiring a piece of equipment but also gaining access to a whole world of possibilities and ideas. Its applications are so extensive that it caters to a wide range of needs, always delivering professional results.

This model stands out for its power and precision. To fully utilize all the options it offers, it is advisable to dedicate ample time to explore its capabilities. Rest assured, it is an incredible machine that won't disappoint.

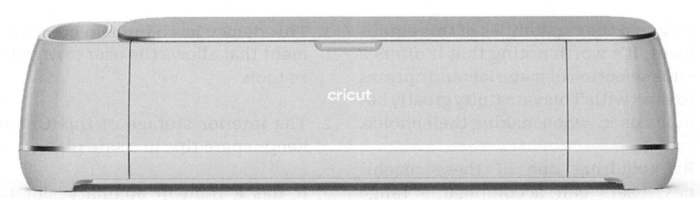

Why Buy This Machine?

For those who are deeply involved in crafting, it can be more than just a hobby that occupies several hours a day. It may even be a passion that they consider turning into a profession. In that case, the Cricut Maker is the ultimate Cricut machine for you.

When you purchase this machine,

One of its remarkable features is the ability to add text, intricate illustrations, foil details, or easy folding lines for cards and 3D projects. It can print and cut on both white and colored paper. With the Cricut Explore 3, you can even print images using your home printer and then cut them out. This feature is particularly amazing for those who create stickers.

Cricut Explore 3

These innovative and creative machines are primarily designed for cutting rather than printing. They feature special elements that facilitate the cutting process for various materials, including paper, fabric, vinyl, and cardboard, among others.

When discussing the Cricut Explore 3, it's important to highlight its standout feature: more powerful motors. This results in up to twice the speed compared to previous versions. It's truly a machine that any entrepreneur would want to have as an invaluable ally.

To grasp the capabilities of this equipment, it's worth noting that it offers a wide selection of materials and options to work with. This versatility greatly benefits users when making their choice.

By acquiring one of these machines, users can accomplish a range of tasks, such as cutting, peeling, and adhering to create delightful cards, as well as crafting captivating layered banners and posters without the hassle of traditional glue.

Furthermore, it can handle large-scale projects like cutting large banners or creating a solar system adorned with countless stars. As the saying goes, for the Cricut, the sky is the limit.

One of the advantages that sets this machine apart and makes it a comprehensive tool for creatives is its proprietary system, Design Space. It serves as the official application used by Cricut cutting machines, providing a dedicated space for users to bring their projects to life.

For those seeking a machine capable of handling extensive projects, the Cricut Explore 3 is an excellent choice.

The small details of the Cricut Explore

1. This device has a built-in compartment that allows the user to organize tools.

2. The interior storage of this Cricut keeps spare tips in a safe place.

3. It has a built-in auxiliary slot to hold devices such as tablets or cell phones.

4. It also comes with two clamps for cutting and marking simultaneously.

Materials

It makes use of the popular Smart Materials, which are fantastic creative supplies available in various forms such as smart vinyl, smart label writing paper, and smart label writing vinyl.

After utilizing the Cricut Explore 3, you're left with three tasks: cutting, peeling, and gluing. This means there's no excuse not to create delightful cards, captivating layered posters, and vibrant banners without the hassle of adhesive.

cuts twice as fast as the Cricut Maker 2 and Explore Air 2.

The standout feature of this new model is its ability to cut without a mat using the new smart materials from Cricut. The best part is that these materials can be directly fed into the machine.

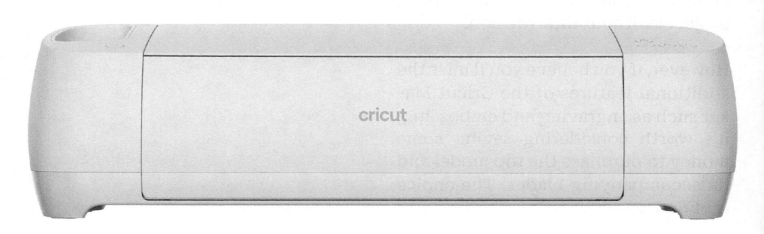

In case you're unaware, the Cricut Explore 3 excels at cutting a wide range of materials with exceptional precision, including cardboard, vinyl, and specialty materials like glitter paper and stabilized fabric. It is compatible with over 100 different types of materials.

The Cricut Explore is one of the latest models in the company's lineup of DIY cutting and processing equipment. This new device can achieve

Why choose the Cricut Explore?

If you're considering purchasing a machine but haven't made a decision yet, let us assure you that the Cricut Explore is the best option if you're seeking a professional cutting plotter that doesn't limit your creativity in your projects.

With this machine, you can achieve precise cuts on a wide range of materials and create incredible results.

It serves as an intermediate option, allowing you to elevate the look of your crafts with a lower investment compared to the Cricut Maker.

If you're certain that cutting, folding, and drawing are your primary focus and that's what you're looking for, then the Cricut Explore is the ideal Cricut machine for you. You'll be able to explore endless possibilities and have hours of fun customizing projects without interruption.

However, if you believe you'll miss the additional features of the Cricut Maker such as engraving and embossing, it's worth considering saving some money to purchase the top model and its accompanying blades. The choice is yours!

Important to Keep in Mind

When placing a piece of paper, it is necessary to ensure it matches the top corner with the top left corner of the machine's cutting mat.

CHAPTER 3

WHICH MACHINE IS BEST FOR YOU? LET'S FIND OUT TOGETHER

In this chapter, we will determine which machine is best for you, for all their models work perfectly. However, each one is created for particular projects. So, find out which one best suits your needs.

Cricut Joy

As mentioned earlier, the Cricut Joy is the latest model to hit the market and is touted as the smallest cutting plotter in history. If convenience is what you're after, this option is excellent because it can be easily carried anywhere you go.

It offers a maximum cutting area of 11 cm (4.33 in) wide, so it's important to consider this detail when making a purchase, as your projects should be designed to fit within these dimensions.

For those who have an insatiable passion for designing and want to indulge in drawing to their heart's content, this device allows you to cut and draw on up to 50 different types of materials, including vinyl, cardboard, paper, and infusible ink materials.

It is perfect for people who:

- Want to take up little space with the machine.
- Make very long projects or simple and quick projects.
- Solve projects at the last minute and are short on time.
- Love to have everything organized with stickers and names since adhesive vinyl is the specialty of this machine.

You can find exclusive projects at Design Space with Cricut Joy. You can utilize the Cricut Joy for practical everyday projects like spice jar labels.

It's a fantastic tool that caters to craft enthusiasts and entrepreneurs who seek to enhance their creations with unique details.

This device enables you to cut, write, and draw on various materials, allowing for customization of objects such as cell phone cases, plastic containers, glass jars, glasses, T-shirts, bodysuits, pants, slippers, or even for decorating spaces.

Additionally, you can create adhesive stickers for helmets, skateboards, flashlights, wooden signs, and acrylic panels, as well as embellish corporate cards, greeting cards, or invitations.

Cricut Explore

As previously mentioned, the Cricut Explore Air was one of their initial releases. However, its significance remains high as it has undergone updates and improvements over time. This plotter can cut over 100 types of materials ranging from cardboard to vinyl, but it has a cutting force of 400 g (0.88 lb.), which is considerably lower than that of the Maker.

In terms of affordability, if you desire a machine of this size without a substantial investment, this option is much cheaper than the Maker while still delivering precise and enjoyable crafting experiences.

The machine itself features a dial where you can select the material to be cut, or you can opt for the "Custom" setting to choose the material directly from the Design Space. Conversely, in the Maker, material selection is done directly within the application.

With the Cricut Joy, the notable difference lies in its size as it can cut materials up to 30 cm wide. The good news is that it also doubles the speed when working with materials like vinyl or cardboard, providing a faster cutting and writing experience, up to two times quicker.

For creative individuals, this new iteration of Cricut machines is straightforward and doesn't differ much from previous versions. The aesthetic differences are minimal, as the core appearance remains the same.

When examining the specifics, the differences are more noticeable from an internal perspective. This latest generation, introduced in 2021, offers higher speed compared to its predecessors.

Furthermore, all Explore Cricut machines are compatible with tools from previous versions, so if you're considering an upgrade, you can do so with confidence knowing that the Explore machines utilize the same tools as their predecessors.

blades come with integrated quick swap sleeves, facilitating the effortless interchange of tools.
Simply press the button on the top and insert the desired tip.

Cricut Maker

It is renowned as the most comprehensive home cutting plotter available in the market, boasting a cutting force of 4 kg (8.8 lb.), enabling it to cut materials up to 2.4 mm thick.

This makes it the perfect machine for individuals working with fabrics, chipboard, and balsa wood, as it delivers unmatched precision. Similar to the Explore model, it can cut through 300 materials, ranging from the softest to the toughest.

If you believe that all these machines are similar at this point, it's important to note that the significant difference with the Cricut Explore lies in its incorporation of a carriage system that allows for seamless adaptation of the new blades. This technology regulates the blade's direction and provides up to 10 times more cutting force.

Another notable feature is that the

CHAPTER 4

CRICUT DESIGN SPACE - THE CRICUT SOFTWARE

Cricut Design Space is the official application utilized by Cricut cutting machines. Regardless of your idea, it is essential to configure and manipulate the device using this specialized software, which is available for both computers and mobile devices, to carry out your projects.

The interface provided to users incorporates user-friendly functions that enable full customization of any design with images. The toolbars are intuitively divided, allowing for easy access to text, photos, and cutting options, making it ideal for projects involving cards, stickers, T-shirts, and more.

This complimentary application executes the cutting and design commands sent by the creative user, so it is crucial to understand how it works and the basic operations to successfully manipulate it and achieve clean cuts.

This program fulfills its purpose through the blades, which apply pressure with impressive precision, enabling work with both simple and intricate designs. It can cut various materials such as paper, adhesive, as well as stronger materials like cardboard and vinyl.

The Benefits of Using Cricut Design Space in Your Designs

With the abundant supply and demand for materials and technology, investing in a specific piece of equipment can be daunting. Additionally, many may hesitate to take the plunge because they are unsure how to navigate such devices through an application. That's why, for those dedicated to crafts or those who find inspiration in them, it's best to consider the most practical option, and this application precisely provides that benefit.

There are numerous alternatives available, ranging from highly specialized to more straightforward options. However, if there's one that offers both practicality and affordability, it's the Cricut machines, which are the most appealing choice. The truth is, unlike others, the Cricut Design Space software required for setup and operation is no more challenging to use than other mobile applications. It boasts several advantages that will prove useful to users with limited experience.

With this application, the complexities of programs like Photoshop, Illustrator, Corel Draw, and others can be set aside, as the Cricut software offers editing, customization, a library, cutting capabilities, and much more for creatives who want to express their ideas in a unique format.

One of the main benefits of this program is that it's free and readily available on the web for any user. Simply download the application from the **design.cricut.com** website and follow the simple steps to complete the installation.

Furthermore, there is a special Cricut Access membership available, which provides unlimited access to templates, images, and other benefits, as described in the following chapter. Cricut Design Space enables you to combine illustrations and fonts, adjust placement, size, colors, and much more using the resources available in the library. Pre-designed templates and ready-made projects are also at your disposal, eliminating the need to start from scratch.

A feature tailored entirely for users is the connection to Access accounts, allowing projects to be saved directly, shared, and customized with other members of the Cricut community. Moreover, a gallery of simple shapes assists users in assembling their designs. All you need is a basic idea and the available options that will enable you to bring your creations to life.

While it operates optimally when connected to the internet, there is also an offline work function for situations where network difficulties may arise, preventing any loss of time due to unsaved projects. For those seeking additional qualities, one of the most useful and noteworthy is its ability to easily handle SVG files from other design programs, such as Illustrator or Inkscape.

The next Cricut Design Space book that you will find in this collection, will provide specific details on these and other features.

CHAPTER 5

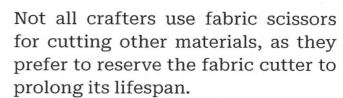

CRICUT ACCESSORIES AND TOOLS

For a designer, it is necessary to have a series of tools and materials because it is with these supplies that new ideas are born. It is the case for many creatives, and one of the favorite aspects of having a Cricut machine is its variety of tools and accessories. In this chapter, we will tell you about the main tools you will have and what they work for.

The Fabric Cutting Blades

Many individuals utilize the fabric blade along with a blade holder, which is compatible with all Cricut machines, including the Maker, Explore, Explore One, Explore Air, and Explore Air 2.

To extend the blade's lifespan when cutting fabric, it is recommended to use it with an interlining. This can be helpful when cutting bonded fabrics or fabrics with backing for ironing.

Not all crafters use fabric scissors for cutting other materials, as they prefer to reserve the fabric cutter to prolong its lifespan.

With this blade, you can easily differentiate between the fine-point blade designed for bonded fabrics and the one intended for other materials. It functions in the same way as the Premium Fine-Point blade and features the distinctive pink color of the FabricGrip mat.

It is advisable to use the blade with the fabric sheet housing attached. Alternatively, it can also be used with a high-end fine-point blade housing. This blade and blade housing are compatible with all Cricut Maker and Cricut Explore machines.

Deep Cutting Blade

This Cricut deep-cutting blade with a blade holder is perfect for cutting thicker materials such as magnets or laminated cardboard.

It consists of a deep-cutting blade and a blade holder.

Operating at a 60° angle instead of the usual 45°, it makes cutting through thicker materials much easier. It is a highly useful tool that is compatible with the entire range of Cricut machines, including the Maker, Explore Air 2, and Explore Air.

You will need the following:

- Magnet
- Stamp material
- Wooden cardboard
- Thick cardboard
- Foam sheets
- Hardened felt
- Cardboard

With the Cricut housing and deep point blade, you can expand the range of materials you can cut for your projects.

This equipment enables users to effortlessly create unique chipboard wall calendars using the Explore machine. It is recommended to use rubber sheets for cutting stamps and making custom magnets.

Deep point blades should be used with the deep point blade housing and are exclusively available in black for identification purposes. All Cricut Maker and Cricut Explore models can make use of this blade and housing.

The Maker, Explore, Explore One, Explore Air, and Explore Air 2 machines all offer support for additional Bonded-Fabric blade configurations.

The Premium Fine Tip Blade

The Premium Fine-Point Blade, made of German carbide steel for enhanced durability and precision, is an excellent companion specifically designed for this edition of the Cricut.

It enables the creation of intricate cuts in various thin to medium materials. Whether it's card stock, vinyl, or paper, the Premium Fine-Point blade is designed to handle the most challenging cuts. These blades are typically available in a gold color and come with a replacement blade. They are compatible with Maker and Explore machines.

It is recommended to use the premium fine-point housing, available in either gold or silver, with the gold premium fine-point blades. All Cricut Maker and Cricut Explore machines support this blade style and housing.

Marking Tool or Scoring Needle

Certainly, the Cricut marking tool makes creating folding lines much easier. It can be placed on the double carriage of the Cricut machine, allowing for simultaneous cutting and marking. This tool is perfect for creating letters, envelopes, boxes, and 3D projects.

With the scoring stylus, you can hold both a cutting blade and a stylus in one hand while using your Cricut Explore machine to cut and mark without the need to switch mats. It is also compatible with the Cricut Maker.

Cricut Roll Holder

With the Cricut Roll Holder, you can easily align materials for precise cuts on long projects. This roll holder is designed to hold and guide rolls of smart materials to the cutting machine. Here are some key details about the roll holder:

- Specific roll holders for Smart materials are available in lengths ranging from 3 meters to 22.8 meters.
- The roll holders come with a blade that can cut the material straight once your project is complete.
- The Cricut Roll Holder is compatible with both the Cricut Maker 3 and Cricut Explore 3.

Cricut's smart cutting machines position the brand as a leader in creative crafting technology, enabling individuals to ideate, create, and customize various items. Whether you want to produce decorative decals, liven up your home's walls, or design custom T-shirts for your loved ones, these machines provide the tools you need.

The Cricut Explore 3 is a fully-featured and highly capable piece of equipment that can cut at speeds of up to eight inches per second. It makes the creative process easier and more enjoyable.

In addition to cutting, Cricut machines offer versatility in craftsmanship by being compatible with additional tools. For example, you can use special Cricut pens (sold separately) to write messages or draw designs on paper and other materials. The scoring tool (also sold separately) allows you to add embossed patterns to crafts or create precise folds on paper, showcasing your creativity.

Another advantage of these innovative machines is their ability to function as laminating tools, adding a unique finishing touch to greeting cards, invitations, and home decorations.

Overall, the Cricut cutting machines, including the Cricut Explore 3, provide a wide range of possibilities for creative projects, making it easier for users to explore their artistic potential.

Smart Iron-On

Cricut's Smart Iron-On is a type of thermoadhesive material designed for use with Cricut cutting machines. It is a thin, flexible material that can be applied to fabrics using heat to create custom designs and graphics on clothing, accessories, and other textile decoration projects.

Smart Iron-On is available in various options, including different colors and finishes such as matte, metallic, or glitter. It is designed to withstand washing and ironing, ensuring that your designs remain beautiful and durable over time.

To use Smart Iron-On with a Cricut machine, you need to select the corresponding material in the Cricut Design Space software, place the material on the cutting mat, and follow the instructions to cut the desired design. After cutting, you can remove the excess material and apply Smart Iron-On to the desired surface using an iron or heat press.

Smart Iron-On is a popular choice among crafting enthusiasts and those looking to personalize their clothing or create unique gifts. It is important to carefully follow the application instructions for best results and ensure proper adherence of the material to the fabric.

Up to 9' in size, Smart Iron-On is available in standard and specialty finishes, including glossy and holographic. The widest cut is 11.7 inches. The Smart Iron-On can be cut up to 4' at once, making it ideal for creating items like family vacation t-shirts or a large quantity of bags to sell online.

New Platen

A wonderful new platen that Cricut unveiled makes it possible to manage lengthy rolls of smart vinyl. It is especially helpful for anyone utilizing a 75-foot reel.

The rolling attachment allows the user to keep the vinyl material perfectly aligned as it is fed into the Cricut Explore 3. In addition, the vinyl can be trimmed neatly after the cut.

The Cricut Smart Material Roll Holder

The Cricut Smart Material Roll Holder is an accessory designed for use with Cricut cutting machines, such as the Cricut Maker 3 and the Cricut Explore 3. Its main purpose is to enable precise positioning and alignment of smart material rolls during cutting projects.

The Cricut Smart Material Roll Holder features an adjustable holder that firmly holds the smart material roll as it is fed into the cutting machine. This helps keep the material straight and aligned, ensuring accurate cuts on large projects.

It is compatible with Cricut smart material rolls, which include Smart Vinyl, Smart Iron-On, and Smart Paper. These smart materials are designed to be used without the use of a cutting mat, allowing the roll to be fed directly into the cutting machine.

The Cricut Smart Material Roll Holder is a useful option for those working on large projects or using Cricut Smart Materials frequently. It helps simplify the material feeding process and achieve accurate, quality results.

Roll Holder for Large Rolls

After discussing the possibilities of working with the huge 75' vinyl rolls on the machine, it's important to explain how to load them into your machine.

You can simply add them and let the roll rest on the table. However, you might want to consider adding a roll holder to your machine. The roll holder attaches securely to the tray of the Cricut Explore 3, allowing you to easily insert the roll of smart material.

To ensure neat and precise cuts on these rolls for your future projects, this version of the Cricut surprises users with a paper trimmer. This machine attachment works well with Smart Vinyl and Smart Iron-on materials.

Vinyl Roll Holder

The vinyl roll holder (sold separately) clips directly onto the front of the Explore Air 3 and holds the vinyl roll for you.

It even has a built-in blade so you can easily cut the vinyl when you're done.

Additionally, the Explore Air 3 has built-in sensors that measure the length of the material, ensuring that you have enough for each project before cutting. This is a great advantage.

Paper Trimmer

If you don't already have one, you may need a wider paper trimmer since the materials are 13 inches wide. Most paper trimmers can only handle up to 12 inches. Fortunately, Cricut has introduced a new paper trimmer that is ideal for this purpose.

Foil Transfer Tool

The Foil Transfer Tool is a versatile set of 3 tools in 1, featuring interchangeable fine, medium, and coarse tips. It comes with 12 gold and silver foil transfer sheets, each measuring 4" x 6" (10.1 cm x 15.2 cm).

These tools are specifically designed to work with the Cricut Explore machine. Please note that they are not compatible with mobile applications and require a computer with Design Space to operate.

Description

Imagine adding a touch of sparkle and elegance to your cards, invitations, gift boxes, and more with stunning foil embellishments. The Foil Transfer Tool is a unique pressure-activated tool that delivers professional-quality results.

With its replaceable fine, medium, and coarse tips, along with the included twelve foil transfer sheets, you can achieve exquisite designs. Simply follow the directions in Design Space, and once your Cricut Explore 3 machine is ready, the magic of sparkle and shine will be revealed.

This tool should be used with Cricut foil transfer sheets, available in various colors. For further information, please visit cricut.com/help/foil-transfer.

Features
- Easy embellishment without the need for heat.
- Polished and long-lasting results.
- Specifically designed for use with Cricut foil transfer sheets.

Cricut Pens

Cricut Pens are special pens designed for use with Cricut cutting machines. These pens allow you to write and draw accurately on a variety of materials, such as paper, cardstock, vinyl, and more.

Cricut pens are available in a variety of colors and thicknesses to suit different creative needs. They are designed to fit into the appropriate slot on the Cricut machine, allowing the machine to write or draw the desired design.

Cricut pens are compatible with Cricut Design Space software, which allows you to select the desired fonts, designs, or illustrations and transfer them to the machine for precise writing or drawing.

They are very useful for adding custom text, embellishments, or hand-drawn details to your Cricut designs. Cricut pens offer crisp, professional results, allowing you to further customize your creative projects. Please note that you need to purchase the original Cricut pens, as the Cricut Joy pens will NOT work on this machine or any Explore models.

In another book that you'll find within this collection, I will provide information about the essential accessories you need to work with your Cricut machine, as well as introduce you to other tools and accessories.

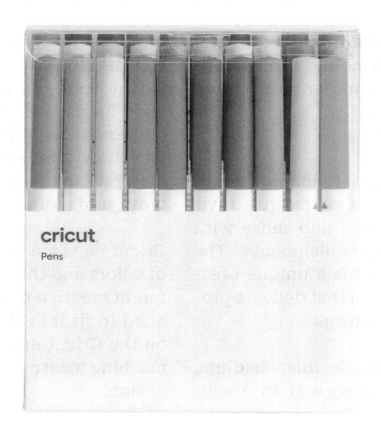

CHAPTER 6

MATERIALS THAT CAN BE USED WITH CRICUT

Cricut is compatible with a wide range of materials that can be used to create custom designs. Regardless of the model of your Cricut machine, it is important to have a good understanding of the available materials. In this chapter, you will learn more about these essential supplies.

Vinyl

Cricut Vinyl is a type of thin adhesive material used to create custom decorations, stencils, and stickers. It is available in different colors, finishes, and sizes and is designed to be used with Cricut cutting machines. Cricut Vinyl can be applied to a variety of surfaces, such as walls, windows, decorative objects, and more. It is water-resistant and can be easily removed without damaging the underlying surface.

Vinyl Cricut is very popular among crafting enthusiasts and allows you to make custom projects with ease. It is known for its durability and versatility as a material.

The New Cricut Smart Vinyl

A permanent and removable version of Cricut Vinyl is available, offering a range of colors, finishes, and lengths, from 0.9 m (2.9 ft) to 22.9 m (75 ft). This allows you to create custom designs and decorations, including personalized t-shirts in various colors and effects. You can cut an image up to 1.2 m (3.9 ft) or repeat shapes up to 3.6 m (11.8 ft). Simply load the material into the machine, and you're ready to start your project!

One notable improvement in the Cricut Explore 3 is the inclusion of new sensors that measure the material before cutting, ensuring that you have enough for your project.

The Design Space software will prompt you to load additional material if more is needed. This feature helps streamline the cutting process and ensures accurate results.

Cricut Paper

Cricut Paper refers to a range of specially designed papers that are compatible with Cricut cutting machines. These papers are created to provide optimal results when used with Cricut machines and are available in various colors, patterns, and finishes.

Cricut Paper is suitable for a wide range of crafting projects, including card making, scrapbooking, and paper-based decorations. It is often used to create intricate designs, cutouts, and embellishments.

The paper is typically lightweight and comes in different thicknesses, allowing for versatility in crafting. Some varieties of Cricut Paper may have special features like textured surfaces or finishes such as glitter or metallic effects, adding an extra touch of creativity to your projects.

To use Cricut Paper with a Cricut machine, you will need to select the appropriate setting in the Cricut Design Space software and load the paper onto the cutting mat. The machine will then precisely cut your chosen design onto the paper, resulting in clean and accurate cuts.

Cricut Paper is widely available and can be purchased in individual sheets or as part of paper packs or kits. It provides crafters with a convenient and reliable option for creating beautiful and intricate paper crafts with their Cricut cutting machines.

The Smart Paper

This paper has an adhesive backing and is great for crafting cards, party decorations, and scrapbooks. Make sure to use the best adhesive before cutting, peeling, and sticking. Smart Paper has a maximum cutting area of 11.7 inches high by 11.2 inches wide.

Cricut Mats

Cricut mats are adhesive mats used with Cricut cutting machines. These mats are designed to hold the material firmly during the cutting process. They are available in several variations, each of which is suitable for specific types of materials.

Cricut mats have an adhesive surface that securely grips the material and keeps it in place as the cutting machine operates. This ensures precise and accurate cuts by preventing the material from shifting during the cutting process.

There are different types of Cricut mats tailored to specific materials such as paper, cardstock, vinyl, fabric, and more. Each mat is designed with the appropriate level of adhesion, ranging from standard to strong, depending on the material's weight and surface texture.

Cricut mats can be refreshed and reused by replacing the adhesive surface when it starts to lose its stickiness. This allows you to extend the lifespan of the mat and achieve consistent cutting results over time.

Before using a Cricut mat, it is essential to clean it thoroughly and ensure it is free from any dust or debris. This helps maintain the mat's adhesion and prevents interference with the cutting process. Additionally, it is important to follow the specific instructions provided for the material you are working with to achieve optimal cutting performance.

Other types of materials

Rest assured that the Cricut Explore 3 is capable of cutting everything that the previous Cricut Explore models can cut, and even more! When using a mat, it can cut various materials, including regular vinyl, sheets, and cardstock.

With the exception of one item, you can use the fantastic accessories that were available with the previous model machines, just as you can with the materials.

For those who plan on using smart materials, it's important to note that a 12-inch trimmer will not be suitable. Instead, a larger 13-inch trimmer is required to cut the materials, which are 13 inches wide.

The deep point blades should be used with the deep point blade housing and are identified by their black color. It's worth mentioning that this blade and housing can be used with all Cricut machines.

I will now present to you a comprehensive list of all the materials that can be used with your Cricut machines. You will undoubtedly be amazed by the vast array of materials available, each offering countless possibilities to create unique objects. **The only limit will be your imagination**.

- Acetate 350
- Adhesive foil
- Adhesive foil, matte
- Adhesive foil, double-sided
- Aluminum foil
- Art/Illustration board
- Balsa - 1/16" (1.6 mm)
- Balsa - 3/32" (2.4 mm)
- Bamboo fabric
- Basswood - 1/16" (1.6 mm)
- Basswood - 1/32" (0.8 mm)
- Bengaline
- Birch, Permanent adhesive
- Boucle
- Broadcloth
- Burlap
- Burnt velvet
- Butcher paper
- Calibration paper
- Calico
- Cambrian
- Canvas
- Carbon fiber
- Cardboard (for intricate cuts)
- Adhesive-backed cardboard
- Cashmere
- Cereal box
- Slate vinyl
- Challis
- Chambray
- Chantilly Lace
- Charmeuse Satin

- Chiffon
- Chintz
- Chipboard (1,5 mm)
- Colored adhesive tape
- Construction paper
- Copy paper - 20 lb (75 gsm)
- Copy paper - 24 lb (90 gsm)
- Copy paper - 32 lb (120 gsm)
- Corduroy
- Corrugated cardboard
- Corrugated paper 329
- Cotton
- Cotton, sized
- Handmade foam
- Crepe Charmeuse
- Crepe de Chine
- Crepe paper
- Crepe satin
- Trimmed card + backing
- Cutting mat protector
- Damask
- Delicate fabrics (such as tulle).
- Delicate fabrics (such as tulle) bonded.
- Deluxe paper
- Deluxe embossed paper sheet.
- Deluxe paper, adhesive-backed
- Denim
- Denim, bonded
- Swiss dotted
- Double cloth
- Double stitch
- Dry-erase vinyl
- Duck cloth
- Duct tape sheet
- Dupioni silk

- EVA foam
- Everyday Iron-On
- Everyday Iron-On
- Mesh Iron-On
- Everyday Iron-On Mosaic
- Express Iron-On
- Extra heavy fabrics (like burlap)
- Eyelet
- Mistake
- Faux fur
- Synthetic leather (paper thin)
- Synthetic suede
- Felt
- Felt, acrylic cloth
- Felt, hand-bonded
- Felt, bonded sheen
- Felt, rigid
- Felt, wool bonded
- Felt, wool cloth
- Flannel
- Flat cardboard
- Fleece, fleece lining
- Flexible foam
- Flocked Iron-On
- Flocked paper
- Aluminum acetate
- Foil Iron-On
- Aluminum Kraft plate - holographic
- Aluminum foil - 0.36mm
- Aluminum foil poster
- Aluminum foil tape-glossy side down
- Aluminum foil tape - glossy side up
- Foulard
- Freezer paper
- Fusible tissue
- Fusible fleece
- Fusible interface
- Gauze
- Gel sheet
- Genuine leather
- Georgette
- Glitter cardboard
- Glitter Kraft foam
- Glitter adhesive tape
- Glitter Iron-On
- Glitter mesh sheet
- Glitter vinyl
- Gossamer
- Grocery bag
- Grois point
- Grosgrain
- Habutai
- Handmade paper
- Heat transfer (non-Cricut)
- Heather
- Heavy card stock - 100 lb. (270 gsm)
- Thick chipboard - 2.0 mm (2.0 mm)
- Heavy fabrics (such as denim)
- Heavy fabrics (such as denim), bonded.
- Thick patterned paper
- Heavy watercolor paper - 140 lb (300 gsm)
- Holographic card stock
- Holographic heat transfer
- Holographic Iron-On
- Iron-On holographic mosaic
- Holographic glossy holographic

Iron-On

- Home spun fabric
- Infusible dye transfer sheet
- Insulbrite batting
- Interlock stitch
- Jacquard
- Pullover
- Jute
- Kevlar
- Khaki
- Kraft Board
- Kraft Cardboard
- La Coste
- Lame
- Laser copy paper
- Lightweight card stock - 163 gsm (60 lb)
- Lightweight cotton
- Lightweight cotton, 2-ply
- Lightweight cotton, 3-ply
- Lightweight fabrics (such as silk)
- Lightweight fabrics (such as silk), bonded.
- Lightweight printed paper
- Bed linen
- Bed linen, bonded
- Lycra
- Magnetic sheet - 1.0 mm
- Magnetic sheet - 0.5 mm
- Board (1.5 mm)
- Matelasse
- Matte vinyl
- Medium card stock - 216 gsm (80 lb)
- Medium fabrics (such as cotton)
- Medium fabrics (such as cotton), bonded.
- Medium garment leather - 4-5 oz. (1.6 mm)
- Melton wool
- Mesh
- Metallic mosaic with Iron-On coating
- Metallic leather
- Metallic poster board
- Metallic vinyl
- Microfiber
- Moiree
- Moleskin
- Monk's cloth
- Mulberry paper
- Muslin
- Mylar
- Natural wood veneer
- Neoprene
- Non-adhesive vinyl - 16 ga.
- Non-adhesive vinyl - 20 ga.
- Notebook paper
- Nylon
- Oilcloth, bonded
- Oilcloth
- Organza
- Ottoman
- Outdoor vinyl, bonded
- Oxford
- Paint chip
- Panne velvet
- Adhesive-backed paper
- Parchment paper
- Party foil
- Stamped glitter cardstock
- Stamped Iron-On
- Pearl paper

- Peau de Soie
- Photo paper
- Pima cotton
- Pique cotton
- Plastic sheeting
- Plastic packaging
- Plisse
- Plush
- Polyester
- Polyester, bonded
- Poplin
- Premium outdoor vinyl
- Premium vinyl - permanent gloss
- Premium vinyl - matte removable
- Premium vinyl - frosted gloss
- Premium vinyl - frosted gray
- Premium vinyl - frosted opaque
- Premium vinyl - holographic
- Premium vinyl - holographic texture 3D
- Premium vinyl - holographic Art Deco
- Premium vinyl - holographic bubbles
- Premium vinyl - holographic crystals
- Premium vinyl - holographic pink bubbles
- Premium vinyl - holographic threads
- Premium vinyl - mosaic
- Premium vinyl - pearl
- Premium vinyl - shiny
- Premium vinyl - textured
- Premium vinyl - textured metallic
- Premium vinyl - true brushed
- Printable fabric
- Printable foil
- Iron-On printable, dark
- Iron-On printable, light
- Printable magnetic sheet
- Printable adhesive paper (clear)
- Printable adhesive paper (white)
- Printable vinyl
- Quilted batting
- Ramio
- Raschel stitch
- Rayon Lyocell
- Ribbing stitch
- Rice paper
- Nylon ripstop
- Sailcloth
- Sandblast stencil
- Satin silk
- Seersucker
- Sequinned
- Shantung
- Shantung canteen
- Shiny leather - 1 mm
- Shiny paper
- Chinese silk
- Silk, linked
- Slinky stitch
- Smart Iron-On
- Smart Iron-On - glossy
- Smart Iron-On - holographic
- Smart paper, adhesive cardboard
- Smart vinyl - matte metallic
- Smart vinyl - permanent
- Smart vinyl - removable
- Smart vinyl - glossy
- Smooth paper with glitter
- Spandex
- Glossy paper
- SportFlex stencil
- Stencil film - 0,4 mm

- Stencil vinyl
- Adhesive paper, removable
- Adhesive note
- Suede
- Tafetta
- Terry cloth
- Fine garment leather - 2-3 oz. (0.8-1.3 mm)
- Tissue paper
- Tool leather - 2-3 oz. (0.8 mm)
- Tool leather - 4-5 oz. (1.6 mm)
- Tool leather - 6-7 oz. (2.4 mm)
- Transfer sheet
- Transparency
- True brushed paper
- Tulle
- Tweed
- Ultra-firm stabilizer
- Vellum
- Velour
- Velvet upholstery
- Velvet
- Vinyl
- Viscose
- Waffle cloth
- Washi Sheet
- Washi tape - 0.06 mm
- Wax paper
- Window adhesion
- Wool crepe
- Wrapping paper
- Ziberline

will provide more detailed information in the upcoming Cricut Materials book of this amazing collection.

There is no doubt that this extensive list of materials will enable you to create a wide variety of products, and we

CHAPTER 7

CRICUT CHEAT SHEET

The Cricut Cheat Sheet is a handy reference guide that provides useful tips, tricks, and instructions for using Cricut cutting machines and related tools. It is a compilation of information and techniques designed to assist users in maximizing their creativity and efficiency when working with Cricut machines.

The cheat sheet typically includes information on machine setup, software navigation, material selection, cutting techniques, troubleshooting common issues, and more. It serves as a quick and convenient resource for both beginners and experienced users, offering guidance and shortcuts to enhance the crafting process.

Whether you're looking for specific settings for different materials, shortcuts for design software, or troubleshooting solutions, the Cricut Cheat Sheet can be a valuable tool to have on hand, providing you with the knowledge and assistance you need to create amazing projects with your Cricut machine.

From the initial setup to mastering specific tools and accessories, this chapter combines a series of valuable tips and recommendations to streamline your usage experience.

The Essential Materials for Cricut Machines

Cricut machines have the capability to cut a wide variety of materials, and the list continues to expand as these machines evolve and more users experiment with new options. While it's challenging to provide an exhaustive list, here are some popular cutting materials to consider:

• Aluminum foil
• Butcher paper
• Cardstock
• Slate vinyl
• Construction paper

- Copy paper
- Cardboard
- Craft foam
- Iron-on vinyl
- Faux leather
- Felt
- Glitter cardboard
- Glitter vinyl
- Infusible ink sheets
- Magnetic sheet
- Natural wood veneer
- Parchment paper
- Permanent vinyl
- Printable adhesive paper
- Removable vinyl

In addition to these materials, there are also **smart materials** available for use with Cricut machines, including stencil film, parchment, washi tape, and wrapping paper. It's important to note that these materials are recommended for use with current Cricut models.

For example, the Cricut Explore 3 is capable of cutting over 100 materials such as cardstock, vinyl, iron-on vinyl, glitter paper, and bonded fabric. On the other hand, the Cricut Maker 3 can cut over 300 types of materials, including paper, vinyl, fabric, wood, and leather, which are commonly used materials. The Cricut Joy, a more compact machine, can cut over 50 materials, including paper, vinyl, iron-on paper, and select faux leather materials.

It's worth exploring and experimenting with different materials to unlock the full potential of your Cricut machine and create unique projects tailored to your creative vision.

Regarding Material Brands

For first-time users, it's important to know that you don't necessarily need to purchase Cricut brand materials to achieve successful results. While Cricut vinyl is commonly used, other brands of vinyl can also yield good outcomes.

Once you've completed your first practice project, it's recommended to acquire more supplies and materials to continue your creative journey. Take the time to determine which materials work best for your specific projects and which ones may not be suitable.

Here are some additional tips for using materials:

- If you prefer working with paper, consider purchasing scrapbooking paper, cardstock, and vellum.
- If you prefer working with vinyl, explore options such as adhesive vinyl, iron-on vinyl, and transfer tape.
- For Cricut's infusible ink projects, you'll need infusible ink sheets or markers, as well as a compatible "blank" item.

Getting started with your first Cricut project is straightforward by following these steps:

1. Begin by selecting one of the many designs available in Cricut Design Space. You can choose a pre-made image or create your own.

2. Next, choose the appropriate cutting material and place it on the adhesive mat. The mat securely holds the material while the Cricut machine cuts the pattern. Insert the mat into the machine by pressing the button.

3. In Design Space, send the selected design to your Cricut cutting machine, ensuring you've chosen the correct material setting.

4. Press the flashing button on the machine to start the cutting process.

5. Once the machine has finished cutting the design, remove the mat from the machine and carefully take the material off the mat.

6. You can now add the cut pieces of paper or vinyl designs to your projects, further enhancing your creativity.

By following these steps, you'll be on your way to creating beautiful projects with your Cricut machine.

What kind of projects can be made with Cricut?

The versatility of the Cricut machine and the variety of compatible materials allow you to experiment and create projects of all kinds. Whether you are a beginner or an expert in crafting, the Cricut machine will provide you with a wide range of creative possibilities to make beautiful and impressive projects.

You can use the Cricut to create a wide variety of craft projects. In this series of books, you will find step-by-step projects that are perfect for beginners and will help you achieve amazing results. These projects will guide you through the process and provide you with inspiration and instructions to create stunning crafts using your Cricut machine.

So whether you want to make personalized cards, custom home decor, unique gifts, or even intricate paper cutouts, the Cricut machine is well-suited to meet your crafting needs. With its precision cutting capabilities and user-friendly design software, you can unleash your creativity and bring your ideas to life with ease.

No matter what type of project you choose, the Cricut machine will help you achieve professional-looking results and take your crafting to the next level. So get ready to explore the endless possibilities and enjoy the process of creating beautiful projects with your Cricut machine.

Here are some of the best Cricut projects for beginners:

- Address envelopes and invitations.
- Stencils for glass engraving.
- Custom painted wooden sign.
- Vinyl decals for car windows.
- Personalized pantry labels.
- Stencils for a painted doormat.
- Quilt blocks and applique shapes.
- Ironed t-shirts and onesies.
- Handmade greeting cards.
- Leather earrings and bracelets.
- Paper banners and party decorations.
- Personalized stickers.
- Monograms for a mug or cup.

An Easy Way to Set Up Your Cricut

Before you begin crafting, you'll need to set up your new machine. To do this, you'll require a computer or mobile device with an internet connection.

Let's briefly go over the **7 steps to set up our Cricut machine** before we can start our first project:

1. Remove the machine from the packaging and place it on a stable surface.

2. Plug the machine into an electrical outlet using the provided power cord.

3. Turn on the machine by pressing the power button.

4. Download the Cricut Design Space app on your mobile device or access Design Space on your computer through the official Cricut website.

5. Create an account or log in to the app or website.

6. Follow the instructions to connect the machine to your device via Bluetooth or a USB cable, depending on the model of Cricut machine you own.

7. Ensure that the machine is updated with the latest firmware. If necessary, follow the instructions to perform a firmware update.

Don't worry if some steps are not clear. This first book was created to give you a comprehensive overview of the Cricut world. In subsequent books, we will delve into specifics, such as creating your account, installing the Cricut Design Space software, and much more. **You will never be left alone.**

How to Cut Paper Safely on a Cricut?

Paper cutting is one of the most popular Cricut projects for beginners. It allows you to familiarize yourself with the machine without the worry of ruining expensive materials. I hope you find this guide on using the Cricut and becoming an expert enjoyable.

1. To start, place the cardstock or paper on the cutting mat provided by the Cricut LightGrip.
2. Next, design your layout in Design Space and feed the materials into the machine.
3. Make sure to choose the appropriate material settings and insert the fine point blade into the machine.
4. Press the "Start" button to begin the cutting process.
5. Once the cut is complete, unload the mat.

Here's a crucial tip for removing the paper from the mat: Flip the mat over and peel the paper off, rather than directly removing the paper. This technique helps prevent the paper from curling. Although it may feel awkward at first, it will become second nature once you get the hang of it.

How to Cut Vinyl?

After completing a few paper projects, you'll be ready to move on to cutting vinyl, which is a great material for beginners after paper. In Cricut crafting, it's important to understand the two main categories of vinyl as they can help you save on material and ensure project accuracy.

The two types of vinyl are heat transfer vinyl and adhesive vinyl. Cricut often refers to its heat transfer vinyl as "iron-on vinyl," but the terms are interchangeable.

1. Adhesive vinyl, similar to a sticker, is applied to projects. There are various types available, including vinyl with both permanent and removable adhesive.
2. On the other hand, heat transfer vinyl has a vinyl layer and a paper backing. Once the vinyl design is

cut, you peel off the backing paper and press the vinyl onto your items using heat.

To safely cut adhesive vinyl, *follow these simple steps:*

1. Create your project in Cricut Design Space or upload a pre-designed file.

2. When working with vinyl, place the paper side down on the cutting mat. Load the cutting mat into the Cricut machine.

3. Go back to Design Space and select the appropriate material settings. Insert the correct blade into the machine. Press the "Go" button to start cutting.

4. After the cut is complete, unload the mat. Use a weeding tool to remove any excess vinyl from the design.

Steps for Cutting Iron-on Vinyl

After completing a few projects with adhesive vinyl, it's worth trying iron-on vinyl, also known as heat transfer vinyl.

Iron-on vinyl is a type of craft vinyl with a heat-activated adhesive.

When heated using a tool like an EasyPress or a home iron, this vinyl adheres to materials such as fabric or other surfaces.

Iron-on vinyl consists of **two layers**: the **vinyl itself** and a **plastic sheet**. If you examine it closely, you'll notice that iron-on vinyl has two sides—one opaque and the other glossy. The plastic sheet covers the shiny side.

Cutting iron-on vinyl is similar to cutting adhesive vinyl, but there are a few important differences to keep in mind:

- Load the vinyl onto the Cricut cutting mat with the "shiny side down."
- Make sure to click the "Mirror" button in Design Space to flip the design horizontally before cutting.
- After cutting the design, use the plastic backing sheet to transfer the design onto your project.

Using Cricut Infusible Ink

Another exciting material to cut with Cricut is the new infusible ink line. You may have come across information about this material, but let us explain what infusible ink actually is. It is Cricut's innovative dye transfer product.

If you're curious about how to use infusible ink, it's perfect for creating vibrant and colorful designs with a smooth, professional finish on various projects. Unlike iron-on vinyl, which uses a heat-activated adhesive to adhere to fabric, infusible ink transfers are fused directly into the fabric. This means that the design will never flake, peel, wrinkle, or crack, as the ink becomes part of the material.

Using infusible ink is just as easy as working with iron-on or heat-transfer vinyl. The process is quite similar. Here are some essential steps to follow when working with infusible ink sheets that you may not be familiar with:

- Select an infusible ink sheet and a compatible blank project.
- Create your design in Cricut Design Space. Load the infusible ink sheet onto the Cricut cutting mat and use your Cricut machine to cut out the design. Remove any excess infusible ink from the design.
- Next, position the infusible ink design on your unfinished item and use a Cricut EasyPress or heat press to apply heat according to the recommended settings.

By following these steps, you'll be able to successfully create projects using infusible ink and **achieve impressive, long-lasting results.**

Want to create cards quickly and easily with your Cricut Explore or Cricut Maker?

Since we haven't covered the details of how Design Space works, it might be a bit premature to discuss creating a small, albeit simple, design. However, in this brief subchapter, I'll provide a general overview of the steps you can take to create a simple card using your Cricut machine.

I'll provide the necessary instructions and tips for using Cricut card kits with your 2 x 2 card mat. It's important to note that the Cricut 2 x 2 card mat is compatible with all card kits that include inserts, sticky cards, and foil cards, and it can produce up to 4 cards simultaneously. With the mat, you can use pre-designed or custom designs in Design Space.

To create Cricut insert cards using pre-designed projects, follow these steps:

1. Log in to Design Space and ensure that you have selected the appropriate machine.
2. Next, choose the "Cards" category or select the "All Categories" option from the drop-down menu.
3. Enter your search term to view a list of pre-made cards that are "ready to create."

Note: The proportions of each card design may be adjusted to match the components of your card kit.

Here is a list of card sizes that are compatible with this mat:

- R10: 8.9 cm x 12.4 cm (3.5 in x 4.8 in)
- R20: 10.8 cm x 14 cm (4.5 in x 4.5 in)
- R30: 11.4 cm x 15.9 cm (4.5 in x 6.5 in)
- R40: 12.1 cm x 16.8 cm (4.7 in x 6.6 in)
- S40: 12.1 cm x 12.1 cm (4.7 in x 4.7 in)

Note: The **"R"** denotes rectangular-shaped cards, while the **"S"** denotes square cards.

Another tip: Many of the pre-designed projects utilize machine-compatible markers. Consider how the marker color will look on the cardstock to ensure you like the combination for the cut-out part, which pertains to the color of the insert.

You can also create special cards by combining markers and foil for added effect.

The Trick to Designing Cricut Sticky Cards

With adhesive cards, a precise cut is usually applied to the backing piece, resulting in small cuts across the cardstock to reveal the contrasting material underneath. It's fortunate that the slots that hold the insert card in place don't need to be left open when using sticky cards.

Here's how to get started:

1. Use the Design Settings specific to your sticky cards to create your designs.
2. From the drop-down menu, choose the size and shape of your card before making any modifications to the design. Make sure it complements the supplies in your card kit. The design will be overlaid with a layer that outlines the card's layout.
3. Ensure that the size of your card matches your design, and add photos and text accordingly. To achieve the best results when removing excess material, make sure your design doesn't contain parts smaller than 3 mm in diameter.

Hide the design layer and the square or rectangular layer before cutting.

We have some advice that can simplify the creation of your sticky cards, just like with any design.

Keep the following in mind:

- Add a square or rectangle in the same color as the cardstock you'll be using underneath your design.

- Use the edit bar on each layer to modify the background and marker colors to showcase your design.

- Remember that sticky cards require a little preparation before cutting. Adhere the backing paper before placing your card in the cutting machine. This will ensure that each piece stays exactly where it's supposed to be.

Here's what you need to know before cutting:

- When you click "Make It," you will be directed to a screen where you may need to select your mat.

- Choose the "Pre-folded Card Mat" option and click "Continue."

- The Design Space application will automatically center and organize the cards on the mat, grouping them by size and color.

- You can rearrange your design placement by selecting and dragging the pieces to the desired empty area. If the design matches the preset size, you can also adjust the card's size using the drop-down option on the far left.

- If you want to create multiple copies of the same card, increase the number of copies in the project.

Cutting and Assembling Cards

Before using your mat, cover the adhesive areas of the mat with the protective mat covers, with the shiny side facing down.

Ensure that the card fits in the upper left corner of the mat.

While keeping the card flat against the top and the fold flush with the edge, slightly open the pre-folded card and slide the back through the mat slot.

Cut the top of the folded card and evenly smooth the top of the card on the mat. Make sure the arrangement of the cards matches the cut preview screen as you repeat the process with as many cards as you like.

Follow the on-screen instructions carefully, using pens or the Cricut foil tool to achieve the desired results.

Important: Make sure the star wheels are properly positioned to grip the mat and prevent markings on your cards. Once the card mat is loaded, press the "Start" button. Remove the card mat when the cutting is complete, and then remove each card individually.

Tip 1: Before removing your cards, check one of the corners to ensure that the cut has been made correctly. If not, you can click "Start" again to start over.

Tip 2: Use a squeegee to lift the corners of each card off the mat after it has been cut. This will help prevent oil spots from your hands on the mat.

More Tips and Tricks

- After removing the card, use the scraper to remove the paper negatives from the mat. Replace the protective mat coverings with the shiny side facing up after scraping the remaining pieces to the top and bottom borders.

- When using insert cards, gently slide the corners of the contrasting insert piece into the card corner slots.

- To remove cut-outs from sticky cards, use tweezers or fingers to delicately grab them with a profiling tool at the cut-outs' tightest corners.

Basic Cricut Terminology

Because you are still new to this fascinating field, you may sometimes come across technical terminologies that can be challenging to understand. Therefore, it is essential to familiarize yourself with these terms before you begin using the machine. By doing so, you can navigate through the equipment with ease and confidence.

Here are some of the most popular terms you should know:

- **Blade**: This is the cutting tool used by the Cricut machine to make precise cuts. There are different blades available depending on the material and the type of cut desired.

- **Burning**: It involves applying transfer tape to vinyl by rubbing the top of the tape with a scuffing instrument.

- **Cardstock**: It is a heavy and sturdy type of paper, often used for making cards, invitations, and other paper crafts.

- **Cut/Cutting**: Refers to the process of using the Cricut machine to precisely cut out designs or shapes from various materials.

- **Design Space**: This is the online software provided by Cricut for designing and preparing projects for cutting. Design Space can be accessed via a computer or mobile device with an Internet connection.

- **HTV**: Heat transfer vinyl, commonly called iron-on vinyl, a vinyl variety that heats up to stick to your product.

- **Infusible ink**: It is a special ink that, when heated, permanently fuses with compatible materials like fabric, resulting in vibrant and durable designs.

- **Iron-on vinyl**: Also known as heat transfer vinyl, it is a type of vinyl that can be applied to fabrics using heat. It is commonly used for creating designs on T-shirts, bags, and other textile items.

- **Layers**: In Design Space, layers refer to individual elements or components of a design that can be stacked or arranged on top of each other. Layers are used to create complex designs with multiple colors or materials.

- **Mat**: This is an adhesive surface on which materials to be cut are placed. Mats can be of different types and sizes depending on the material used.

- **Mirror**: Clicking "mirror" reverses the design, so it is cut as a "mirror image." You should do this to ensure your iron-on projects come out correctly. (You do not need to mirror regular adhesive vinyl projects, only iron-on and infusible ink).

- **Print then Cut**: This feature allows users to print an image or design using a printer and then have the Cricut machine precisely cut around the printed area, resulting in detailed and intricate designs.

- **Score/Scoring:** It is the process of creating a crease or indentation on materials like paper or cardstock without fully cutting through them. Scoring is commonly used for creating folds in card-boxes, and other folded projects.

- **Test Cut**: Before committing to the complete project, performing a tiny test cut is important when utilizing a new material for the first time. By doing so, you may verify that your material settings are right.

- **Upload/Uploading:** Allows users to import their own images or designs into Design Space for use in their projects.

- **Vinyl**: It is a thin, adhesive material used for creating stickers, decals, and decorative designs. It can be applied to various surfaces, such as walls, windows, and vehicles.

- **Weeding**: It is the process of removing excess or unwanted material from a cut design. This is typically done with vinyl or other materials that have intricate or small details.

- **Weld/Welding**: In Design Space, welding is the process of merging two or more individual shapes or letters together to create a single continuous shape. This eliminates any cut lines or gaps between the welded elements.

I hope this helps clarify the main terms used in the context of Cricut! For those who are just starting with a Cricut machine, it is important to know that cheat sheets are valuable resources that provide helpful guides and information.

Starting a project without sufficient relevant information can be challenging, so having access to cheat sheets can make the process much smoother.

CHAPTER 8

TIPS AND TRICKS (AND MAINTENANCE)

By now, you may have gained a better understanding of the Cricut world, and perhaps you have even started experimenting with some projects. However, it's crucial to recognize that tips and tricks for using the Cricut machine remain valuable not only at the beginning or for specific projects. In this chapter, we will provide you with information about the Cricut and its maintenance.

Cricut Maintenance:

Over time and with usage, any machine can accumulate dust, paper particles, and grease. It's common to see the grease from the machine building up on the carriage rail. Here are some tips for cleaning your Cricut machine:

- Before cleaning, always disconnect your machine from the power source.

- Use a soft and clean cloth along with a glass cleaner to wipe the plastic surfaces of your machine.

- Static electricity can cause dust or paper particles to gather on or inside your machine. Gently remove these specks with a clean cloth.

- While a certain amount of oil is necessary for the machine to operate properly, if you notice an excessive buildup on the carriage rail, wipe it off using a cotton swab, tissue, or soft cloth.

- Take care of the cutting sensor light by using a small, dry, and clean paintbrush to gently sweep and clean it on your Cricut Explore or Cricut Maker machine.

- Keep your work surface clean: Before starting a project, make sure your work surface is free from residue of previous materials. Remove any fragments or excess residue to avoid interference with your cuts.

- Regularly change the blades: Worn-out blades can compromise the quality of your cuts. Be sure to replace the blades when they become dull or marked. Follow the manufacturer's instructions to properly replace the blades.

- Use the correct materials: Only use the materials recommended for your Cricut machine. Using inappropriate materials may damage the machine or affect cutting performance.

- Proper storage of accessories: Store spare blades, tools, and accessories appropriately. Keep them clean and well-organized for easy access and to preserve their lifespan over time.

- Firmware updates: Ensure that you install available firmware updates for your Cricut machine. Updates can improve performance and address any known issues.

- Follow the manufacturer's instructions: Carefully read the instruction manual provided with your Cricut machine and follow the manufacturer's recommended guidelines to ensure correct and safe usage of the machine.

Important: Avoid spraying the cleaning solution directly onto the machine, and refrain from using acetone or nail polish remover, as they can cause permanent damage to the plastic surfaces of the machine.

CONCLUSION

We have reached the end of this first book, and I hope you found it interesting and satisfying to read. The purpose of this book was to provide you with a comprehensive overview of the Cricut world. We discussed the different machines available to date, their differences, the materials we can use, and the tools that can help us enhance our designs.

We learned that for creating various designs, we need the Cricut Design Space, which is the software that allows us to create our projects and send them to the Cricut machine for execution. I have provided you with tips on how to maintain the efficiency of your Cricut machine at all times, and we have explored the commonly used terms in this field together.

In the upcoming books, we will delve into each topic covered in this introductory book in great detail.

The aim of this series of books is to share all my knowledge about this world with you and empower you to navigate it effectively, allowing your imagination to soar.

The Cricut machine offers limitless possibilities for your creativity. Additionally, by scanning the QR code provided, you can access my website where you will find numerous bonuses tailored for you. You can also join my community and follow me on social media. My team and I will always be available to assist you.

TABLE OF CONTENTS

Chapter 1
What Cricut Design Space Is

57

62

Chapter 2
Downloading and Installing Design Space on Windows and IOS

Chapter 3
Cricut Design Space Subscription Explained

70

72

Chapter 4
The Various Areas of the Cricut Design Space

Chapter 5
How to Import Images Into Cricut Design Space

81

89

Chapter 6
SVG File and Cricut Machine

Chapter 7
Working With Colors

92

94

Chapter 8
Crafting Success: Your Cricut Design Space Project Guide

BOOK 2 - CRICUT DESIGN SPACE

CHA PTER 1

WHAT CRICUT DESIGN SPACE IS

Knowing and learning how to use the Cricut Design Space application, which is essential for manipulating Cricut machines, is not as difficult as you may think. In this chapter, we will cover everything about the core aspects of this program that every creative individual should be aware of.

First and foremost, it is important to understand that this program provides the necessary tools to carry out projects independently, regardless of the user's expertise. The "Cricut" machines are designed primarily for cutting, not printing, contrary to what many may assume. These devices are equipped with special blades that can cut various materials such as paper, fabric, vinyl, cardboard, and more.

The Cricut machine is an ideal tool for executing DIY projects and crafts, and it is highly sought after by graphic designers and entrepreneurs who recognize the potential business opportunities it offers. Understanding how the Cricut Design Space works is particularly important, especially if your designs or projects have a minimalist aesthetic. Additionally, it is worth mentioning that the technical knowledge required is relatively straightforward compared to other software applications. Both the mobile app and desktop program offer a similar and intuitive interface.

What You Should Know About Cricut Design Space

Any creative individual, designer, or entrepreneur with an interest in crafts has likely encountered Cricut at some point. This art form requires a specialized cutting device, and Cricut Design Space serves as the official application for Cricut cutting machines. It is essential for carrying out projects and configuring and manipulating the device. The program is available for both computers and mobile devices.

Regarding its user interface, it offers simple functions that allow for full customization of designs with images. The toolbars are divided and dynamic, making it easy to locate options for images, text, and cuts. This makes it particularly suitable for projects involving cards, stickers, T-shirts, and more.

Considered a complementary application, it executes the cutting and design commands sent by the user. Therefore, understanding how it works and mastering basic commands is crucial for achieving clean and successful cuts. The program offers various alternatives, ranging from specialized to simpler options. However, if practicality and affordability are key considerations, Cricut machines are undoubtedly the most attractive choice.

These machines operate using blades that apply precise pressure, allowing for the cutting of simple or complex designs. They can handle various materials, such as paper, adhesive materials, cardboard, and vinyl.

Unlike complex software programs like Photoshop, Illustrator, and Corel Draw, the Cricut Design Space software required for setup and operation is user-friendly and no more difficult to use than other mobile applications. It offers advantages that inexperienced users will find beneficial.

Gone are the days of struggling with the complexities of advanced software. The Cricut app has been specifically designed to provide editing, customization, library access, cutting tools, and more, catering to the needs of creatives and bringing their ideas to life in a unique format.

cricut®

Design Space® for Windows®

Set up a new Cricut product, browse projects, start designing, and more.

Cricut Design Space is free, and will be forever

Another advantage of the program is that it is **free and accessible online for all users**. Simply download the application from the website *design.cricut.com*, and follow the simple steps to complete the installation (we will see it together in the next chapters how to install it step by step).

Additionally, there is a special Cricut Access membership available, providing unlimited templates, images, and other benefits.

Cricut Design Space simplifies the process of combining images and fonts, offering options for placement, size, colors, and more, utilizing the resources available in the library. It also provides pre-designed templates and pre-made projects, eliminating the need to start from scratch.

A feature designed with users in mind allows for seamless integration with Access accounts. This enables users to save, share, and customize projects directly with other members of the Cricut community. The system includes a gallery of simple shapes, assisting users in assembling their designs.

All you need is a basic idea and knowledge of the available alternatives to bring your creations to life.

One of the most useful and relevant features is its ability to handle SVG files from other design programs effortlessly. You will delve deeper into this topic later on.

While optimal operation is achieved when connected to the internet, there is also an offline mode available for instances when network connectivity is problematic. This feature saves time for unsaved projects.

However, it's important to understand from the outset that using the program requires meeting certain minimum system requirements in order to produce excellent quality products with Cricut machines.

The minimum specifications for a computer to install the program are at least 370 MB of available storage space. For saving projects, a minimum of 4 GB of hard disk space is required.

Another important detail to consider, which may impact certain users, is that this tool is not compatible with Chromebooks or Unix/Linux computers. However, system requirements and updates for computers, phones, and tablets may change over time. Therefore, it is essential to check the software's availability for the specific device you intend to use.

Cricut Design Space-Specific Requirements for Operating Systems

To ensure a smooth installation process and address any doubts you may have, it's important to be aware of the specific requirements for each operating system:

For Mac:
- Cricut Design Space is compatible with MacOS 11 or later.
- Your computer should have a minimum of 4GB of RAM, a processor running at 1.83 GHz, 2GB of free disk space, an accessible USB port, Bluetooth capability, and a screen with a minimum resolution of 1024x768 pixels.
- For optimal internet performance, a broadband connection with a minimum download speed of 2 to 3 Mbps and a minimum upload speed of 1 to 2 Mbps is recommended. Standard data plans can be used.

For iOS:
- The minimum requirement is iOS 14 or later.

- Your device should be compatible with the features of Design Space.
- For internet connectivity, it is recommended to have a broadband connection with a minimum download speed of 2 to 3 Mbps and a minimum upload speed of 1 to 2 Mbps. Standard data plans can be used.

For Windows:
- The operating system should be Windows 10 or later.
- Your CPU should have a similar AMD or Intel Dual-Core processor, 4GB of RAM, 2GB of free disk space, a USB connector, and at least one Bluetooth connection.
- Additionally, your computer should have a built-in screen with a minimum resolution of 1024x768 pixels.
- For optimal internet performance, a broadband connection is preferred, with a minimum download speed of 2 to 3 Mbps and a minimum upload speed of 1 to 2 Mbps. Standard data plans can be used in other cases.

For Android:
- If you are using a smartphone or tablet to operate a Cricut, the system requirements are Android 9.0 or higher.
- The performance will depend on the quality and capabilities of your device, as well as your internet connection.

- Notable devices that meet the requirements include the Google Pixel series, Samsung Galaxy S, Galaxy Note, Galaxy Tab A, and Galaxy Tab S series, Motorola Droid G, Z, E, Turbo, or Moto series, and LG G, K, or V series.
- For internet connectivity, it is recommended to have a broadband connection with a minimum download speed of 2 to 3 Mbps and a minimum upload speed of 1 to 2 Mbps. Standard data plans can be used.

To ensure your device meets the necessary specifications, it is advisable to specifically check if the Design Space application requires higher specifications or new updates.

Please note that these requirements and device compatibility may change over time, so it's always important to verify the latest information from the official sources.

CHA PTER 2

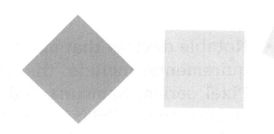

DOWNLOADING AND INSTAL-LING DESIGN SPACE ON WIN-DOWS AND IOS

Once you grasp the advantages of this program and have a device that meets the requirements, the next step is to install the software. This chapter will guide you through this process.

First and foremost, it's important to note that the Cricut Design Space mobile or desktop application can be downloaded for free on devices running Windows, Mac, iOS, and Android operating systems.

When you choose the download option, the system will provide you with a file containing straightforward instructions that you need to follow.

The subsequent steps outline the installation process for various devices:

How to Create a Cricut Account

Before we delve into the process of installing the software used to create our projects, let's take a step-by-step look at how to easily create a Cricut account. This is necessary for logging in and gaining access to our workspace, where we can save our projects and upload our images.

To create a Cricut account, follow these simple steps:

1. Visit Cricut's official website at **https://www.cricut.com/**

2. Click the "Sign In" or "Register" button located at the top of the page.

3. You will be redirected to the login/registration page. If you don't have an account, click on the **"Create Cricut ID"** link. Fill out the registration form with the required personal information. Typically, you will need to provide your name, email address, and create a secure password.

Carefully read the terms of use and privacy policy, then check the confirmation box to accept them.

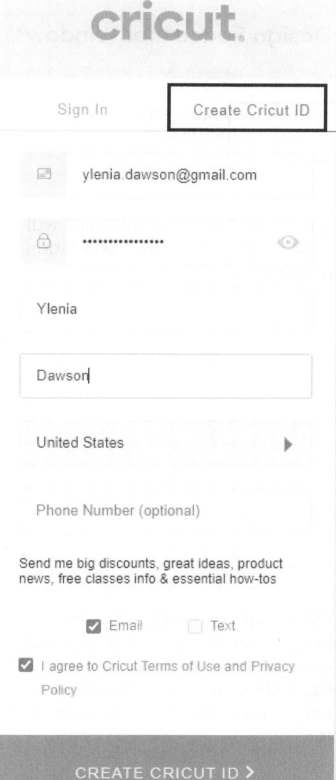

4. Click the "**Create Cricut ID**" button to complete the registration process.You may receive a verification email at the email address you provided during registration.

5. Open the email and follow the instructions to verify your account. (just cick on "Verify Email"). Once your account is verified, return to the Cricut website and log in using the email address and password you selected during registration.

6. You should now have access to your Cricut account and can utilize all the features offered by the platform.

Important: Remember to keep your login credentials secure and use a strong password to protect your account.

Downloading and Installing Cricut Design Space on Windows

Installing the Cricut Design Space software on computers is actually quite simple and only requires the use of a web browser. Just follow these steps:

1. Open the **design.cricut.com** page in your browser.

2. Select the "**Download**" link. A file will start downloading through your browser.

3. To launch the downloaded file (the name is **CricutDesignSpace.exe**), either click on it or locate it in your download folder. Your system will display a popup asking for your trust in the program. Grant the necessary authorizations.

4. A new configuration interface will appear, showing the installation progress.

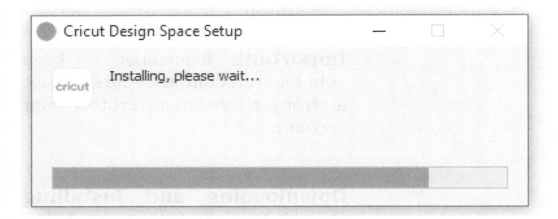

5. Log in with your Cricut username and password.

6. After that, you will see a Design Space icon on your desktop and taskbar. Double-click the icon or right-click and select "Run" to launch the software on your computer.

Important Aspects of Cricut Design Space on Windows:

- You don't need to log in with your Cricut account every time you use Design Space. The software is designed to remember your username and password unless you have previously logged out.

- It is advisable to save your work regularly since Design Space does not have an auto-save feature.

Uninstalling Cricut Design Space on Windows:

If you encounter problems with the Design Space application on your desktop computer and cannot resolve them, it is recommended to uninstall the program.

Cricut Design Space can be uninstalled like any other application on your PC. The following procedure was performed on a Windows 10 computer, but the steps will be the same if you have Windows 11:

1. Close Design Space, as well as any other applications and files you have open on your computer. This is important to ensure a successful uninstallation.

2. Click on the Start button and type

"Add or Remove Programs" option. Another window will open, displaying a list of applications and their characteristics.

3. Find the Design Space application in the list and select the "Uninstall" option that will be located at the top of the window.

4. The system will initiate the uninstallation process, and once it is completed, it will prompt you to restart your device.

Downloading and Installing Design Space on Mac

As mentioned earlier, the Cricut Design Space software is multi-platform, meaning it can be installed on various operating systems.

To install the Design Space software on a Mac computer, **you need to follow these steps:**

1. Find the official Cricut website and select the Download option. Keep in mind that each browser has its own interface, so the location of the options may vary.

2. If you're using a Mac, you may receive a popup asking for permission to launch a program downloaded from the internet. To proceed, choose Open.

3. After the download is complete, you'll see a .dmg file. You can either double-click on it or find it in the Downloads folder on your device.

4. To complete the installation, add Design Space to the Apps folder by dragging the Cricut icon. You can create a shortcut by dragging the application to the dock.

5. Double-click on Cricut Design Space in the Applications folder to launch it. You will be prompted to log in with your Cricut username and password.

Uninstalling Cricut Design Space on Mac:

If you wish to uninstall the Cricut Design Space tool, just follow these steps:

1. Open Finder and select the Applications option.

2. Locate the Cricut Design Space application and click on it.

3. Drag and drop the Cricut application into the Trash by holding down the mouse button.

4. In the Trash, click on the Settings icon. Then select the Empty Trash option and confirm that you want to permanently delete the files.

5. Once the process is complete, the files will be completely deleted. You may need to restart your device to remove any remaining traces.

Download and Install Design Space on iOS

For those who prefer not to use the Design Space application on their desktop, there is a tool available that is compatible with iOS devices. **Just follow the steps below:**

1. On your iOS device's home screen, tap on the App Store icon.

2. This will open the App Store, where you should search for the Cricut Design Space application (look for the white and green logo with the letter "**C**" in the center).

3. Tap on the "Get" button to authorize the download of the application. You may need to enter your iTunes password to confirm the process.

4. Please note that the download may take a few minutes, and it will be influenced by your internet connection.

5. Once the download is complete, the application will start and prompt you to complete the Cricut machine configuration, which will provide you with an overview of the application.

6. If you do not wish to set up the machine's preferences or connect to iTunes, you can click on the "X" in the top right corner. This will load the home page, and you will be taken to the canvas when your Cricut session begins, allowing you to start creating.

Uninstalling Cricut Design Space on iOS:

If you need to remove the Cricut Design Space app from your iOS device, please follow these instructions:

- Press and hold the Design Space icon until your device vibrates.

- Select the "X" (Delete) option that appears, which will remove the app from your iOS device.

Note: If you have downloaded images, fonts, or saved projects directly on your device instead of the Cricut Cloud, uninstalling the app may delete those resources. If you want to keep the content on your device, try downloading the Design Space app again.

Downloading and Installing Cricut Design Space on Android

An application is available for download from the Play Store for devices running the Android operating system. It's a simple process to get it, just follow these instructions:

1. Tap the app icon on your device's home screen to open the Play Store.

2. In the Play Store, search for the Cricut Design Space app. Look for the white and green logo with the "C" of Cricut in the center.

3. Select the "Install" option to begin downloading the app to your device.

4. Once the download is complete, the Design Space app's home screen will appear. Simply log in to access all the features and tools for designing Cricut projects with ease.

Uninstalling the Program on Android:

If you wish to uninstall the Cricut Design Space app, follow these instructions:

1. Open the "Settings" menu either from the top bar icon or the device's menu screen.

2. Select the "Applications" option from the Settings menu.

3. Look for the "Downloads" tab or the "Application Manager" option.

4. Locate and select "Design Space" from the list of applications. This will take you to another window where the "Uninstall" option will be available.

5. It is recommended to restart your device once the uninstallation process is complete.

Special Case: What to do if you're using Windows 7?

Windows 7 is no longer supported by Microsoft, which means it no longer receives security updates or support for new applications. This is why Design Space is incompatible with Windows 7 computers. It's recommended to update both your operating system and computer to ensure compatibility with the Design Space software. Updating will address performance issues, installation errors, and other inconveniences that may affect your user experience and results.

In Case Something Doesn't Work

If you encounter any issues or have suggestions for improving the Cricut Design Space experience, it is highly recommended to submit feedback using the Feedback tool in the Account menu. Here are the steps for both Windows/Mac and iOS:

From Windows/Mac:

1. Go to the menu, select Account, and then choose Comments.
2. Enter your email address and provide a detailed description of the difficulty you're experiencing or the suggestion you'd like to share.
3. If you wish to attach an image to support your comment, you can use the paperclip icon at the bottom right of the window to attach screenshots or videos that can help better understand the problem or suggestion.
4. Finally, select Submit to send your comment.

Note: When reporting a problem, including a screenshot of the issue is important. If you need help taking screenshots, refer to your device's user manual.

From iOS:

1. Select the Account menu in the application and tap Help & Feedback > Send Feedback.
2. The system will open a feedback form where you can enter your email address and provide a detailed description of the issue or improvement suggestion.
3. When reporting a bug, be sure to provide as much detail as possible, describing the problem and the steps you took to reproduce it. This will help developers narrow down the issue and address its root cause.
4. As you near the end of the form, you will see an option to attach a photo or video.
5. Finally, select Submit to send the form to Cricut.

Note: When reporting a problem, including a screenshot of the issue is important. If you need assistance with taking screenshots, consult your device's user manual.

CHAPTER 3

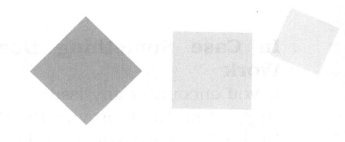

CRICUT DESIGN SPACE SUBSCRIPTION EXPLAINED (DO I HAVE TO PAY TO USE CRICUT DESIGN SPACE?)

As mentioned in previous chapters, Cricut Design Space is a free-to-use and licensed program. However, in this chapter, you will learn about a paid membership option called Cricut Access, which provides unlimited access to Cricut's resource libraries and stores.

The Cricut Access Subscription Types

To begin with, you should know that there are three types of subscriptions, and we will explain the features of each:

Free Subscription:
- Over a thousand images
- 15 fonts
- On-demand digital purchases
- Over 250 ready-made project templates

- Maximum of five collections

Value: Included with the Cricut account.

Standard Subscription:
- Over 200,000 images with unlimited use
- Over 700 fonts
- 10% discount on licensed images
- 2 unlimited collections
- Thousands of project templates
- 10% discount on purchases (including machines)
- Priority attention for members

Value: $95.88/year ($7.99/month).

Premium Subscription:
- Unlimited use of over 200,000 images
- Unlimited use of over 700 fonts
- 10% discount on licensed images
- Unlimited collections
- 10% discount on purchases
- 20% discount on all materials
- Free or low-cost shipping on certain products
- Specialized attention for subscribers

Value: $119.88/year ($9.99/month).

Choose the subscription that best suits your needs and unlock the full potential of Cricut's resource libraries and stores.

Some Cricut Access Benefits You May Not Know About

- **10% Discount and Exclusive Offers:** Subscribers to the official Cricut website can enjoy a 10% discount and access exclusive offers. Whether you're looking for new machines or supplies, Cricut Access Standard or Premium membership can help you save on your creative projects.

- **Discounts on Licensed Content:** With Cricut Access, you can enjoy discounts on projects featuring popular licensed content from Disney®, Marvel®, Star Wars™, Harry Potter™, and more. Customize premium Cricut designs at a reduced cost, with savings of up to 10% or 50% on purchases of images, fonts, ready-made projects, and digital patterns.

- **Special Protection Policies:** Cricut Access members benefit from special protection policies for file sales within the Cricut community. This ensures a secure and trusted environment for purchasing and sharing creative files.

- **Free Shipping for Orders Over $50:** If your order exceeds $50, you may be eligible for free shipping. This can provide additional savings when purchasing Cricut products and materials.

- **Automated License Acquisition and Setup:** When downloading Design Space on desktop, Mac, Android, or iOS devices, Cricut Access offers automated license acquisition and setup. This streamlined process ensures a hassle-free experience for accessing the software.

- **Mystery Boxes with Cricut Cutie:** Cricut Access members can participate in the Mystery Box program, which features special Cricut collectible figures known as Cricut Cuties. These exclusive items add a fun and collectible aspect to your Cricut experience.

Discover these exciting benefits and more by becoming a Cricut Access member today!

CHAPTER 4

THE VARIOUS AREAS OF THE CRICUT DESIGN SPACE (DESIGN PANEL, HEADER, ZOOM, LAYERS, ETC.)

The Design Space is where creatives bring their projects to life. In this chapter, we will explore how to add and update projects, photos, text, and much more within the Design Space. It is the ultimate hub for all your creative endeavors.

The Layout of the Design Panel

When you open the Cricut Design Space app, you will see a screen similar to the image below. From here, you have several options to choose from:

1. Select the type of Cricut machine you are using (in my case, the Explore 3).
2. Create a new project.
3. Access your list of projects and the images you have added.

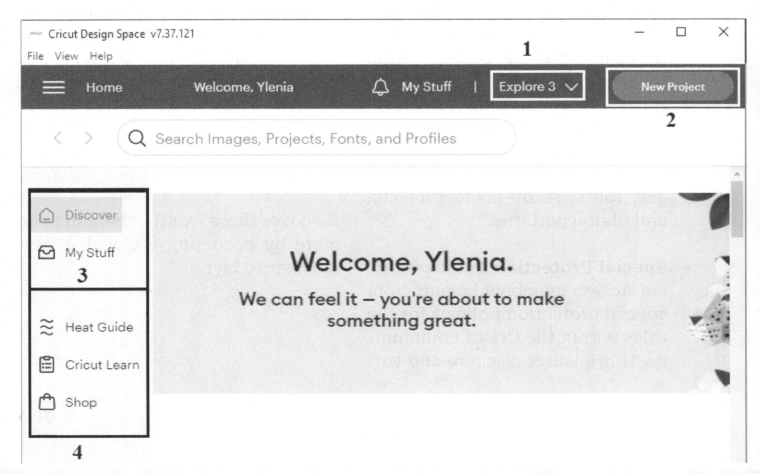

4. Explore the Cricut shop and find guides about the Cricut world.

Once you have selected the appropriate machine, click on the **"New Project"** button. A new window will appear, which is the workspace of the Design Space where you can create your projects. Together, we will explore this workspace so that you can confidently navigate and utilize all its features.

The Layout of the Design Space Canvas

The Design Space Canvas is the central component of the Cricut Design Space software, serving as the primary workspace for creating your designs. Within this canvas, you have access to a wide range of options and features that allow you to customize and bring your designs to life.

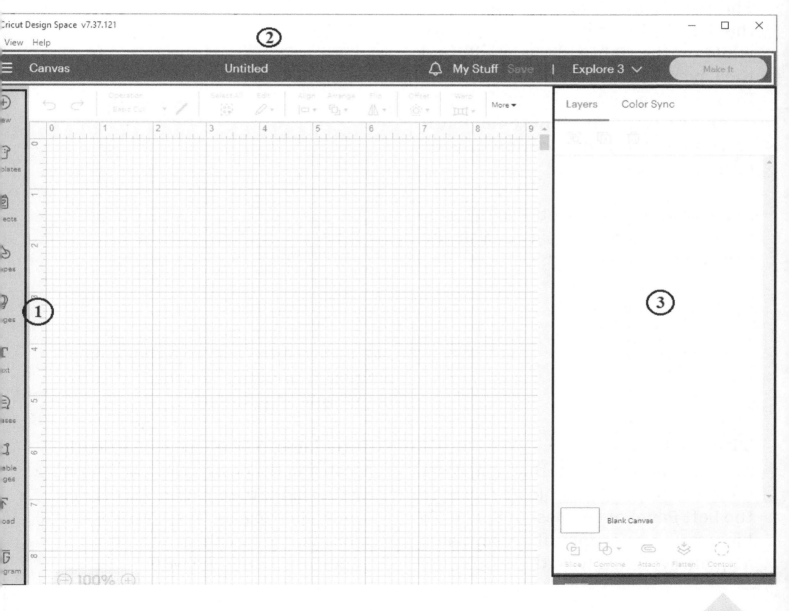

When exploring the Cricut Design Space interface, you will inevitably come across the canvas area. This space opens when you click "New" and is key because it is where all your creations will be arranged. It is precisely where you organize elements, apply effects or edits, and load fonts and images—everything related to the design itself.

The panels with tools are located in the upper left area of this canvas, while on the right side, you will find the Layers options for the images. Before creating any design with Cricut machines, it is important to familiarize yourself with the location of each option or tool

For ease of use, this section can be divided into three main parts, as shown in the figure on page 73:

- the left panel (1)
- the header panel (2)
- the right panel (3)

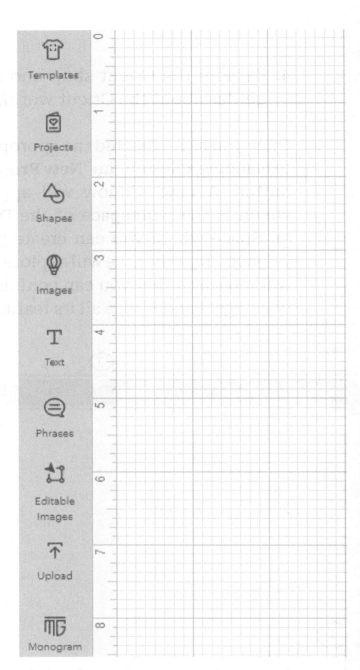

Let's delve into them together, analyzing each in detail to ensure you become well-acquainted.

The Left Panel
The common options that empower creatives to initiate projects reside in the Left Panel of the Design Space. To kickstart your journey, it's essential to acquaint yourself with these options.

- **Templates**: These are conveniently located in the design panel and serve to streamline the creation of mockups while allowing for easy project size adjustments to enhance the visualization of the finished work.

- **Projects**: This section provides users access to a membership program that simplifies the utilization of this tool. It's where you can organize your list of completed projects and templates with customizable ideas, ensuring a polished and professional finish to all your creations.

- **SHAPES**: If you're looking to create figures using basic shapes, this feature offers a variety of options, including squares, rectangles, circles, triangles, pentagons, and more.

- **Images**: This option comes with a user-friendly search engine that simplifies the discovery of ideas, news, templates, and visual resources. If you wish to create new resources, this feature offers a comprehensive set of tools to assist you.

- **Text**: Activating this option brings up a top panel with various alternatives and formatting choices to meet any need. While some fonts may require payment, Standard and Premium subscribers enjoy unlimited access to fonts at no extra cost.

- **Phrases**: In Cricut Design Space, the term "Phrases" denotes pre-designed text components or quotations that you can incorporate into your crafting and design ventures. These phrases are frequently adorned and themed, rendering them appropriate for a wide array of events, ranging from birthdays and weddings to holidays and beyond.

- **Editable images:** At times, you might come across an image in Design Space that's nearly perfect, but there's a name, number, or greeting you wish to tweak to make it just right for your needs. That's why hundreds of images have been included in Design Space, with the option to edit them. This way, you can customize the name, change the occasion, or adjust a sentiment. When an editable image is placed on the canvas, any text you can edit will be highlighted in blue. Once you've made your edits, the blue highlighting will disappear.

- **Upload**: Typically, when working with designs created in other programs like Illustrator or Photoshop, this function becomes indispensable. It enables you to import these works (or your images in general) for editing and eventual cutting in Design Space.

- **Monogram**: Cricut Design Space offers a "Monogram Maker" feature that allows users to easily create personalized monograms. Monograms are often used for decorative purposes, particularly in crafting and design projects.

The Right Panel

In this panel, you can view and learn how to manipulate any template, which is important to understand because it's where you'll find options for customizing the design. It's also referred to as the layers panel, and it's an essential tool for creating highly customized projects. It includes functions such as Group and Separate, Duplicate, Delete, Split, Merge, Link, and Merge Layers. In the upper part, you'll find the functions for Group and Separate, Duplicate, and Delete, while all the others are located in the lower part.

Top Area (1)

- Group/Separate (Ctrl + G) - Group multiple layers, images, or text together to enable them to move and resize as a single unit on the drawing area. Separating a set of layers, images, or text allows them to move and resize independently of each other on the drawing area. When it comes to text, selecting "Separate" once permits each text layer to move and resize independently while keeping the letters grouped together.

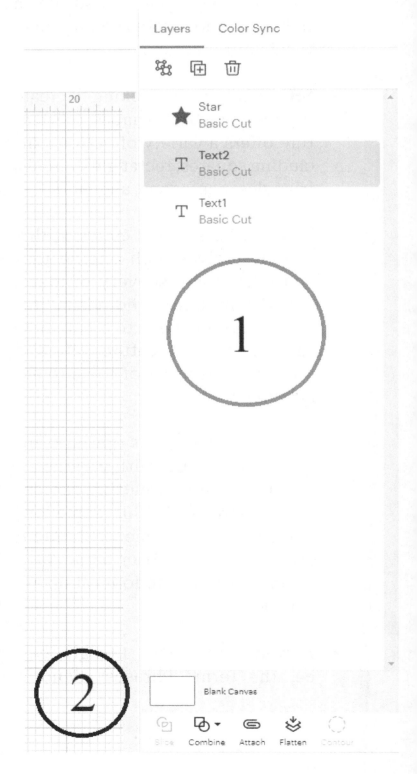

- Duplicate (Ctrl + D) - Quickly copy and paste an object in a single step to create multiple instances of the same object.
- Delete (Delete or Backspace) - Erase the selected object from the drawing area.

Bottom Area (2)
- Slice: Used to divide two elements.
- Combine: Employed to combine two or more elements.
- Attach: This option allows you to apply multiple actions to the same object.
- Flatten: It transforms a cut section into an element for printing and subsequent cutting; this is a handy tool.
- Contour: This function is applied when it's necessary to hide specific parts of a selection

The Top Panel
This panel is central and essential for achieving results in Design Space. It contains the options for editing and organizing shapes on the canvas.

It is further divided into two sub-panels: one for saving, cutting, and naming projects, and the other for editing the elements on the canvas. When beginning any project, configuring the machine you'll be working with is an indispensable step. Depending on the selected device, the tools can be automatically adjusted, streamlining the production or cutting process on the chosen material. Many of the options available in this menu are related to adjusting the size of elements, including flip, arrange, rotate, align, and more.

Subpanel 1: Project Characteristics
This subpanel facilitates navigation from the canvas to your profile, allows you to access your projects, and lets you send completed works for the cutting process. Specifically, it includes the Project name and My Projects. The Save Project option has been explained previously.

- **Machine**: This option provides a menu for selecting the type of device to be used. Choosing the correct machine is crucial, as it prompts the program to configure specific settings for the Cricut Joy, Maker, or Cricut Explore Machine.

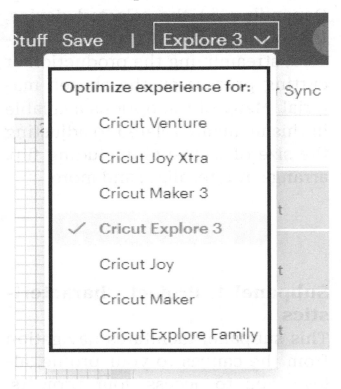

- **Toggle menu**: This option opens another menu packed with useful features for customization. You can change your profile image, account details, and manage your Cricut Access subscription. Other **vital functions** include **calibrating the machine and its blades**, as well as updating the device's firmware to ensure it doesn't have any security vulnerabilities.

- **Simple edits**: This feature provides a user-friendly way to make adjustments to images and resources. It introduces Anchors or corner points that appear when you click on images. These areas allow you to resize the image by clicking on them and adjusting the dimensions. It also includes a lock to maintain proportions and an X that removes the image entirely.

- **Make It**: This action finalizes your work and sends the design to virtual cutting "mats." A screenshot illustrates how all the design elements are arranged and grouped by color. Once you've defined the location and size of each part, you can proceed with the final cutting steps using the Cricut machine.

Important usage information: Even with a subscription, certain terms and conditions apply to the correct use and reproduction of the materials available in the library. Primarily, the illegal sale and distribution to third parties are prohibited, as well as the use of some images exclusively reserved for members. This option outlines Cricut's platform terms and protective policies for sales.

Subpanel 2: Edit Menu

This subpanel presents a range of advanced options for editing elements and customizing them to suit each user's needs. It provides actions to organize, edit, and customize fonts and images on the canvas.

Here are some of the functions found in the Edit subpanel:

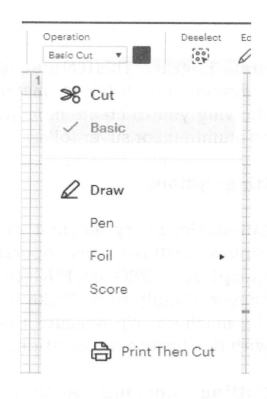

- **Undo and Redo**: These options allow you to correct any mistakes made on the canvas. The Undo button lets you backtrack to fix unintended deletions or modifications.

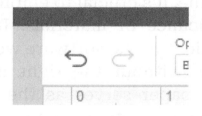

- **Operation**: Depending on the chosen machine before starting the project, this item configures cutter operations based on their type. You can assign basic cuts, perforations, corrugation, sheeting, engraving, standard printing, or cuts.

Drawing Options

- **Draw-Foil:** This option allows you to achieve stunning foil finishes, a recent addition to Cricut Design Space. It's an aluminum foil transfer kit, conveniently integrated into the application. You'll find options for fine, medium, and intricate finishes.

- **Draw-Pen**: With this option, you can write on Cricut designs. All you need are external devices or digital pens supported by the system. The pen's color outlines the canvas layers when the design is selected, and upon pressing the Make It button, Design Space will write or draw instead of cutting.

- **Draw-Engrave:** This feature enables engraving on different materials, allowing you to create monograms on aluminum or silver foils.

Cutting Options

- **Cut-Basic:** Every element on the canvas features this operation, except for JPEG or PNG format images. Simply press Make It, and the machine will execute the cut with this basic configuration.

- **Cutting-Punching:** Achieve the crisp tear-off effects often seen on tickets, coupons, and cards with perforating blades. These blades produce uniform, perfect cuts that make it easy to tear the material.

- **Cut-Wave:** Generating perfect lines can be challenging in Design Space, which is where this feature comes in. It creates wavy effects without requiring additional accessories like rotary or fine-tipped blades.

- **Score:** Similar to score lines, this attribute, when applied to a layer, makes elements appear dotted or dashed. It involves using a marker pen or marker wheel and pressing Make It. Instead of cutting, the machine now "scores" the materials in the tray.

Printing Options

- **Standard Print and Cut:** This feature is invaluable for cutting patterns. It draws the shapes and then cuts the material with precision.

- **Printing:** Ideal for those who want to ensure their design is error-free. You can connect to the printer and produce a pattern for verification before proceeding with cutting.

Supplies

In addition to mastering the software and general operation of the Cricut machine, it's crucial to emphasize the significance of materials. Becoming proficient in the software won't yield results without the right materials. While paper serves as the base for quicker projects, colored cardboard, cardboard, vinyl, and other readily available supplies can be expertly handled.

Regarding additional tools, having spare blades, both linear and corrugated, and a Cricut pen will make it easier to enhance your designs.

CHA PTER 5

HOW TO IMPORT IMAGES INTO CRICUT DESIGN SPACE

The starting point for any user is the vast array of images offered by Cricut Design Space in its gallery. Prepare to embark on an exciting journey in this chapter as we unveil the secrets of harnessing the power of program images and the art of importing your most cherished ones. Unleash your creativity and craft mesmerizing items that will leave both friends and potential customers utterly enchanted by your skills.

Exploring the Riches of the Cricut Library

The Design Space program provides users with a treasure trove of resources to fuel their creative endeavors. The Cricut Library alone boasts over 200,000 files, including photographs, elements, and templates, all primed for customization.

For those images that come with an additional cost, you have the liberty to use them before making a purchase, ensuring they seamlessly fit into your design. This is a handy detail you can leverage to your advantage.

To dive into this treasure trove, simply log in to Design Space and start a new project.

Note: On Mac desktop computers, you'll find the Images menu on the left side, while in the mobile app (for Android and iOS), it resides in the bottom corner of the screen.

- Upon opening this menu, a window unfolds, revealing a wealth of featured images from the Cricut Library.

- In the upper right corner, you'll spot a Search bar designed for locating items using keywords or codes.

Images Menu

When you navigate to the Images menu, you'll discover a Quick Menu offering a variety of search options.

- **Categories**: Easily select from free images, the most popular ones among the Cricut community, image sets, and more.

- **Themes**: Images are categorized according to the theme you desire, whether it's birthdays, anniversaries, seasons, and more.

Alternatively, you can simply click "Browse All Images" to explore the complete image library.

Browse All Images

Highlighted Categories	Subject	Graphics	Theme
Featured	Animals	Banners & Flags	Cards
Recently Added	Arts & Entertainment	Decorative Elements	Causes
Popular	Clothing & Accessories	Letters & Numbers	Celebrations
Free	Fantasy	Mandalas	Holidays
Image Sets	Food & Drink	Shapes	Organization
	Home & Garden	Symbols	Seasons
	Nature	Tattoos	Sympathy
	People	Zentangles	
	Phrases	Zodiac Signs	
	Places & Travel		
	Religion		
	Sports & Recreation		
	Structures		
	Transportation		
	Workplace & Professions		

- **Subjects**: Tailor your search by choosing images based on genres like animals, fantasy, sports, and more.

- **Graphics**: Quickly locate images by their graphic style, including tattoos, zodiac signs, and more.

By accessing this menu, you gain access to the vast array of images that the Cricut world offers. You can search for images by:

- **Free Images**

- **Editable Text**

- **Operation Type**
1. Cut only
2. Draw Only
3. Print and the Cut
4. Cut + Draw

- **Layers**
1. Single
2. Multi

- **Project Type**
1. For Watercolor Markers
2. Stencil
3. 3D
4. Cards
5. Etc

- **Material**
1. Acetate
2. Chipboard
3. Crepe Paper
4. Etc

- **Language**
1. Afrikaans
2. Arabic
3. Etc

- **Available Offline**
1. Downloaded (These are the images we imported)

- **Licensed Content**
1. Disney
2. Marvel
3. Etc

☐ Free

☐ Editable Text

My Stuff   +

Operation Type   +

Layers   +

Project Type   +

Material   +

Language   +

Available Offline   +

Licensed Content   +

Some useful options within this bar that will streamline your experience

- **Categories**: Clicking this option organizes library items based on the category you select, with pre-defined choices offered by the platform.

- **Cartridges**: Cricut cartridges are collections of images. Clicking this item unveils a list of over 400 cartridges, conveniently sorted alphabetically. This simplifies searches, allows for batch image selection, easy insertion into projects, and seamless editing as per your requirements.

Additional Actions Available in the Summary Option:

- **Image Mosaic:** This feature provides visualizations of the image displayed on the canvas.

- **Information:** As the name suggests, this item contains vital image data and other pertinent details, such as access levels (owner, subscriber, free, or available for purchase), the cartridge or image set, resource availability, assigned serial numbers, dates, times, formats, and more.

- **Cricut Access Content**: This section, accompanied by its symbols and characteristics, holds information about Cricut Access action plans, whether you're using a paid membership or the free version.

- **Upgraded Printable Images:** These resources are prepped for printing and cutting with the machine, featuring stylish decorative patterns. No configuration tweaks are needed to achieve beautiful designs.

- **The Bounding Box:** Selecting any element triggers the appearance of the Bounding Box, which, in turn, reveals the Quick Edit menu at each corner. Among the actions available in the Quick Edit menu are:
1. Deleting the image (Up + Left).
2. Rotating the image (Up + Right).
3. Locking or unlocking proportions (Down + Left).
4. Resizing (Down + Right).

How to import images in Cricut Design Space

Importing images into Cricut Design Space is remarkably simple. Navigate to the Upload menu and select "Upload Image" (you can also import a pattern fill).

Upload

🖼 Image	🔲 Pattern fill

Upload an image to use in designs.

Compatible file types: .jpg, .gif, .png, .heic, .bmp, .svg, or .dxf

(Upload Image)

Recent Uploads   View All

Next, click "Browse" to search for the image you wish to import. Alternatively, you can directly drag and drop your file onto the dotted screen.

The next step before importing is selecting the upload type, and finally, importing it into the Canvas area.

Drag & drop file here

or

Browse

.png, .jpg, .gif, .svg, .dxf, .heic or .bmp

The final step involves selecting the option that best corresponds to the complexity of your image. This ensures that you have the most suitable tools to work with your image.

Select image type

Your image will be uploaded as a single layer .

Select the option that best matches the complexity of your image. This ensures you get the best tools to work with your image.

Simple

High-contrast colors and transparent or monochrome background.

Moderately complex

Simple details and color, with good contrast between subject and background.

Complex

Fine detail, blended colors, or low contrast between subject and background. This image is more challenging to work with.

Specific Functions for Images

The following glossary of functions breaks down the essential actions applicable to images in Cricut Design Space projects, making it a breeze for Cricut enthusiasts and hobbyists to bring their custom designs to life.

Edit menu

- **Select All**: This action lets you manipulate all the elements on your canvas at once with a single click. For intricate creations with numerous layers, shapes, drawings, and images, individually handling them can be a hassle. Selecting everything saves valuable time.

- **Edit**: This function makes significant changes to elements and offers a dropdown menu with important options. It enables you to copy an element to create an exact duplicate, cut or delete the canvas to start fresh, and paste elements copied or cut from the canvas.

Offset menu

The Offset tool in Design Space allows you to create proportional outlines in fonts, photos, and shapes, adding a highlighted effect to elements that's perfect for stickers, vinyl pieces, and more. Here are some of its submenus:

- **Distance**: Specifies the measurement of the offset in numbers, with a maximum of one inch in any direction.

- **Corner**: Choose between round or square corners to achieve elegant finishes in your designs, perfect for projects like cards, edited photographs, and collages.

- **Weld Offsets**: This option is for those who prefer a single outline for their design, while deselecting it allows you to outline every detail.

Align menu

The Align options in Cricut Design Space help you organize selected elements on your canvas by aligning them in your chosen direction. Here are the submenus in this category:

- **Align Left**: Positions all selected elements perfectly aligned to the left

- **Align to Bottom**: Aligns elements to the bottom to determine their final placement

- **Align Right:** The rightmost element determines the final position of the rest of the selections

- **Center Horizontal**: Aligns resources horizontally, ideal for both text and images

- **Align Top**: Places selected elements at the top, next to the farthest element in that direction

- **Center**: Ensures even distribution, particularly useful for elements of the same size, allowing you to position them better on the canvas both vertically and horizontally

- **Center Vertically:** Ideal for organizing columns and ensuring proper alignment

Distribute menu

For this action to work, you need to select more than three elements. Pressing it evenly spaces the selected elements, greatly improving the design quality. Otherwise, moving each element one by one would be tedious and imprecise.

- **Distribute Horizontally**: Determines the spacing between elements by using elements on the left and right as reference points.

- **Distribute Vertically**: Similar to horizontal distribution, but it uses elements at the top and bottom as reference points to space the elements evenly.

Arrange menu

Designing in Cricut often involves working with layers, meaning that each element is placed in front of or behind others. The Arrange option helps you organize elements on the canvas.

- **Send to Background**: Moves an object or figure to the bottom of the canvas, placing it behind other elements.

- **Send to Front**: Places an object in front of other elements on the canvas.

- **Move Backward**: Moves the selected object one step backward without sending it to the bottom.

- **Move Forward**: Similar to Move Backward, but it moves the object one step forward.

Flip menu

The Flip option is essential for mirroring elements in your designs. It allows you to move an object while keeping its central anchor point. Cricut Design Space offers two options:

- **Flip Horizontal**: Creates a left-to-right mirrored effect.

- **Flip Vertical**: Achieves a similar effect vertically, creating a reflection-like effect often used for shadows.

Size menu

Size options are crucial when designing. Shapes and resources often come in default sizes that may not fit your vision or require resizing for improved results. The bounding box options are a simple way to deal with this, but when precision is essential, click the button and adjust the object's dimensions.

Remember to use the padlock function that appears when selecting an image. It allows you to lock or unlock the ratio, preventing distortions and preserving image quality. Other Options available on this menu:

- **Rotate**: Rotate elements from a specific angle, allowing you to set an anchor point and change the location from that point.
- **Position**: An advanced tool for selecting an object on the canvas and moving it by clicking on the desired location. It's excellent for aligning multiple objects quickly.

CHAPTER 6

SVG FILE AND CRICUT MACHINE

By now, you might be wondering about SVG files and their vital role in the world of Cricut machines. In this chapter, we'll delve into their significance and unravel everything you need to know. First, let's grasp what vector formats entail and why they're indispensable for Cricut Design Space in creating cut files that neatly divide your designs into layers based on color.

Regrettably, regardless of whether your file incorporates images, photos, or gradients, Cricut Design Space can no longer generate files with separate layers for each shape and color. Cricut machines rely on a code with instructions, akin to G-code, to execute various actions and achieve the desired cuts. To produce the instruction code for a specific cut, you must import a 2D design into Cricut's Design Space software.

This program is known for its compatibility with certain 2D file formats, including JPG, PNG, BMP, and GIF, along with the versatile scalable vector graphics format, SVG. Developed in 1999 for web image storage and 2D data in vector format, SVG allows you to scale 2D digital assets like drawings and images up or down without sacrificing quality, thanks to its geometric, rather than pixel-based, attributes.

About SVG Files

SVG stands for Scalable Vector Graphics. It is a widely used vector image format for two-dimensional graphics with support for interactivity and animation. SVG files are based on XML (Extensible Markup Language) and are used to describe the shapes, colors, and layout of images rather than relying on a grid of pixels like raster image formats (e.g., JPEG, PNG, GIF). SVG files are resolution-independent, meaning they can be scaled up or down without losing image quality. SVG files are commonly used for a variety of purposes, including web graphics, logos, icons, charts, maps, and illustrations. SVG files are ubiquitous on the internet, and their utility extends beyond just Cricut machines to similar CNC cutting devices. While many platforms host SVG files, the best ones stand out for the following reasons:

Considerations When Choosing a Design:

- **Abundant Variety**: Look for platforms offering a wide range of designs. While some websites provide only a handful of free designs, the top repositories boast hundreds, if not thousands, of files spanning various genres and applications.

- **User-Friendly Interface**: A clean, user-friendly interface is crucial for easy navigation. Efficient navigation tools like search bars and filters streamline the process of finding the perfect template.

Exploring Free Design Websites

Now, let's explore some highly recommended sites for discovering free designs.

1. **Free SVG**: This user-friendly SVG file library offers over 164,000 free and downloadable designs. No account is required, and designs are categorized using tags, encompassing everything from flowers, plants, animals, signage, to everyday items. It even allows you to select your preferred file size for downloads, offering SVG or PNG formats in both small (300 pixels) and large (2400 pixels) sizes.

2. **SVG Repo**: This site serves as a repository for SVG files, boasting an impressive collection of over 300,000 free vectors without the need for subscriptions or fees.

3. **Craft House SVG**: With around 580 free SVG files, Craft House SVG is a great option for Cricut enthusiasts. It covers designs such as plants, animals, and celebratory phrases. For those seeking even more options, the site offers additional SVGs available for individual purchase or in bundles.

4. **DesignBundles**: While this site provides approximately 560 free files, it also features bundles of SVG files available for download. The number of SVG files surpasses the free selection since many are included in these design bundles.

5. **SVG Designs**: This subscription-based website allows you to download three free SVG files weekly without a subscription fee. It offers a sizable selection, with nearly 500 free designs. Additionally, it hosts paid designs, many of which are contributed by individual users rather than the company.

6. **Printable Cuttable Creatables**: This repository of SVG files boasts over 380 free designs, including logos, icons, and text. Beyond the free options, the site also provides premium designs. One of its notable advantages is that designs are downloaded as ZIP files containing various file formats, such as SVG, PDF, DXF, and PNG. The user interface is fairly intuitive and well-organized, although the category list can appear a bit cluttered.

7. **Dreaming Tree**: Dreaming Tree offers at least 150 free projects, with even more available for purchase. The site provides video tutorials and information on required supplies and compatible machines. Most projects are compatible with Cricut machines, making it a valuable resource for enthusiasts.

8. **Simply Crafty SVGs**: This platform offers both standard 2D options and intriguing "3D SVG files." The 3D SVGs are project collections that include multiple SVG designs for assembling 3D objects, such as lamps or chocolate egg cartons. The designs cover a wide range and include boxes, bags, cards, and Christmas decorations. There are around 109 free designs available, encompassing various gifts, boxes, cards, ornaments, and other creative projects.

BONUS FOR YOU

Discover a treasure trove of complimentary goodies waiting just for you within these pages. Unlock your first delightful surprise with a simple scan of this QR code. Dive into a world of freely available SVG files, yours for the taking!

CHAPTER 7

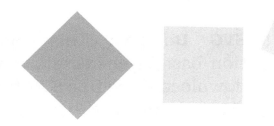

WORKING WITH COLORS

After delving into the fundamentals and discovering the special features tucked away in Cricut Design Space, brace yourself for a vivid exploration of color manipulation in this chapter.

Where to Work With Colors in Design Space?

You'll find your color-crafting haven within the image editing realm. Here, the buttons that wield the magic of hues await your command:

- **Material Colors Option**: Effortlessly harmonize your project's shades by tapping into the Material color palette. A quick checkmark here, and your chosen layer will proudly wear the selected hue.

- **Common Colors**: Dive into a realm of established color schemes, carefully curated for your artistic journey.

- **Advanced**: This option grants you the power to input a hexadecimal color code of your choice or embark on a chromatic adventure with the custom color picker and slider.

- **Drawing Attributes**: When the "Draw" line type is your weapon of choice, select a Cricut pen type from the drop-down menu. Behold a list of vibrant colors at your disposal for that chosen pen type.

- **Fill**: Choose a color or pattern to grace your Print and Cut image layer. Accessible when the Cut Line Type is chosen.

- **No Fill**: This signifies that no fill adorns the selected image layer, earmarking it for slicing. In the event a fill is applied, you can effortlessly revert the layer to a cut-only state.

- **Print**: Opt for "Print" to unveil a world of color and pattern choices, seamlessly followed by the precision of cutting.

- **Fill Sample**: Elevate your image layer's fill game with the Fill Sample option, introducing additional fill properties.

- **Fill Attributes**: Before embracing the Print, then Cut journey, pick your photo's color or pattern fills.

- **Original Work**: Revert your Print layer's fill status back to its pristine state with this option.

- **Color**: Exercise your creative autonomy by selecting print and material colors for cutting. Dive deep with the custom color picker via hexadecimal input or pick from a palette of fundamental colors.

- **Pattern**: Infuse your text or image layer with a captivating pattern fill. Focus your pattern search with a color filter, then fine-tune the pattern's scale and orientation using the Edit Pattern tools.

- **Select All/Unselect**: In the Layout, these options offer the superpower of simultaneous selection or deselection of all elements.

Color Synchronization Tool

Behold the Color Sync tool, perched enticingly on the left side of your canvas. In its concise menu, it promises simplicity.

Drag and drop different layers together to synchronize their hues. This nifty feature streamlines intricate projects with multiple colors, ensuring you cut all elements of the same color in one graceful sweep. Time-saving brilliance, especially when juggling diverse materials!

Can You Alter Pen Colors in Cricut Design Space?

You're not alone in wondering. The answer is a resounding "yes." Changing the pen type is a breeze; just select the drop-down box within that menu. The pen type you opt for dictates the thickness of lines in your image. Get ready to paint your creativity with a spectrum of possibilities!

CHAPTER 8

CRAFTING SUCCESS: YOUR CRICUT DESIGN SPACE PROJECT GUIDE

When diving into your creative journey with the Cricut program, it's essential to remember some key steps and expert tips.

Let's break them down for you:

1. Launching into Cricut Design Space

- To embark on your crafting adventure, fire up the application or program on your chosen device.
- At the top of the screen, you'll spot your canvas options, including the crucial "My Projects" category.
- Keep an eye out for a box sporting a + sign enclosed in a circle that reads "New Project."

Pro Tip: For extra guidance, Cricut offers a treasure trove of video tutorials covering various machines and techniques.

2. Mastering the Main Menu Functions

Familiarize yourself with the functions at your disposal in your inaugural Cricut project:

- **Calibration**: This feature fine-tunes your blade for precise cuts, particularly handy when deploying the Print then Cut function or Cricut Maker's blade.
- **Go to Settings**: This menu lets you choose grid preferences—full, partial, or none—as well as whether you prefer metric or imperial measurements.
- **My Projects**: Located right at the top row, this is where all your saved projects reside. You can peruse them all by hitting the green "View All" button and continue editing or crafting.
- **Ready to Make**: Explore a selection of pre-designed projects that fellow crafters have deemed fantastic.

3. Choosing Your Machine Type

- In the top-right corner of your window, you'll find the option to specify your machine type. This choice allows you to customize settings based on your specific machine.
- The machine selection window offers seven menu options: New, Templates, Project, Images, Text, Shapes, and Upload.

4. Exploring Key Functions

Delve into the primary functions you'll likely use in your Cricut project:

- **Templates**: Perfect for visualizing how your design will appear on your chosen material, aiding with spacing and sizing.
- **Images**: Access Cricut's vast image library to select from thousands of images to incorporate into your project.
- **Filters for Efficient Image Search**: Refine your search with the Filters tool to avoid sifting through endless options. Simply click the + sign next to each filter to open it, click the box to choose a filter, and voilà—your search becomes more precise.

5. Tailoring Line Types to Your Machine

- Your choice of line type depends on your Cricut machine. Different pens and blades produce distinct line styles.
- The Cricut Maker, for instance, offers eight line types, including Cut, Marking, Draw, Engrave, and more. Each corresponds to specific tools used for different crafting magic.

6. Making the Most of the Attach Tool

The Attach tool is a handy feature to familiarize yourself with. It's particularly useful when working with printable images, ensuring elements stay together as intended.

7. Streamlining Your Craft with the Outline Tool

The Outline tool is an often-overlooked gem. It allows you to remove or conceal unwanted portions or cut lines, especially useful when dealing with intricate designs.

TABLE OF CONTENTS

Chapter 1
Cricut Blade

97

104

Chapter 2
The Best Accessories
You Can't Live Without

BOOK 2 - CRICUT ACCESSORIES

CHAPTER 1

CRICUT BLADE

Welcome to this chapter, where we'll dive into the world of Cricut machine accessories and the remarkable tools they bring to your creative endeavors. Prepare to be inspired!

Printing and Cutting in the Design Space

The Print, then Cut option allows you to infuse your creations with a vibrant spectrum of colors, marking the beginning of the enchantment. Your home printer can be employed to print your photographs, and then you can simply sit back and witness the precision with which the computer cuts the images.

The best part is that no scissors are required. In this functionality, the quality and capability of the accessories truly shine. Once you insert printable images into your project or switch the operation type of your images to Print, select "Do it," and immediately witness the magic unfold.

Types of Cricut Blades

It's crucial to acquaint yourself with the various types of blades before commencing any project. Cricut plotters can be categorized into two main groups. On one hand, you have the Maker and the Explore, which share many accessories and blades. On the other hand, there's the Cricut Joy, a machine with its own set of accessories that are incompatible with the Maker or the Explore.

Before delving into the specifics of Cricut blades, bear in mind that each blade requires its adapter, typically color-matching the blade for easy identification of the necessary blade holder.

It's a well-established fact that blades or tips deteriorate over time, but you can always opt for the well-known spare parts or replacements. However, it's important to note that these replacements do not include a blade holder; you only need to replace the tip.

Now, let's delve into the various types of blades, analyzing their purposes and determining which types of machines these blades are compatible with.

Cricut Joy Blade and Housing

This blade is versatile, suitable for a wide range of crafting projects, and compatible with various crafting materials, including Cricut Joy's specialty materials like Smart Materials. With this blade, you can infuse a distinctive foil shine into all your projects, making it ideal for use with foil transfer sheets. This tool is compatible with a variety of materials, including paper, cardstock up to 270 grams, photo paper, and the "Smart Label Writable" vinyl line.

Blades for the Cricut Joy

Despite being the smallest machine in the brand's lineup, the Cricut Joy packs a punch when it comes to functionality. As previously mentioned, it has its own unique set of blades that are exclusive to this machine.

Premium Fine Tip Blade

This is the go-to blade for intricate and detailed cuts. Thanks to its fine tip, it delivers highly precise cuts, even for the most intrica-

te designs. This blade is compatible with hot-melt adhesive vinyl, paper, cardboard, vinyl, and other thin to medium-weight materials.

Stabilized Fabric Blade

Undoubtedly, the best choice for complex cuts, especially when working with interlaced fabrics, felt, or fabrics with heat-adhesive vinyl coatings. You can identify it by its pink color, which matches the special fabric cutting mat, also in pink.

Deep Cutting Blade

Constructed from durable, hard steel, this blade is designed for tackling complex cuts in materials up to 1.5 mm thick, such as thick cardboard (300 grams—10.5 oz), cardboard, Eva foam, glitter vinyl, rigid felt, and certain fabrics.

Foil Transfer Tool

This is one of the most well-known blades, used for adding foil details to various materials. It includes three interchangeable tips (fine, medium, and coarse), allowing you to work on a wide range of designs, from the simplest to the most intricate.

QuickSwap Tools

Also known as a housing or blade holder, this accessory enables you to swiftly change the blade or tip for your specific needs. It includes tools for creating folding lines, an embossing tip, an engraving tip, a piercing blade, and a wavy blade, each offering great versatility for your projects.

Marking Wheel and Double Marking Wheel

These two wheels apply ten times more pressure than a marking pencil, making them the perfect choice for creating sharp creases. The marking wheel, in particular, creates a single crease and two parallel lines, ideal for marking denser materials like thicker cardboard or cardboard.

Engraving Tip

This tip allows you to create personalized engravings, texts, or drawings on thin metal sheets, leather, soft metals, acrylics, or plastics.

Embossing Tip

If you're looking to add embossed designs, this tool is essential for adding dimension and relief to your projects.

Perforating Blade

This blade generates evenly distributed perforation lines, making it easy to tear cleanly. It's perfect for creating curved shapes.

Keep in mind that this blade should be used with the FabricGrip mat, which is made of a stronger and denser material. It's also recommended that designs made with this blade be at least 1.9 cm (0.74 in) or larger due to the blade's shape. Because of its sliding action, the blade may leave a mark on the mat and reduce its lifespan if used for very tight turns.

Rotary Blade

Compatible exclusively with the Cricut Maker, this blade delivers clean, precise, and customizable cuts in various materials, including fabrics. Its sliding movement allows you to cut soft, less dense fabrics without the need for protective materials. Additionally, you can use it to cut other materials such as tissue paper or cork.

Wavy Blade

This is one of the most unique tools, allowing you to bring your designs to life by creating decorative edges on any project. It can be used on most materials, including paper, vinyl, and cardboard, among others.

Extra Deep Knife Blade

If you own a Cricut Maker and need to make detailed cuts in thick materials, this blade is ideal for the job. It can slice through corrugated paper, balsa wood, and chipboard with its 2.4 mm blade.

Frequently Asked Questions About Blades

If something is unclear, here are some frequently asked questions:

Can I always use the fabric blade when cutting stabilized fabric?

No, you should always use the rotary blade if you have a Cricut Maker. The other blade, called the "stabilized fabric" blade, is designed specifically for fabrics that have been previously interlaced; it doesn't perform well with untreated fabric. Using the rotary blade ensures clean cuts on any fabric, whether stabilized or not.

Please note that the stabilized fabric blade is intended for the Explore series machines. If you have a Maker, you won't need it.

Can I use any fabric blade?

The stabilized fabric blade is the same as the fine-point blade; the only difference is the color. You can use any new fine-point blade and designate it for fabric use only.

Can I use the deep-cut blade in the normal blade holder?

No, you cannot use the deep-cut blade in the normal blade holder because the deep-cut blade holder is slightly shorter than the fine-point blade holder. This design allows more of the cutting edge to be exposed and provides more room for cutting through thicker materials.

However, if you're not cutting thick materials and only need the cutting edge for detailed cuts, you can use deep-cut blade replacements in the silver, gold, or pink blade holder.

Do I need the deep-cut blade if I have the knife blade?

No, you don't need the deep-cut blade if you plan to cut very dense materials. Additionally, if you're cutting rubber, the deep-cut blade isn't necessary.

However, if you're working with rubber or Eva foam, a thinner blade is more suitable. The sharp edge can also deliver excellent results for intricate or detailed designs on standard materials like paper and vinyl.
What is the difference between the normal blade and the premium blade?

The premium blade offers greater durability and resistance compared to the standard blade. Furthermore, the silver and gold blades are identical and can be used interchangeably.

THE BEST ACCESSORIES YOU CAN'T LIVE WITHOUT

As is well-known, Cricut machines come with many accessories that perform exceptionally well. But there are always some that are essential, and you'll discover them in this chapter.

Machine Mat

The machine mat is undoubtedly one of the best accessories for Cricut users. It is also referred to as a mat or cutting. There are three types commonly used:

Regular Adhesive Mat or "Standard-Grip" (Green)

This type of mat is perhaps the most widely used. It works perfectly with various medium weight materials, including cardboard, textured paper, vinyl, patterned paper, heat transfer vinyl and infusible transfer sheets. The mat ensures a solid interface between the material and the Cricut plotter, ensuring the material stays in place during the cutting process,

making it easy to remove the cut pieces.

It's advisable to cover the mat with a transparent sheet when not in use to protect it. Conduct an easy test cut paper pieces extending its lifespan.

Strong-grip Mat (Purple)

The "Strong-grip" mat provides an exceptionally strong adhesive, ideal for heavy materials such as thick cardboard, glitter cardstock, magnetic materials, reinforced fabrics, balsa wood, and more.

It is also perfect for use with the Cricut Maker's Knife Blade, allowing thicker wood and 3D foam types. You can even create interior cardstock items with this mat and blade combination. Each adds a premium cushion giving a beautiful bevel, to prevent any potential damage.

103

CHAPTER 2

THE BEST ACCESSORIES YOU CAN'T LIVE WITHOUT

As is well-known, Cricut machines come with many accessories that perform exceptionally well, but there are always some that are essential, and you'll discover them in this chapter.

Machine Mat

The machine mat is undoubtedly one of the best accessories for Cricut users. It is also referred to as a mat or matting. There are three types commonly used:

Regular Adhesive Mat or "Standard-Grip" (Green)

This type of mat is perhaps the most widely used. It works perfectly with various medium-weight materials, including cardboard, textured paper, vinyl, patterned paper, heat transfer vinyl, and ink-infusible transfer sheets. The mat acts as a vital interface between the material and the Cricut plotter, ensuring the material stays in place during the cutting process and making it easier to remove the cut pieces.

It's advisable to cover the mat with a transparent sheet when not in use to protect it from dust and any remaining cut paper pieces, extending its lifespan.

StrongGrip Mat (Purple)

The StrongGrip mat provides an exceptionally sticky surface, ideal for heavy materials such as thick cardboard, glitter cardstock, magnetic materials, reinforced fabrics, balsa wood, and more.

It is also perfect for use with the Cricut Maker's Knife Blade for cutting thick wood and foam paper. You can even create interior cardstock frames with this mat and blade combination. For added protection, consider using a transparent cover to prevent any potential damage.

Soft Adhesive Mat or "LightGrip" (Blue)

The LightGrip mat features sufficient adhesive strength to secure lightweight materials like printer papers, vellum, thin scrapbook papers, and washi sheets. It's an excellent choice for materials that don't require strong adhesion. As with the other mats, using a transparent protector is recommended to safeguard the mat's surface. A spatula can be handy for removing cut photos, and a scraper helps eliminate any excess bits. And, of course, it's advisable to use the recommended material for each type of mat.

FabricGrip Mat (Pink)

This mat is specially designed for fabrics and boasts a lightly adhering surface, making it ideal for various fabric types. What's more, it doesn't leave any glue residue on the fabric. If you have a passion for sewing, this mat is perfect for holding fabrics securely during the cutting process, and they can be easily removed once cut. It's constructed from strong yet flexible material that can withstand the pressure of cutting blades. Suitable materials for this mat include the stabilizing fabrics for the Cricut Explore and non-reinforced fabrics for the Cricut Maker. These mats are indispensable tools for your Cricut machine, each designed to optimize your crafting experience depending on the materials you're working with. Happy crafting!

How to Use the Mats

1. **Prepare the Fabric:** Begin by cutting the fabric to the size you need, ensuring it fits within the mat's dimensions so that it doesn't extend beyond the bonding area. If any part of the fabric is left outside the adhesive area, you can slide it under the wide rubber rollers on either side of the roller bar and hook it into the machine. It's also a good practice to iron the fabric if it's excessively wrinkled. Folds or bubbles can lead to inaccurate cuts, so the fabric should lie flat on the mat.

2. **Place the Fabric on the Mat:** The Design Space app can assist you in correctly aligning the fabric based on the warp's direction. "Warp" refers to the threads running parallel to the fabric's edge. If the piece number is vertical, position the mat so that the number runs from top to bottom. If the numbers are offset to one side, place the fabric on the mat so that the warp runs from right to left. Place the printed side face down on the mat to make it easier to see the fabric marker's traces. However, if your fabric doesn't have a distinct "pretty" side, use the side you want to showcase.

3. **Secure It in Place:** Position the fabric on the adhesive area of the mat and press it down firmly with your hands. If you notice any loose threads or inadequate adhesion, use a roller to secure it further. A note of caution: when working with elastic fabrics, avoid stretching them while adhering, as this could cause wrinkling or distortion during cutting. If you observe any wrinkles or stretching, gently lift and reposition the fabric.

4. **Select the Appropriate Blade:** In Design Space, you have the option to choose the appropriate blade based on your selected material. For the FabricGrip mat, the rotary blade or stabilized fabric blade is ideal.

5. **Remove the Fabric:** Once the cutting process is complete, it's advisable to remove the excess fabric. Avoid excessive handling of the adhesive side, as the grease from your hands can reduce its effectiveness. You can use a pair of wide-tipped tweezers to lift the fabric. For fabrics with loose weaves that tend to fray, a spatula can be used to remove the cuttings from the mat.

These cutting mats are available in two sizes: 12" x 12" and 12" x 24". The choice between them depends on the scale of your projects. It's worth noting that using adhesive spray to restore stickiness is not recommended, as the exact adhesive composition is unknown, and it may not be suitable for all materials. Cricut has designed these mats with precision to ensure you can match the right one with each material, guaranteeing precise and perfect results.

For those who haven't yet acquired a cutting plotter, the fabric mat and soft adhesive mat are already included when you purchase the pink or champagne Cricut Maker. The Cricut Explore Air 2 comes with a soft adhesive mat only.

Card Mat

The term "card mat" refers to the Cricut Joy's card mat. The Joy Card Mat is a reusable mat specifically designed for card making. It's perfect for quickly customizing cards for occasions such as birthdays, weddings, parties, and more. Cricut Joy's card-making kits, known as "Insert Cards," make it easy to die-cut your cards even when folded, without damaging the cardstock. You can also enhance your cards with cardstock featuring special effects to highlight the cut-out message.

XL Scraper

The XL Scraper is undoubtedly a valuable tool for quickly applying larger projects to surfaces and cleaning cutting mats. It excels at working with vinyl, cleaning your cutting mats, and handling other surfaces. Additionally, it's highly effective at cleaning large areas and applying materials to larger surfaces. This tool is compatible with all electronic cutting machines manufactured by Cricut. In case you weren't aware, the Cricut scraper is specifically designed to remove waste from cutting mats, thus extending the mat's lifespan. Moreover, it can be used to smooth materials on the mat, eliminate creases and air bubbles, and polish materials like vinyl.

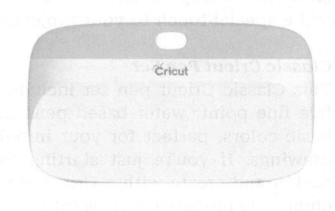

Cricut Pens

Now, let's talk about another essential tool—Cricut pens. These pens come in various ink types, including fine-point pens, gel pens, markers, and more, allowing you to add typography, logo designs, and artwork to cards, gifts, and other creative projects. The larger Cricut machines, the Maker and Explore series, also come with interchangeable pens that can be used with any machine. If you own the more compact and portable Cricut Joy, it features a dedicated pen line. However, other companies also offer pens designed for use with Cricut machines, and you can even purchase an adapter to use your regular pens with the machine.

The Cricut Maker or Explorer Pens

Meet the lineup of pens that will add a special touch to your projects:

Classic Cricut Pen Set
This Classic Cricut pen set includes five fine-point, water-based pens in basic colors, perfect for your initial drawings. If you're just starting to sketch and create with a Cricut machine, you probably don't want to invest heavily in a comprehensive pen collection right away.

These pens are ideal for crafting party invitations and decorations or adding a handwritten appearance to any project. The ink dries completely in just 24 hours, resulting in a lasting pattern.

- Thickness: 0.4 mm
- Suitable for all projects

Cricut Opaque Gel Pens
Cricut's new opaque gel pens come in eye-catching pink, white, orange, blue, and yellow and are designed to work on dark materials, including stickers, cards, and vinyl. You can create stunning designs, illustrations, and messages with these pens. Additionally, they work well on light materials.

- Thickness: 1.0 mm
- Great for art projects

Cricut Glitter Gel Pens
Elevate your art and cards with Cricut's new glitter gel pens, available in a range of rainbow colors: red, orange, yellow, green, blue, purple, pink, light blue, brown, and black. These pens provide a smooth finish with sparkling effects to enhance your cards and invitations. They are also perfect for creating intricate art, with 0.8mm nibs for precise, clean line art.

These pens are excellent for experimenting and having fun.

- Thickness: 0.8 mm
- Ideal for cards and gifts

Cricut Ultimate Fine Point Pen Set

The ultimate fine point pen set from Cricut includes 30 pens with a 0.4mm tip, available in various colors. This set allows you to add phrases to scrapbook pages, frame art, or personalize cards and invitations with handwritten script. For frequent Cricut users, collector packs offer substantial cost savings compared to purchasing several smaller packs of five pens.

- Thickness: 0.4 mm
- Perfect for cards and illustrations

Cricut Extra-Fine Point Pen Set

The Cricut Ultimate extra-fine point pen collection offers a variety of colors, but the tips are smaller at 0.3 mm. These pens are particularly useful for writing or drawing on smaller craft projects and materials, such as labels or gift tags. They are fantastic for occasions when you want to give invitations a handcrafted feel.

- Thickness: 0.3 mm
- Ideal for labels and gift cards

Cricut Gel Pen Set

Cricut gel pens are perfect for adding a touch of elegance to your projects.

They have a 1.0mm thickness and feature a twist ball instead of a felt tip. It's not recommended to use them on glossy or textured materials as they may appear bolder and brighter. However, they work wonderfully for adding flair to paper and card projects. These pens are available in complementary color sets, and purchasing larger multipacks leads to long-term savings.

- Thickness: 1.0 mm
- Great for invitations and cards

Martha Stewart Glitter Gel Pen Set by Cricut

Introducing the Martha Stewart Glitter Gel Pen Set by Cricut, which adds an extra sparkle to your creations. This set, inspired by the renowned craftsman Martha Stewart, features three colors: gold, silver, and a deeper metallic gray. These pens provide a distinctive touch to wedding invitations and other special projects. What's even better is that they become permanent after drying, are water-based, acid-free, non-toxic, and safe for design and creativity. These unique gel pens are fantastic and enjoyable to use.

- Thickness: 0.8 mm
- Ideal for special invitations

Cricut Washable Fabric Pen

As the name suggests, the Cricut washable fabric pen is designed for fabric. You may often find the need to mark your fabric with drawings before cutting, and being able to erase those marks is essential. This pen simplifies the less enjoyable aspects of sewing, such as pattern marking and fabric cutting. It's a handy tool for using sewing designs with the Cricut Maker. It's easy to control with Cricut Design Space, but it's primarily intended for use on cotton.

- Thickness: 1 mm
- Suitable for fabric and garment designs

Cricut Assorted Pen Set

The Cricut assorted pen set allows you to vary the thickness of text and artwork in your creations. This is especially useful when crafting calligraphy text designs. The set includes three different thicknesses, available in black and silver: two extra-fine 0.3 mm Cricut pens, one 1 mm pen, and two 2 mm calligraphy pens. This variety allows you to select the best pen for your design, whether it's a card, banner, or something else. These pens are a valuable addition, particularly if you're creating labels for your products for branding and customer delivery.

- Thickness: 0.3mm, 1mm, 2mm
- Perfect for calligraphy

Cricut Infusible Ink Markers

The latest additions to the Cricut range are Infusible Ink markers and felt-tip pens. They use a heat-activated method to apply specially formulated ink to fabrics like T-shirts, bags, and more. Although they can be used on other materials, Cricut recommends their heat presses, as they offer a variety of T-shirts, bags, coasters, and mugs that have been proven to work well with Infusible Ink products. These markers are convenient, simple, and a preferred choice for permanent transfers that won't bleed, wrinkle, or crack, making them perfect for T-shirts and other materials.

- Thickness: 1.0 mm or 0.4 mm
- Suitable for fabric prints

Craft World 0.4 Tip Fine Point Pens

Craft World's 0.4 tip fine point pens offer an excellent alternative to Cricut pens. Many companies manufacture pens designed to fit Cricut machines, but Cricut pens can be expensive, especially with regular use. This multipack from Craft World is a reliable choice for the Cricut Maker and Cricut Joy, offering 30 pens in various colors. However, it's worth noting that these pens may not be as vibrant as Cricut pens. Typically, they come with a sturdy plastic base to keep the pens secure and hygienic.

- Thickness: 0.4 mm
- Great for general use

Craverland Pen Adapters for Cricut

If you opt for non-Cricut pens, you'll need Craverland pen adapters. This collection includes 40 adapters designed for various popular pen brands, including Sharpie, Crayola, Papermate, Stabilo, Staedtler, BIC, and Cricut. It's important to note that Cricut does not officially support these adapters, and using pens other than Cricut's may void your machine's warranty. Therefore, consider carefully before using an adapter.

- Various thicknesses
- Not recommended for use with non-Cricut pens

Cricut Pens for Cricut Joy

These are the Cricut pens designed for the Cricut Joy:

Cricut Joy Pens

It is widely known that the Cricut Joy machine is the smallest and most portable in the Cricut lineup. It also offers a line of official, smaller Cricut Joy pens. These pens are a bit pricey but of high quality, making them among the top choices for Cricut Maker and Cricut Explore users who want to experiment with cutting out words and drawings without a significant investment.

- Thickness: 0.3 mm
- Suitable for beginners

Cricut Joy Glitter Gel Pens

These are the Glitter Gel pens produced by Cricut for the Maker and Explore machines but adapted to fit the Cricut Joy (although they have the same 0.8 mm tip size). These pens are typically available in the same colors as the range for the larger craft machines: red, orange, yellow, green, blue, purple, pink, light blue, brown, and black.

The Cricut Joy breaks the norm by including 10 pens in the Glitter Gel pen set for Cricut's small, portable craft machine. This offers great value, and the smooth, flowing finish these pens provide will give your cards, decals, and paper crafts a high-quality finish.

- Thickness: 0.8 mm
- Ideal for cards, stickers, and labels

Cricut Joy Gel Pen Assorted Pack

For the price, this is the best Cricut Joy pen set available. Unfortunately, unlike Cricut pens for the Maker and Explore that come in packs of five, fifteen, and thirty, Cricut Joy pens are only available in sets of three. This means that if you want to use a variety of colors and styles, Cricut Joy pens can quickly become expensive.

Thankfully, you can save money by purchasing this gel pen set instead of buying the four individual packs of three separately. Additionally, you get two different thicknesses that can add variety to your card designs, doodles, and sketches.

- Thickness: 1.0 mm, 0.8 mm
- Great for regular use with more color options

Cricut Joy Metallic Markers
Cricut Joy metallic markers are an excellent choice for writing on dark cardstock or paper as they allow you to create striking contrasts with bold text. These markers, with a 1.0 mm tip, are not suited for small print but look fantastic when used in larger sizes on cards, flyers, or event invitations.

There are two different packs, each including a silver marker.

One pack pairs it with violet and copper colors, while the other includes gold and a shimmering metallic blue. Both options provide a beautiful and elegant design alternative for any project you have in mind.

- Thickness: 1.0 mm
- Ideal for event invitations

Cricut Joy Infusible Ink Pens
Cricut Joy Pens with infusible ink are a valuable addition to the Cricut accessory lineup. As mentioned in our list of the top Cricut pens for the Maker and Explore machines, Cricut has produced several Infusible Ink pens designed exclusively for use with the Cricut EasyPress to print on fabrics.

One drawback of Cricut Joy is that each box contains only three pens. Consequently, if you need to use a variety of colors, even though there are numerous color combinations available, it can get quite expensive.

- Thickness: 0.3 mm
- Ideal for textile designs

Xinart Double-Ended Pens for Cricut Joy
In addition to offering 33 colors, the double-ended Xinart pens for Cricut Joy also come in two different thicknesses.

They offer one of the widest ranges of colors among Cricut pen sets. Despite the extensive variety, some colors may still be hard to find.

Considering that official Cricut Joy pens are only available in sets of three, this package offers great value.

- Thickness: 0.4 mm and 1.0 mm (double-ended)
- Great for general crafts

Applicator and Remover Set
This two-in-one tool set extends the life of your Cricut mat and is typically used with the Cricut Maker. You can easily identify the Cricut applicator and remover set by the white-colored remover. The Cricut Roller firmly adheres materials to your cutting mat and is perfect for pressing fabric, vinyl, hot melt vinyl, and inking pads for making prints. It's a must-have tool if you own a Cricut Maker.

Scoring Stylus
The scoring stylus, or scoring pen, is a valuable tool for creating folding marks with your Cricut machine. For those of you who own an Explore machine, rest assured that it is compatible with your machine.

By default, whenever you include any scoring lines in your designs, and in the case of owning a Maker, the Design Space application will prompt you to load the scoring stylus. This tool is used to mark fold lines on various items such as cards, envelopes, boxes, 3D crafts, and more. Cricut cutting machines seamlessly handle both the scoring pen and the cutting blade, allowing for both marking and cutting in a single motion.

Ruler
This accessory provides quick, clean cuts with a safety guard and easy-to-read measurements. It's an 18 cm aluminum cutting ruler with a stainless steel edge. Its mint color adds a touch of style to your crafting, and it simplifies cutting, making it fast, easy, and safe. The laser-etched measuring markings ensure legibility and clarity throughout the lifespan of your project.

Weeder

The weeder tool is perfect for removing small cuts, including single vinyl and iron-on negatives from the backing sheet or for extracting small negatives from a cut cardstock image. This versatile tool, known as the weeder, is great for picking up small pieces, making them ready for easy application to your projects. You can use the tool's tip for punching tiny holes or its curved portion to secure delicate cuts on the carrier sheet while removing surrounding parts.

TrueControl Kit

The TrueControl knife set can significantly assist you in your crafting endeavors. This kit includes five extra blades and a convenient storage cartridge for keeping track of and disposing of worn blades. It provides you with enhanced control and superior results. With its various components, you can work on a wide range of materials, including paper, cardstock, thin plastics, canvas, and more, with remarkable precision and accuracy. It comprises:

- TrueControl Cutter.
- 5 high-quality steel blades in a storage cartridge.
- Blades crafted from high-quality steel, featuring sharp edges and piercing tips.

Basic Tool Kit (to buy in bulk everything you need to get started)

These essential starter tools are indispensable for your Cricut crafting session:

Scissors

Cricut Scissors feature stainless steel blades that have been hardened for strength, ensuring smooth and consistent cutting on all materials.

The micro-pointed blade enhances accuracy, and the ejectable sheath offers blade protection.

Tweezers

Cricut tweezers feature a reverse-grip design that allows for easy lifting and securing in one motion. Squeeze the handle to open and release pressure to close. The smooth inside points help protect your fabrics from tearing or other damage.

Spatula

The spatula assists in removing extra parts around a cut image, especially helpful for vinyl images and hot melt vinyl projects. It's also perfect for delicately removing tiny negative parts from cut cardstock images.

Scraper and Scraper Set

These scraper tools simplify your work, aiding in lifting your images from the Cricut machine's surface. These tools are prepped and ready to use, so you only need to focus on removing your artwork from the Cricut machine. The Cricut scraper tool excels at removing residue from edges, while the squeegee helps with precise design application. They enable you to complete projects quickly without ripping or tearing, resulting in professional-quality work.

Cricut Spatula and Scraper

These two tools are ideal for easy use with your Cricut machine. They make it easy to tear and clean cutting mats. The spatula even comes with an interchangeable cap in various colors, and the craft scraper tool is imported.

Rotary Cutter

Cutting fabric with your Cricut machine is faster, easier, and more enjoyable with a rotary cutter. It features a quick-release button for safe blade activation when not in use and an ergonomic grip that ensures precise control. Cricut rotary cutters are suitable for both right- and left-handed individuals. The superior carbon steel rotary blades, available in sizes 45 mm and 60 mm, deliver precise, controlled cuts on various materials. The tool includes a quick-release sliding blade cover for added safety when not in use.

Cricut Glue Gun

The Cricut glue gun boasts a compact, ergonomic design for comfort, precision, and control. It minimizes glue drips, strings, and backflow, keeping your workspace clean and organized.

TABLE OF CONTENTS

Chapter 1
Materials

117

126 **Chapter 2**
Blades

Chapter 3
Mats

129

131 **Chapter 4**
Smart Materials

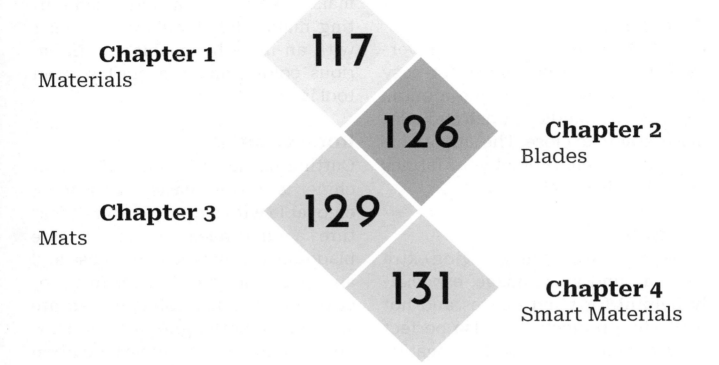

BOOK 4 - CRICUT MATERIALS

116

CHA PTER 1

MATERIALS

If you own a Cricut machine, you're probably curious about what materials it can cut. To fully grasp the world of machine materials, dive into this chapter.

Cricut machine mats have indeed been optimized for a wide range of crafting materials. Each machine mat provides just the right grip to firmly secure your material during cutting and then allows for easy removal afterward.

Cricut Explore and Cricut Maker machine owners, your creative possibilities are virtually limitless. These incredible machines can handle everything from thick leather to delicate tissue paper.

However, it's important to note that while Cricut Explore and Cricut Maker machines can cut a diverse array of materials, they may not accommodate every single substance. In such cases, it's advisable to conduct a test cut using a similar material setting, as long as the material is less than 2.0 mm thick for the Cricut Explore and 2.4 mm for the Cricut Maker. The stiffness of the material can also influence the maximum thickness.

Please be aware that the Cricut Explore and Cricut Maker machines are not suitable for cutting materials like fondant or other food-related items, as they are not certified as food-safe.

Cricut Maker 3

In the upcoming section, prepare to be dazzled as I unveil the exhaustive roster of materials your Cricut Maker 3 machine can seamlessly use. Get ready to discover a treasure trove of possibilities, including some materials that might have been flying under your creative radar until now:

- Acetate
- Adhesive foil

- Metallic foil, matte
- Double-sided adhesive foil
- Aluminum foil
- Art/illustration board
- Balsa - 1.6 mm (1/16")
- Balsa - 2.4 mm (3/32")
- Bamboo cloth
- Basswood - 1.6 mm (1/16")
- Basswood - 0.8 mm (1/32")
- Viscose
- Birch, permanent adhesive
- Loop
- Plain cotton
- Burlap
- Printed velvet
- Caliper paper
- Calico
- Batiste
- Canvas
- Carbon fiber
- Cardboard (intricate design)
- Adhesive cardboard
- Cashmere
- Cereal box
- Slate vinyl
- Rayon
- Batiste fabric
- Chantilly lace
- Satin charmeusse
- Chiffon
- Chintz
- Cardboard (1.5 mm)
- Colored adhesive tape
- Construction paper
- Copy paper - 75 gsm (20 lb)
- Corduroy
- Corrugated cardboard
- Corrugated paper
- Cotton
- Stabilized cotton
- EVA foam
- Crepe Charmeuse
- Crepe de Chine
- Crepe paper
- Satin with crepe backing
- Mat protector
- Damask
- Stabilized delicate fabrics (such as tulle)
- Deluxe paper
- Foil deluxe embossed paper
- Blend
- Fusible denim
- Swiss stitch
- Double fabric
- Double knit fabric
- Dry erase vinyl
- Cotton canvas
- Adhesive tape sheet
- Silk dupioni
- Everyday iron-on
- Everyday thermo adhesive mosaic
- Everyday heat transfer vinyl mesh
- Express hot melt
- Super-heavy fabrics (such as burlap)
- Eyelet
- Faya
- Synthetic hair - synthetic fur
- Synthetic leather (very thin)
- Synthetic chamois
- Felt

- Felt, acrylic fabric
- Stabilized craft felt
- Stabilized felt with glitter
- Rigid felt
- Stabilized wool felt
- Felt, wool fabric
- Flannel
- Flat cardboard
- Fleece fabric
- Flex rubber
- Velvety hot melt adhesive vinyl
- Velvet paper
- Acetate with Foil
- Foil heat adhesive vinyl
- KraftfFoil- holographic foil cardboard
- Foil paper - 0.36mm
- Foil cardboard
- Foil tape - glossy side down
- Foil tape - glossy side up
- Fular
- Freezer paper
- Hot melt adhesive fabric
- Hot melt fleece
- Heat-sealable interlining
- Gabardine
- Gauze
- Gel sheet
- Genuine leather
- Georgette
- Glitter cardboard
- Glitter foam EVA
- Glitter adhesive tape
- Hot melt glitter vinyl
- Glitter vinyl hot melt adhesive mesh
- Glitter vinyl
- Gauze
- Food grade bag
- Grois stitch
- Ottoman
- Habutai
- Handmade paper
- Heat transfer (not Cricut)
- Heather gray
- Thick card stock - 270 gsm (100 lb)
- Thick cardboard - 2.0mm
- Heavy fabrics (like denim)
- Stabilized heavy fabrics (such as denim)
- Heavy patterned paper
- Thick watercolor paper - 300 gsm (140 lb)
- Holographic card stock
- Holographic hot melt vinyl
- Holographic hot melt adhesive
- Holographic hot melt mosaic
- Holographic hot melt adhesive with glitter
- Holographic hot melt mosaic with glitter
- Holographic glitter vinyl
- Hand spun fabric
- Infusible ink transfer sheet
- Insulbrite wadding
- Interlock fabric
- Jacquard weave
- Jersey
- Jute
- Kevlar
- Khaki
- Kraft cardboard

- Lacoste
- Lamé
- Laser copy paper
- Lightweight card stock - 176 gsm (65 lb)
- Lightweight cardboard - 0.37mm (0.37mm)
- Lightweight cotton
- Lightweight cotton, 2-ply
- Lightweight cotton, 3-ply
- Lightweight (silk-like) fabrics
- Stabilized lightweight fabrics (like silk)
- Lightweight printed paper
- Linen
- Stabilized linen
- Lycra
- Magnetic sheet - 0.5mm
- Magnetic sheet - 0.6mm
- Passe-partout (1.5mm)
- Matelase
- Matte vinyl
- Medium-thickness cardboard, 216 g (80 lb)
- Medium-thickness fabrics (like cotton)
- Stabilized medium-thickness fabrics (like cotton)
- Melton wool
- Mesh
- Metal - 40 gauge fine copper
- Metallic hot melt vinyl mosaic
- Metallic leather
- Metallic cardboard
- Metallic vinyl
- Microfiber
- Moiré
- Moleskin
- Monk's cotton
- Mulberry paper
- Muslin
- Mylar
- Natural wood varnish
- Neoprene
- Non-adhesive vinyl - 16 gauge
- Non-adhesive vinyl - 20 gauge
- Notebook paper
- Nylon
- Fusible, waterproof fabric
- Waterproof fabric
- Organza
- Ottoman
- Outdoor vinyl, fusible
- Oxford
- Paint flake
- Panne velvet
- Adhesive paper
- Parchment paper
- Party foil
- Glitter-stamped card stock
- Hot-stamped adhesive vinyl
- Pearlized paper
- Paduasoy
- Photo paper
- Pima cotton
- Pique cotton
- Plastic fabric
- Plastic packaging
- Pleated
- Plush
- Stabilized polyester

- Poplin
- Cardboard
- High-quality outdoor vinyl
- Premium vinyl
- Premium vinyl - frosted glossy
- Premium vinyl - frosted grey
- Premium vinyl - opaque frosted
- Premium vinyl - holographic
- Premium vinyl - holographic 3D texture
- Premium vinyl - holographic art DAco
- Premium vinyl - holographic bubbles
- Premium vinyl - crystallized holographic
- Premium vinyl - holographic bubbles pink
- Premium vinyl - holographic threads
- Premium vinyl - mosaic
- Premium vinyl - pearlized
- Premium vinyl - shiny
- Premium vinyl - textured
- Premium vinyl - textured metallic
- Premium vinyl - true brushed
- Printable fabric
- Printable foil
- Hotmelt adhesive vinyl, dark printable
- clear printable thermal adhesive vinyl
- Printable magnetic sheet
- Printable adhesive paper (transparent)
- Printable adhesive paper (white)
- Printable vinyl
- Quilt wadding
- Ramio
- Raschel fabric
- Lyocell rayon
- Knitted fabric
- Rice paper
- Nylon ripstop
- Canvas
- Sandblast stencil
- Silk satin
- Seersucker
- With sequins
- Shantung
- Shantung satin
- Shiny leather - 1mm
- Glossy paper
- Chinese silk
- Silk, fusible
- Tight knit
- Lycra
- Glossy paper
- SportFlex hotmelt vinyl
- Stencil plastic - 0.4mm
- Vinyl template
- Removable adhesive paper
- Adhesive note
- Chamois
- Taffeta
- Tattoo paper
- Towel cloth
- Garment leather thin - 1.3 mm (2-3 oz.)
- Tissue paper
- Worked leather - 1.6 mm (4-5 oz.)

- Worked leather - 2.4 mm (6-7 oz.)
- Foil transfer sheet
- Transfer sheet
- Transparency
- True brushed paper
- Tulle
- Tweed
- Ultra-strong stabilizer
- Vellum
- Velvet
- Velvet upholstery
- Corduroy
- Vinyl
- Viscose
- Gauze
- Honeycomb fabric
- Washi sheet
- Wax paper
- Window adhesive
- Woolfcrepe
- Gift wrapping paper
- Zibeline

Cricut Explore 3

Of course, the Cricut Explore is no exception. We've got a wealth of materials at our disposal here too. Are you prepared for yet another extensive catalog of options?

- Adhesive Foil
- Metallic foil, matte
- Aluminum foil
- Release paper
- Calibration paper
- Cardboard (intricate design)
- Cardboard, adhesive backing
- Blackboard vinyl
- Construction paper
- Copy paper - 75 gsm (20 lb)
- Copy paper - 90 gsm (24lb)
- Copy paper - 120 gsm (32 lb)
- EVA foam
- Mat protector
- Deluxe paper
- Foil deluxe embossed paper
- Deluxe paper with adhesive backing
- Denim, stabilized
- Adhesive tape sheet
- EVA foam
- Everyday Ion-On
- Everyday hot melt mesh
- Everyday hot melt mosaic
- Express hot melt
- Synthetic leather (very thin)
- Synthetic chamois
- Felt, stabilized wool
- Felt, wool fabric
- Flat cardboard
- Velvet paper
- Acetate with foil
- Foil vinyl thermo adhesive
- Kraft foil
- Foil paper - 0.36mm
- Foil cardboard
- Thermo adhesive fabric
- Genuine leather
- Glitter cardboard
- Glitter EVA foam
- Hot melt glitter vinyl
- Hot melt glitter vinyl netting

- Glitter vinyl
- Food grade bag
- Heavy card stock - 270 gsm (100 lb)
- Thick patterned paper
- Thick watercolor paper - 300 gsm (140 lb)
- Holographic hot melt adhesive
- Holographic hot foil mosaic
- Holographic hot melt adhesive with glitter
- Holographic hot melt mosaic with glitter
- Holographic glitter vinyl
- Infusible ink transfer sheet
- Kraft cardboard
- Laser copy paper
- Lightweight card stock - 176 gsm (65 lb)
- Lightweight card stock - 0.37mm (0.37mm)
- Lightweight patterned paper
- Magnetic sheet - 1.0 mm
- Magnetic foil - 0.5 mm
- Passe-partout (1.5 mm)
- Medium-thick cardboard, 216 g (80 lb)
- Metallic heat-seal vinyl mosaic
- Metallic leather
- Metallic cardboard
- Mylar
- Natural wood varnish
- Notebook paper
- Rubber, stabilized
- Paint flake
- Parchment paper
- Party foil
- Hot-stamped adhesive vinyl
- Photo paper
- Polyester, stabilized

- High-quality outdoor vinyl
- Premium vinyl - permanent glossy
- Premium vinyl - removable matt
- Premium vinyl - frosted glossy
- Premium vinyl - frosted grey
- Premium vinyl - frosted matt
- Premium vinyl - holographic
- Premium vinyl - holographic 3D texture
- Premium vinyl - holographic Art Deco
- Premium vinyl - holographic bubbles
- Premium vinyl - holographic crystallized
- Premium vinyl - holographic pink bubbles
- Premium vinyl - holographic threads
- Premium vinyl - mosaic
- Premium vinyl - pearlized
- Premium vinyl - shiny
- Premium vinyl - textured
- Premium vinyl - textured metallic
- Premium vinyl - true brushed
- Printable fabric
- Hotmelt printable dark vinyl
- Clear printable hotmelt vinyl
- Printable adhesive paper (clear)
- Printable adhesive paper (white)
- Printable vinyl
- Glossy leather - 1 mm
- Glossy paper
- Silk, stabilized
- Smart Iron-On
- Smart Iron-On - glitter
- Smart Iron-On - holographic
- Smart paper, adhesive cardboard
- Smart vinyl - matte metallic
- Smart vinyl - permanent
- Smart vinyl - removable
- Smart vinyl - glossy

- Smooth paper with glitter
- Glossy paper
- SportFlex® hotmelt vinyl
- Stencil plastic - 0.4mm
- Vinyl template
- Adhesive note
- Tattoo paper
- Transparency
- True brushed paper
- Vellum
- Washi sheet
- Washi tape - 0.06mm
- Wax paper
- Window sticker
- Gift wrapping paper

Cricut Joy

Cricut's little one may have a shorter list of compatible materials compared to its larger siblings (as we explored in the previous book when dissecting the machine models). However, don't be fooled – this fantastic model still opens up a world of creative possibilities with its impressively extensive range of compatible materials

- Corrugated cardboard
- Flat cardboard
- Metallic cardboard
- Cardboard
- Glitter cardboard
- Insert card, card stock
- Medium thickness card stock, 216 g (80 lb)
- Hot melt vinyl
- Everyday hot melt mosaic
- Everyday hot melt mosaic
- Hot melt adhesive vinyl mesh with glitter
- Holographic hotmelt
- Holographic hot melt mosaic
- Holographic hotmelt with glitter
- Infusible ink transfer sheet
- Smart Iron-On
- Smart Iron-On, glitter
- Smart Iron-On, holographic
- Smart Iron-On, embossed
- SportFlex hotmelt vinyl
- Leather
- Synthetic leather (very thin)
- Paper
- Deluxe paper
- Deluxe paper with adhesive backing
- Deluxe paper with metal embossing
- Aluminum foil, 0.36 mm
- Pearlized paper
- Glossy paper
- Smart label writable paper
- Glossy paper
- True brushed paper
- Plastic
- Acetate with embossed metal
- Vinyl
- Foil Adhesive - metallic vinyl
- Chalkboard vinyl
- Dry erase vinyl
- Holographic vinyl with glitter

- Premium Vinyl
- Premium vinyl, frosted gloss
- Premium vinyl, frosted grey
- Premium vinyl, frosted opaque
- Premium vinyl, holographic
- Premium vinyl, holographic with 3D texture
- Premium vinyl, Art Deco holographic
- Premium vinyl, holographic bubbles
- Premium vinyl, holographic frosted film
- Premium holographic spun holographic film
- Premium vinyl, mosaic
- Premium vinyl, pearlized
- Premium vinyl, textured
- Premium vinyl, metallic textured
- Premium vinyl, true brushed
- Smart label writable vinyl
- Smart vinyl, holographic embossing
- Smart vinyl, matte metalized
- Smart vinyl, permanent
- Smart vinyl, temporary
- Smart vinyl, glossy
- Vinyl stencil
- Glossy plastic chipboard
- Window sticker

CHAPTER 2

BLADES

One of the key aspects that sets Cricut machines apart is the precision of their blades. Just as there are specific materials for each Cricut machine, understanding the tools designed to cut these materials is essential. When you opt for a trusted brand like Cricut, you're unlocking the full potential of your machine. So, let's dive into the world of Cricut blades and explore their incredible versatility.

Types of Cricut Blades

It's important to note that different Cricut blades are tailored for specific tasks, much like the various brushes a painter uses for different strokes. In the world of crafting, having the right blade for each material and cut can make all the difference.

Cricut Fine Tip Blades

These fine point blades are your everyday workhorses, and they come color-coded for quick material identification:

- **Premium Blade**: This precision cutter handles fine to medium-thickness materials like paper, cardboard, or vinyl. In previous versions, it came in gold or silver.

- **Deep Cutting Blade**: If you're working with thick materials like felt, EVA foam, or cardboard, this black deep-cutting blade delivers precise results.

- **Fabric Blade**: Designed exclusively for fabric cutting, it's best to reserve this rosy blade solely for fabric projects. It's worth noting that while all these blades have fine tips, the gold-colored Premium Blade and the black Deep Cutting Blade are not interchangeable, as indicated by their adapter colors. The Fabric Blade, however, does work with the Premium's gold adapter.

- **QuickSwap Blades**: QuickSwap blades are engineered for the Cricut Maker, offering increased cutting force across a range of materials. These blades live up to their name, allowing you to swap them out with just a push of a button:

- **Rotating Blade**: This unique blade combines sliding and rotating movements to effortlessly cut fabric without the need for stabilizing materials. It pairs perfectly with the pink mat, designed for fabric crafting.

- **Knife Blade**: Built for dense materials up to 2.4 mm thick, such as balsa wood or plywood, it requires you to move all track wheels aside to avoid leaving marks.

- **Marking Blade**: Ideal for marking folds or creases in light materials like paper, cardboard, or acetate, this blade is rotary in design.

- **Double Marking Knife**: Creating two deep parallel lines for folds or creases in thicker materials like cardboard, this rotary knife adds dimension.

- **Embossing or Debossing Knife**: Adding texture and depth to your creations, this blade creates elegant debossed patterns on various materials.

- **Engraving Blade**: Unleash your creativity by adding fine decorative engravings to metals, leather, plastics, and more.

- **Perforating Blade**: Crafting intricate perforations for tear-away projects like notepads or assembly kits, this blade ensures clean cuts, even in curves.

The Right Blades for Every Machine

Let's clarify which Cricut blades are compatible with each machine:

- **Cricut Joy**: Currently, the Cricut Joy has a versatile, multi-purpose blade that handles all supported materials, including paper, cardboard, vinyl, and Smart Materials with precision.

- **Cricut Explore Air**: For the Cricut Explore range, which includes the Cricut Explore Air 2 and Cricut Explore 3, all fine-tip blades are compatible.

- **Cricut Maker**: The Cricut Maker, along with the latest Cricut Maker 3, is a versatile powerhouse. It accommodates all blades, including fine-tip ones and QuickSwap blades. This flexibility gives the Cricut Maker a distinct edge over the Cricut Explore."

CHAPTER 3

MATS

The mats designed for Cricut machines have been carefully crafted to work seamlessly with a variety of common crafting materials. Each machine mat is equipped with the perfect level of grip to secure your material firmly during cutting and allow for easy removal once your project is complete.

Here's an overview of the different types of mats you should be familiar with:

LightGrip Machine Mat
This reusable adhesive cutting mat is tailored for lightweight materials and is compatible with the Cricut Maker and Explore cutting tool series. It's ideal for working with:

- Printable paper
- Thin cardstock
- Vellum
- Construction paper
- Vinyl

StandardGrip Machine Mat
The StandardGrip mat boasts reusable adhesive and serves as the perfect cutting surface for a wide range of medium-weight materials, making it a go-to choice for the Cricut Maker and Explore machine series. It excels with:

- Cardstock
- Patterned paper
- Embossed cardstock
- Heat-transfer adhesive vinyl
- Vinyl

StrongGrip Machine Mat
For heavyweight materials, the StrongGrip mat is the way to go. This reusable adhesive mat is specially crafted for use with the Cricut Maker and Explore machines. It's excellent for cutting:

- Thick cardstock
- Glitter cardstock
- Magnetic material
- Dense cardboard

- Cardboard
- Reinforced fabric
- Leather

FabricGrip Machine Mat

Combining lightweight adhesive with enhanced strength and density, the FabricGrip mat is designed to handle a wide array of textiles. It's tailored for use with the Cricut Maker and Cricut Explore machines, particularly when paired with a rotary blade or stabilized fabric blade. This mat enables you to work with virtually any fabric, securely holding it in place during cutting and releasing it effortlessly.

Tips for Using Cricut Machine Mats

Here are some valuable tips for effectively using Cricut machine mats:

1. When storing the mat, keep the transparent liner cover on to protect it from dust and debris.
2. For gentle removal of cut images, utilize a putty knife and a scraper, both included in the Cricut Basic Tool Kit or Cricut Essential Tool Kit.
3. Always follow the recommended material types for each mat to achieve optimal performance and results.

CHA PTER 4

SMART MATERIALS

In this chapter, you're about to dive into the world of smart materials—game-changers that turbocharge your Cricut machines, making them faster, more efficient, and capable of tackling longer designs. If you've ever felt limited by your machine's speed or maximum cutting size, get ready for an exciting option.

The beauty of these supplies lies in their simplicity. Once loaded into your Cricut Explore 3 or Cricut Maker 3, they're ready to roll. There's a range of smart materials to explore, including Smart Paper Adhesive Board, Smart Vinyl, and Smart Iron-On.

What you should know about Smart Materials:

- With Smart Materials, you can cut single images or multiple designs measuring up to 29.7 cm (11.7 in) wide and a staggering 3.6 m (12 ft) long on the Cricut Explore 3 and Cricut Maker 3. For other materials, the mat size sets the limit on your design's dimensions.

- Smart Materials sport a special backing and can be fed directly into your Cricut Explore 3 or Cricut Maker 3 without needing a cutting mat.

- The app plays its part too, guiding you on when to load your Smart Materials and even estimating how much you'll need. Once loaded, the machine measures the material to ensure it's sufficient for your project. There's a small margin left above and below your design to allow the rollers to grip and load the material effectively.

- The software takes these margins into account when calculating your Smart Materials requirements. To ensure you've got enough for your design, hold off on trimming until the cutting process is complete.

- Loading Smart Materials is a breeze. Align the Smart Material with the machine's left-side material guide, slide it under the mat guides, and across the rollers.

Tips for Cutting Smart Vinyl

- Avoid trimming the material until the machine completes the cut.

- Make sure to select the appropriate Smart Vinyl setting that matches your specific material, whether it's temporary, permanent, glossy, and so on.

- Keep a clearance of 25 cm (9.8 in) behind the Cricut machine to ensure smooth material movement.

- When feeding materials into the machine, ensure they're straight and aligned with the left material guide on the machine.

- As the material comes out of the back during the measuring process, roll the vinyl to maintain a tidy workspace.

- Remember, the Cricut Explore 3 and Cricut Maker 3 can churn out repetitive cuts up to 12 feet (3.6 meters) long, making them versatile for any project.

Tip: For Smart Materials without a cutting mat, they should be at least 15.24 cm (6 in) long. You can go smaller if you place them on a cutting mat.

The Program Provides You With Information on Smart Materials

The Cricut Design Space program offers invaluable insights into your materials. As soon as you select your machine, the application provides information on Smart Materials compatible with your Cricut machine, along with handy tips and tricks tailored to specific materials.

Application Tips
- For most types of vinyl, regular transfer tape works perfectly. However, opt for StrongGrip transfer tape when dealing with textured vinyl like gloss.

- Transfer tape comes in rolls of 12 feet (3.6 m), 21 feet (6.4 m), and 75 feet (22.86 m) for applying to long designs.

- Consider cutting your finished design into smaller sections before applying the transfer tape; it simplifies the application process.

- After applying the transfer tape, smooth both the front and back for optimal results.

- Smart Vinyl packaging is eco-friendly and recyclable.

Tips for Cutting Smart Iron-On

- Hold off on trimming until the machine completes the cutting process.

- Choose the Smart Iron-On configuration that matches your specific material, whether it's glitter, holographic, and so on.

- Maintain a 25 cm (10 in) clearance behind the Cricut machine for seamless material movement.

- When feeding materials into the machine, ensure they're straight and aligned with the left material guide on the machine.

- As the heat-seal vinyl (Smart Iron-On) comes out of the back during measuring, roll it to keep your workspace tidy.

- You can cut virtually any design with the Cricut Maker 3 and Explore 3, spanning up to 12 feet (3.6 meters).

Tip: For Smart Materials without a cutting mat, they should be at least 15.24 cm (6 in) long. You can go smaller if you place them on a cutting mat.

Application Tips

- Refer to the Heat Transfer Guide for detailed instructions on applying Smart Iron-On.

- Select the Smart Iron-On material in the heat transfer guide for proper setup; the Smart Iron-On coating is slightly thicker, requiring different time and temperature parameters.

- In most cases, the liner's adhesive will keep your design in place on the surface. To ensure it stays put during ironing, use heat-resistant tape.

Tips for Drawing and Cutting Smart Paper Adhesive Cardstock

- Hold off on trimming the material until the machine finishes the cutting process.

- When feeding media into the machine, ensure it's straight and aligned with the left material guide.

- Smart Paper adhesive cardstock pairs perfectly with all Cricut Explore and Cricut Maker pens and markers.

- Allow the ink to dry before handling the design.

- Before sending a project to the machine with drawing lines, position the drawing layer using the Attach tool.

- The software will prompt you to load the pen.

Application Tips
- Peel the backing by hand and apply the design to your project.

- Note that transfer tape, which can damage the paper's surface, is not suitable for Smart Paper sticky cardstock.

- Smart paper adhesive is suitable for smooth cardstock, kraft paper, deluxe paper, and other non-textured paper materials. Avoid using it on glass, plastic, or rough paper.

- If needed, you can temporarily reposition sticky Smart Paper.

Create in Record Time With Smart Materials

Unlock the potential to speed up your cutting machine with Smart Materials. It's often said that the only thing you can't create with the Cricut Maker is more time. Thanks to smart materials, the Cricut Maker 3 can cut up to twice as fast without compromising precision or power. Get ready to create like never before.

Frequently Asked Questions About Smart Materials

Here is a series of questions regarding Smart Materials:

Why are Smart Materials considered smart?

Smart Materials are considered intelligent due to their ability to be loaded directly into the machine without the need for a cutting mat, maintaining alignment automatically. This feature allows for uninterrupted cuts of up to 3.6 meters (11.8 ft), letting you focus on the fun part – designing.

What is Smart Paper Adhesive Cardboard?

Smart Paper allows you to load sheets into the machine without a mat. It's as simple as peel and stick for flawless die-cutting. Create colorful banners, multi-layered paper crafts, and delightful cards without the mess of glue.

Is 3D crafting possible with Smart Materials?

Yes! With the Cricut Maker 3, you can now utilize the Knife Blade to cut denser and thicker materials. This makes it an ideal accessory for creating dimensional projects like mockups and home decor.

What should I do if Smart Materials appear wrinkled during loading?

The Cricut Explore 3 and Cricut Maker 3 attempt to stretch the material by measuring it before cutting. If the material remains misaligned after measuring, simply unload and reload it.

What can I do with leftover Smart Materials?

Smart Materials for Cricut Explore 3 and Cricut Maker 3 must be at least 15.24 cm (6 in) long for the machine to align them without a mat. For smaller cut-outs, make use of a cutting mat. Keep in mind that the machine leaves a small margin of material above and below your design.

Can Smart Materials be used with older Cricut Explore and Cricut Maker models?

Using Smart Materials with older Cricut Explore or Cricut Maker machines is not recommended. The Cricut Explore 3 and Cricut Maker 3 models have been meticulously designed, optimized, and extensively tested for compatibility with Smart Materials. Therefore, these machines are the only ones capable of utilizing Smart Materials. While older machines may accommodate Smart Materials if placed on a cutting mat, there's no guarantee they will perform as expected. Using them can lead to material jams, less accurate cuts, or damage to machine parts over time.

What exactly are Smart Materials?

Smart Materials are consumables compatible with Cricut Maker 3 and Explore 3 cutting machines. These materials allow for the creation of images or repetitive cuts measuring up to 29.7 cm (11.7 in) in width and 3.6 m (12 ft) in length. Please note that the mat size determines the maximum design size for all other materials.

What are the benefits of Smart Materials?

Smart Materials are consumables designed to work with Cricut Maker 3 and Explore 3 cutting machines. These materials enable the creation of images or repetitive cuts measuring up to 29.7 cm (11.7 in) in width and 3.6 m (12 ft) in length. The mat size sets the limit on design size for all other materials.

How should I prepare Smart Materials for cutting?

Smart Materials come ready for loading into the machine. Align the Smart Material with the material guide on the machine's left side, then pass it beneath the mat guides and over the rollers. Finally, press the load button. If you don't use all the material in one cut, trim the excess and save it for future projects. When cutting material for future use without a mat, make straight cuts rather than angled ones. Smart material cut-outs smaller than 15.24 cm (6 in) or larger than 33 cm (13 in) should be placed on a cutting mat.

How can I flatten Smart Materials if they become wrinkled during loading?

In the case of the Cricut Explore 3 and Cricut Maker 3, try stretching the material while measuring it before cutting. If the material remains misaligned after measuring, unload and reload it.

Recognizing Smart Materials by Description

You can identify Smart Materials based on three key aspects: cutting pressure, multi-cutting capabilities, and the type of blade used for cutting.

HOW IS YOUR READING GOING?

We have reached the midpoint of our book, traversing through the major facets of the wonderful Cricut universe, endeavoring to provide you with clear and concise information to help you become self-sufficient swiftly.

By now, you should have garnered a clear understanding of many crucial aspects, such as the Design Space, accessories, and materials compatible with your Cricut machine. In the forthcoming chapters, we will delve pragmatically into step-by-step project examples, and I will furnish you with a list of project ideas, categorized by difficulty level—from beginner to advanced.

I trust that what you've perused so far has been engaging. Below, you'll find a QR code to scan, which will direct you to my page where an array of bonuses await your download.

I wish to reiterate the importance of your book review—it's invaluable to me. Towards the end of the book, you will find instructions on how to leave your review swiftly and effortlessly.

TABLE OF CONTENTS

Chapter 1
What's New in Cricut Maker 3?

139

142

Chapter 2
Unboxing Cricut Maker 3

Chapter 3
The Main Differences With Cricut Maker 2

145

148

Chapter 4
Is choosing Cricut Maker 3 the Right Decision for You?

Chapter 5
Pros and Cons

152

BOOK 5 - CRICUT MAKER 3

CHA PTER 1

WHAT'S NEW IN CRICUT MA-KER 3?

When discussing the best craft machines for entrepreneurial ventures or crafting household products, it's essential to mention this remarkable equipment. That's precisely what we'll explore in this chapter.

When it comes to innovative stationery projects, stamping, decoration, or designs, it's impossible not to acknowledge the Cricut Maker 3. This machine simplifies crafting, particularly for beginners who are just starting to explore its capabilities.

To highlight some of its advantages, this machine can cut materials of varying thicknesses and is designed to handle everything from delicate fabrics to robust materials like leather or vinyl.

Invest your time and money in Smart Materials and make the Cricut Maker 3 a valuable addition, especially since it's compatible with the latest Smart Materials offerings.

Revolutionary Materials

Without the need for a cutting mat, you can place fresh materials directly into the machine, maintaining perfect alignment without requiring manual adjustments. This groundbreaking capability allows for single cuts of up to 3.6 meters, a first for Cricut machines.

Since there's no elaborate setup required with this machine, users can focus on what they do best—creating. Since its introduction, this machine has proven that the only thing it can't create is more time.

A Swifter Machine

Thanks to the robust motor in the Cricut Maker 3, you can now adjust the cutting speed. With Smart Materials, it can cut up to twice as fast as before, all without sacrificing power or precision. This feature makes it the ultimate intelligent cutting machine, perfect for all craft enthusiasts.

Much like its predecessor, the Cricut Maker 3 can cut through over 300 different types of materials, including options like leather and balsa wood, as well as delicate paper. However, what sets it apart is its ability to cut at astonishing speeds and handle substantial cuts in a single pass, making it a truly unique piece of machinery.

Get to Know Its Features and Functions

Here is a list of the standout features of this machine:

- **Efficiency Boost**: When you're short on time and need to bring your creative ideas to life quickly, the Cricut comes to the rescue. It rewards creativity by increasing your work speed. In a nutshell, this Maker version is here to provide solutions and answers for entrepreneurs.

- **Integrated Material Sensors**: The Cricut Maker 3 boasts built-in sensors capable of measuring your material's length. This function ensures that you have sufficient material for your project even before the cutting process begins, offering a significant advantage.

- **Compatibility with Special Materials**: This Cricut is designed to work with a wide array of materials, including but not limited to:

1. *Smart Vinyl*: Available in permanent or removable options, it comes in various colors and styles, with lengths ranging from 1 meter to 23 meters (3.2-75.4 ft) approximately.

2. *Sticker Cardstock (Smart Paper™ Sticker Cardstock)*: This material is prepped for cutting, peeling, and sticking. You can create stickers, fun cards, eye-catching banners, impactful posters, and layered paper projects without needing glue.

3. *Textile Vinyl (iron-on)*: Design personalized t-shirts and other items with this incredibly versatile crafting material, available in various colors and styles. You can cut a single image up to 1.2 m (4 ft) or repeated forms up to 3.6 m (10 ft).

4. *Vinyl Roll Holder*: This vinyl roll holder, often sold separately, attaches directly to the front of the machine and holds the vinyl roll for you. It's a handy accessory, even featuring a built-in blade for easy vinyl cutting once your project is completed.

Additionally, you can cut various specialty materials, including:

- Acetate
- Aluminum foil
- Balsa wood
- Burlap
- Slate vinyl
- Wooden cardboard
- Craft foam
- Faux leather
- Glitter adhesive tape
- Magnetic sheets
- Cardboard
- Suede
- Vellum
- Washi sheet

- **Extensive Tool Selection**: The Cricut Maker 3 offers a wide variety of tools, including a blade for thick materials, a rotary blade for materials without backing, and the popular QuickSwap family of tools. These tools can perform tasks such as scoring, adding professional-level decorative effects, embossing, punching, as well as creating waves or vines. Additionally, a fine point blade is already included with the machine, ready for use straight out of the box.

- **3D Project Capability**: With the Knife Blade, the Cricut Maker 3 can now cut denser and thicker materials, making it perfect for dimensional projects such as models and home décor.

- **Print and Cut Functionality**: You can use your home printer to print graphics, and then the Cricut Maker 3 can precisely cut them out. This feature is fantastic for creating stickers. The largest printable and cuttable size, currently supported, is 8.5" x 11".

- **Creativity with Fabric**: If you're passionate about sewing but hesitant to tackle your projects, the Cricut Maker 3 can assist you with one of the most challenging aspects: marking and cutting pattern pieces. The rotary blade, available separately, is a valuable tool. Moreover, the Cricut Maker 3 can be used to accurately cut out appliqué and quilting components. The best part is that you can find a plethora of fun patterns in the Design Space.

CHAPTER 2

UNBOXING CRICUT MAKER 3

In the previous chapter, we discussed the new features of this machine. However, many people are curious about what comes with it in terms of details and physical accessories. In this chapter, we'll delve into what's included in the Cricut Maker 3 box, along with other presentation details of this equipment.

What's included in the Cricut Maker 3 box?

- The Cricut Maker® 3 machine.
- A premium fine-tip blade and an adaptor.
- A free trial subscription to Cricut Access™ (This applies to new subscribers).
- Access to at least 100 ready-to-make projects online.
- Materials for making practice cuts (smart vinyl).
- A welcome card.
- A USB cable.
- The power adapter.

Currently, the machine is available in white with silver, but we don't rule out the possibility of it coming in more colors in the future.

Once you have the machine and are familiar with the accessories and their functions, you can gain a broader perspective on whether you need to invest in a new machine in the future or consider upgrading your equipment.

Additionally, you can use it with Cricut's non-smart materials and mats.

Cricut Maker 3 Features You Need to Know About

Here's a list of functions and other essential aspects of this machine that make it truly special:

Cutting Area: If there's one feature that creators often seek with great enthusiasm, it's the cutting area. The Cricut Maker can cut materials up to 30.5 cm (1 ft) in width and 61 cm (2 ft) in length.

Cutting with a Drag Blanket: It's important to note that cutting using a drag blanket is recommended, as you cannot cut rolls or materials directly. This equipment offers drag blankets with varying adhesion levels, distinguishable by color. They are of high quality and budget-friendly. For the Cricut Maker, there are two options: a blue blanket with low adherence and a special pink one designed for fabrics.

Depth and Cutting Force: Despite its compact size, this cutting plotter can handle materials up to 2.4 mm thick and exerts a force of 4 kg (8.8 lb). It can cut anything from thin vinyl to more robust materials like balsa wood.

Blades and Blade Holders: When discussing what sets the Cricut Maker apart, the blades and blade holders take the spotlight. Quality is paramount in all things Cricut, and these components are no exception. All parts are self-adjusting and constructed from metal.

There are two main types of blades

- Normal blades feature the classic rotating blade found in plotters. They are easily replaceable by pressing up and removing the blade from its housing. Various models and qualities exist, including the fine tip, which comes as a standard option, or the deep cut.

- Rotary blade holders feature a metal-toothed wheel and fit into the B carriage of the Maker. This ingenious mechanism allows for the use of specialized tools such as the rotary fabric blade, the craft blade for denser materials, or the creasing and marking tools. The fabric blade is included with the Maker.

Another notable detail is the option to insert markers or the marker tool into the carriage. When you purchase your Maker, you'll receive a black fine-tip marker.

The Cricut Maker is perhaps the most versatile device available today, as it can be employed in various ways without restrictions. As you explore each function and tool, you'll discover the ideal working methods that suit your needs.

Furthermore, Cricut has introduced a new line of smart materials that seamlessly work with the Cricut Maker 3 without requiring a cutting mat. This is a game changer for crafters creating larger-than-average designs.

In the past, you were limited to cutting designs the size of the standard 12" x 12" (30.5 cm x 30.5 cm) mat or the 12" x 24" (30.5 cm x 61 cm) long mat. But now, with Smart Materials, you have the option to cut designs up to 12 feet (30.5 cm) wide and up to 12 feet (3.6 meters) long.

CHAPTER 3

THE MAIN DIFFERENCES WITH CRICUT MAKER 2

When a new Cricut Maker hits the market, it's only natural for users to wonder: What sets this machine apart from its predecessor?

The answers lie in the detailed analysis of each machine, which we will delve into in this chapter.

When comparing past Cricut Makers with the Cricut Maker 3, several key differences come to light, distinguishing Cricut's classic digital craft-cutting machine from its latest iteration. What remains remarkable is that both machines share the ability to cut, mark, and engrave over 300 materials, including paper, fabric, and wood.

As many may know, Cricut offers other machines like the Cricut Explore 3 and Cricut Joy, which are making waves as the newest and most powerful cutting machines in the market. Both utilize Cricut Design Space for project planning and offer compatibility with 13 tools and blades, making Maker 2 and Maker 3 stand out as top choices among Cricut enthusiasts.

Design

The Cricut Maker 3, while slightly larger than the original Cricut Maker by a few millimeters, maintains a sleek and unnoticeable design difference. However, it is slightly heavier, weighing in at 6.9 kg (15 lb) compared to the Maker 2's 4.8 kg (10.5 lb). So, if mobility is a priority, you might find the original Maker a tad lighter.

The button layout remains the same, offering functions to load and unload materials, power the machine on and off, and start and stop cutting operations. While the choice of color may not be the most critical factor, it's still a significant design consideration.

For those unfamiliar, the original Maker is available in various colors, including pink, blue, and a charming frosted gold. In contrast, the Maker 3 is now offered only in a subdued blue hue.

Both Maker 2 and Maker 3 include integrated tool storage and a convenient spot to place your tablet while you work, ensuring they blend seamlessly into any workspace.

Pricing

Both the Cricut Maker 2 and Cricut Maker 3 come at budget-friendly price points. If pricing is a deciding factor for your purchase, you may lean towards the Maker 2, which is slightly cheaper in the market. We understand that budget considerations play a pivotal role, and your choice will depend on your investment and whether the Maker 3's additional features align with your needs.

Smart Materials

One significant distinction when comparing the Cricut Maker with the Cricut Maker 3 is the latter's compatibility with smart materials, a feature absent in the original model. Cricut's smart materials allow you to work continuously on projects up to 12 feet

long without the need for a cutting mat. In contrast, the Cricut Maker, due to mat size limitations, can only cut materials up to 24 inches in length and does not support Smart Materials.

While you can still use Maker 3 for other materials such as infusible ink and standard cardboard in larger projects, the ability to cut without a mat can be a game-changer.

Which Machine Is the Right Fit?

Both the Maker and Maker 3 can handle nearly any creative project, including working with metal and wood.

Cutting Speed

One notable difference lies in cutting speed. The Cricut Maker 2 has always excelled at swiftly cutting vinyl, but the Maker 3 stands out by performing at twice the speed, enabling you to complete projects in record time. If you're accustomed to crafting throughout the day or run a small business with high demand, the Maker 3 ensures every minute counts. The Maker 3 introduces a more potent adapter that enhances production speed, making it even more impressive. If you don't plan to fully utilize these added speeds, sticking with the original Maker might be more practical, especially if you primarily work with smart materials.

Cutting Dimensions
In terms of cutting dimensions, the Maker can cut materials up to 12 inches wide, while the Maker 3 extends that slightly to 13 inches.

Ease of Use
Cricut machines are renowned for their user-friendliness, and one contributing factor is their excellent Design Space app, offering pre-designed projects.

Several aspects of the new Cricut Maker remain consistent. Both machines are compatible with all 13 attachments, providing versatile functionality, including cutting, marking, writing, and engraving. Both can also print, followed by cutting, on both white and colored paper, a feature only available on the Explore 3, which supports fewer tools than other Cricut models.

The Maker 3 retains the same robust tools for engraving, etching, and more, while also offering the capability to cut over 300 materials with commercial-quality precision.

Connectivity
Connectivity remains consistent between Maker and Maker 3, with both supporting Bluetooth and USB. The retention of the USB port in the Maker 3 is particularly welcome, especially if you need to use the machine in the absence of an internet connection.

Choosing Between Cricut Maker 2 and Cricut Maker 3

When making this decision, it's crucial to consider the primary distinction between Maker and Maker 3: the latter's compatibility with smart materials. The Maker 3 can cut smart materials twice as fast as the original Maker and does not require a cutting mat for continuous cutting up to 12 feet.

For newcomers, the Maker 3 offers an advanced experience with faster cutting and broader access to Cricut's range of materials. If you already own the Maker 2, consider whether upgrading to the Maker 3 is justified. It's a worthwhile investment if you intend to fully utilize Smart Material compatibility, as it speeds up production and eliminates the need for a mat."

CHAPTER 4

IS CHOOSING CRICUT MAKER 3 THE RIGHT DECISION FOR YOU?

Let's explore it together. By now, you're probably pondering whether the Cricut Maker 3 is the perfect choice for you. In this chapter, we'll embark on this discovery journey together, step by step.

With this equipment, creative minds can craft an array of items, from paper crafts, iron-ons, leather creations, and vinyl stickers to sewing projects, crafts, and wooden models, as demonstrated.

This machine boasts an extensive range of tools, accessories, and more, a feature that's undeniably appealing from a shopper's perspective, especially when it includes powerful blade tools and electric cutting pens and scores. Among its accessories, the new rotary blade stands out for its ability to swiftly and accurately cut a wide variety of materials without requiring backup.

Moreover, it simplifies quilting and sewing tasks. This machine offers a vast selection of computerized sewing, marking, and cutting patterns for sewers to choose from.

While utilizing the Maker 3, you have the freedom to upload and use your photos and fonts in various common file formats.

Projects You Can Accomplish with Your Cricut Maker 3

When evaluating if the machine you're eyeing is the right fit for you, it's essential to consider the range of products it can offer. That's why we've compiled an extensive list of what you can achieve with the Cricut Maker 3, unveiling the diversity of projects:

- *Vinyl Decals and Stickers:* Cutting vinyl decals and stickers is a popular pastime among creative individuals, and the Cricut Maker allows you to do this and more. Simply design in Cricut Design Space, set the machine in motion, remove excess material, and transfer the design to your desired surface.

- *Sewing Patterns*: Another significant advantage is the machine's extensive library of sewing patterns, accessible upon purchase. You can select your desired pattern, and the Maker will cut it out for you, including patterns from Simplicity and Riley Blake Designs. No more manual pattern cutting! Plus, it comes with a washable fabric marker to indicate where pattern pieces fit.

- **Fabric Cuts**: The inclusion of the new Rotary Blade is a standout feature of the Maker 3. Thanks to its unique sliding and rolling motion and robust 4 kg force, the machine can cut almost any fabric. In the past, specialized fabric cutters were necessary since desktop cutting machines couldn't handle thicker textiles. Many love the Maker for its integrated design, and it comes equipped with a fabric cutting mat for cutting a wide range of fabrics without a backing.

- **Balsa Wood Cuts**: The Cricut Maker 3 can cut materials up to 2.4 mm thick with its remarkably strong blade. This means you can now use thick materials for crea-

tive projects that were previously impossible with Cricut machines.

- **Cutting Thick Leather**: Thick leather can also be cut with this machine, allowing you to tackle projects that include this material.

- **Personalized Cards**: Crafting paper and cards is now faster and easier than ever, thanks to the machine's strength and precision. Your handmade cards will benefit from the enhanced quality.

- **Jigsaw Puzzles**: With the capability to cut significantly thicker materials than before, the Maker 3 opens up possibilities for creating your jigsaw puzzles.

- **Christmas Ornaments**: The machine's rotary blade, capable of cutting through any fabric, is perfect for crafting holiday decorations. Explore the sewing pattern collection for Christmas-themed patterns, cut them out of felt or your chosen fabric, and stitch each piece separately.

- **Quilts**: Thanks to a partnership between Riley Blake Designs and Cricut, a range of quilt patterns is available in the sewing pattern collection. This means you can precisely cut your quilt sections with the Maker 3 before stitching them together.

- **Felt Dolls and Stuffed Animals**: The sewing pattern collection includes patterns for felt dolls and garments. These creations are sure to be cherished additions to any collection.

- **Custom T-Shirts**: Cutting heat-transfer vinyl to transfer your designs onto fabric is a breeze with the Cricut Maker 3. It takes just a few simple steps to create a transfer: design it in Design Space, then iron it onto the shirt after instructing the machine to cut the heat transfer vinyl.

- **Baby Clothes**: While the Cricut Maker's mat size is limited to 12" x 24", making it unsuitable for cutting adult clothing designs, it's perfect for baby apparel patterns.

- **Doll Clothes**: Just as you can create dresses and other baby items, you can also make doll clothes.

- **Fabric Appliqués**: The fabric blade, designed for cutting intricate fabric designs like appliqués, is available for purchase. Unlike the rotary blade, the bonded fabric blade requires the material's backing to be attached for efficient cutting.

- **Typefaces**: The Cricut Maker's adaptable tooling system is its standout feature. This feature ensures compatibility with all tools and blades from the Maker 3 family and any future tools and blades produced by Cricut.

- **Jewelry**: If you're interested in both jewelry making and craft cutting, give it a try. The Cricut Maker 3's strength lies in its ability to cut thicker materials, ideal for intricate jewelry patterns. While you might not be cutting gold, silver, or diamonds anytime soon, you'll have access to a lovely selection of leather earrings.

- **Wedding Invitations**: Invitations can significantly impact your budget. However, you can cut down on expenses by creating items like invitations yourself. The Cricut Maker is perfect for crafting beautiful invites. In addition to cutting intricate paper designs, you can use the calligraphy pen to add an elegant touch.

- **Wedding and Restaurant Menus**: You can use your Maker to create decorations for the big day, not just for pre-wedding activities. The possibilities are endless, but starting with menus, place cards, and favor tags is a great idea. Keep the design consistent across your stationery to maintain a cohesive theme.

- **Coloring Books**: If you're looking to save money, why not make your coloring books with the Cricut Maker? All you need is paper, playing cards, and a creative pattern. Instruct the Maker to craft your custom coloring book using the Fine Tip Pen tool.

- **Coasters**: Crafting your coasters offers the freedom to use standard, plain holders made of thin paper and scored with a stylus or get creative and design teacup-shaped coasters inspired by Alice in Wonderland.

These are just some of the many creative possibilities the Cricut Maker 3 offers. Whether you're a seasoned crafter or just starting, this machine can bring your ideas to life with precision and ease.

CHAPTER 5

PROS AND CONS

Cricut Maker 3 offers many advantages, but it also has its downsides. In this chapter, we will discuss a series of pros and cons associated with the Cricut Maker 3 that every user should be aware of.

Pros

1. **Ease of Use**: The Cricut company has ensured that using their machines to create projects is as enjoyable as possible. After creating your design, simply click the 'Do it' button in the upper right corner of the design canvas screen. The software will guide you in setting up the correct tools and cutting.

2. **Compatibility with Unbranded Materials**: While Cricut offers a wide range of branded materials, including vinyl, cardstock, natural wood veneer, and aluminum foil, the Cricut Maker 3 can also work with various non-branded mate-

rials. As long as you have a cutting mat to adhere to and adjust the pressure settings to suit what you're cutting, you can experiment with virtually anything.

3. **Business Opportunities**: For many crafters, the dream is to support themselves financially while doing what they love, and the Cricut Maker 3 has made that dream a reality for most. Whether it's your handmade goods or packaging and branding materials, the professional look achieved with a tool like the Cricut Maker 3 can greatly benefit your business. There are virtually no limits to the types of businesses you can start with the help of the Cricut Maker 3. Using Design Space with a Cricut machine can expedite and simplify the process of delivering personalized goods, making it an ideal choice for entrepreneurs. Your Cricut Maker 3 can pay for itself if you find the right product to sell to customers, quickly putting you in a profitable position.

Cons

Here is a list of cons associated with the Cricut Maker 3 machine:

1. **Cost**: The Cricut Maker is relatively expensive for many crafters, but it is worth the investment. There are few tasks this machine can't handle, and when you consider the money it can save you on projects or the potential to start your own small business, the initial purchase cost becomes more justifiable.

2. **Additional Tools and Materials**: While the Cricut Maker 3 comes with a fine point blade and some materials for test cuts, accessories such as adaptable tools, cutting mats, and the Cricut roll holder for smart materials must be purchased separately.

3. **Size**: The Cricut Maker is not a small machine, which is understandable given its capabilities. However, this means that if space is limited in your crafting area, it may be a bit of a squeeze. When closed or not in use, the machine measures 15 x 54 x 18 cm (5.9 x 21 x 7 in). When in use, you need to ensure at least 14 cm (5.5 in) clearance above the machine for the lid to open and at least 25 cm (9.8 in) clearance behind the machine for the mats to pass through without obstruction. The front 'door' of the Cricut Maker can be opened over the edge of a table or shelf without significant impact, but care is needed when loading the mats.

4. **Software Limitations**: Some users find the Design Space software to be somewhat rudimentary. It is best suited as a machine controller and lacks the complexity for designing intricate or high-quality items within the application. It primarily serves a commercial function for Cricut, often promoting additional purchases and subscription options.

While it's true that the Cricut universe offers a wide array of materials and accessories for this machine, you can manage costs effectively by selecting accessories based on your specific needs and projects. Understanding what you want to create and what is required can help you avoid unnecessary expenditures.

TABLE OF CONTENTS

Chapter 1
What's New in Cricut
Explore Air 3?

155

162

Chapter 2
Unboxing   Cricut
Explore Air 3

Chapter 3
The Main Differences
With   Cricut   Explore
Air 2

164

166

Chapter 4
Is Cricut Explore 3 the
Right Choice for You?
Let's Evaluate It To-

Chapter 5
Pros and Cons

170

BOOK 6 - CRICUT EXPLORE AIR 3

CHA PTER 1

WHAT'S NEW IN CRICUT EXPLORE AIR 3?

Among the new cutting plotters from the Cricut brand, we can't overlook the Explore Air 3, a device perfectly compatible with Smart Materials. In this chapter, you'll get all the details.

Features of Cricut Explore Air 3

Considered one of the most powerful, precise, and user-friendly Cricut tools ever, the Cricut Maker's predecessor was already a versatile all-rounder and a household name in the realm of cutting plotters. This new machine has introduced additional functionalities to make it even more comprehensive.

It's important to note that both the Cricut Maker 3 and the previous models are renowned for their versatility and high performance. Whichever one you choose, you'll achieve success in customizing your projects and achieving professional results from the comfort of your home. The Cricut Maker 3 comes in a pastel blue color.

Quick Mode in Cricut and How to Use It

The innovative Quick Mode feature enables you to cut and write up to 2 times faster. It's accessible with settings for vinyl, adhesive vinyl, and cardstock in Design Space.

Once your design is ready, navigate to the cutting screen and click "Make it." You'll be amazed at how this machine cuts and delivers a flawless product. Quick Mode is available only when you've selected a compatible material on the Dial or in Design Space. Simply choose the Quick Mode button.

It's worth noting that Explore 3 doesn't support Quick Mode when using Smart Materials without a mat.

155

For matless materials, this machine is optimized to cut and write twice as fast as in Quick Mode.

Both the Cricut Maker 3 and Cricut Explore 3 automatically manage cutting speeds, rendering Quick Mode unnecessary. Keep in mind that these machines produce more noise when using Quick Mode, which is completely normal.

If you find that Quick Mode leads to inaccurate cuts or drawings, consider switching back to Normal Mode for your specific projects.

Accessories for the Cricut Explore 3

When you invest in machines like these, it's natural to want to know all the details. First, there's no need to worry about the blades because the Explore 3 is fully compatible with Explore Air 2 blades.

Blades and Tools Found in the Cricut Explore 3

Here's an overview of what comes with Cricut machines:

- **Fabric Blade**: The Cricut fabric blade, with its blade holder, is perfect for cutting fabric with your Cricut Maker or Explore machine. It's compatible with all Cricut machines and is identified by its pink color, used with the pink mat. The manufacturer recommends using it for cutting fabric with interfacing to prolong the blade's life.

- **Premium Fine Point Blade**: The Premium Blade is a high-quality fine point blade, a valuable addition for achieving perfection in your work. It's constructed with German carbide steel for durability and precision. Designed to handle tough cuts in various materials, including cardboard, vinyl, and paper, among others. This blade, identifiable by its gold color, includes a replacement blade and is compatible with Maker and Explore machines.

- **Rotary Blade**: Specially designed for cutting fabric and equipped with an adapter, the rotary fabric blade, known as Rotary Blade, allows you to cut delicate fabrics and materials for your sewing projects. This tool is exclusively compatible with Cricut Maker and Cricut Maker 3 machines. Crafted from premium stainless steel, it offers the strength required for the job. For exceptional results, it's recommended to use a dedicated fabric cutting mat (pink) and a specialized washable fabric marker.

- *Marking Tool*: This marking tool, used by Cricut machines, facilitates simultaneous cutting and marking of fold lines.

- *Roll Holder for Smart Materials*: Personalizing your Cricut projects is now easier than ever. These machines come with a roll holder for large vinyl runs. The Cricut Roll Holder allows you to align your Smart materials for precise cuts in lengthy projects, ranging from 3 meters to 22.8 meters (10 feet to 65 feet). It also includes a blade for straight cuts once you've completed the job.

Making Projects in Record Time

This equipment is designed to enhance the speed of your cutting machine. The new Cricut Explore Air 3 boasts more powerful motors, enabling it to cut up to twice as fast as before on Smart materials, all without compromising precision or power.

Works With Other Materials

The Cricut Explore 3 seamlessly works with both the new Smart Materials and the materials you're accustomed to using. These materials don't require a cutting mat to load or enter the machine; they position themselves automatically.

Thanks to this innovation, you can now create cuts up to 12 feet long at once for the first time. Another advantage is that you can focus on the most critical parts of your project because there's no preparatory work required.

Here's a basic overview of the Smart Materials available at launch:

- *Smart Vinyl*: Smart Vinyl from Cricut allows you to work on both permanent and removable projects. It offers a wide range of colors, effects, and material lengths ranging from 3 to 75 feet.

- *Smart Iron-On Textile Vinyl*: Design unique t-shirts for yourself or your team by selecting colors and effects. Cut a single image up to 4 feet long or repeat shapes up to 12 feet long. Personalize your t-shirts with ease.

Smart Paper Adhesive Cardstock: This cut-and-peel-and-stick material enables you to create entertaining cards, eye-catching banners, powerful posters, and layered paper crafts without messy glue.

- **Long-distance Work**: With the Cricut Explore 3, you have the creative freedom to cut enormous banners or even an entire solar system of stars, thanks to the ability to use Smart Materials to cut up to 12 feet (3.6 m) at a time without needing a mat. Simply load the materials and start cutting. This machine is equipped with sensors that measure the material before cutting to ensure you have enough for your project. The Design Space program will prompt you to load more material if needed. To keep the materials aligned from start to finish, it also includes material guides on the front and interior of the machine.

- **Endless Creative Possibilities**: Cricut Explore 3 opens up a world of creative possibilities by working with over 100 materials, including cardstock, regular and iron-on vinyl, and specialty materials like glossy paper and bonded fabric. Whether you're crafting T-shirts for a team or creating exceptional-ly long banners to support them, this machine has everything you need.

- **Decorate with Ease**: For cards and 3D creations, you can easily add flawless lettering, intricate graphics, foiled accents, or simple folds.

Frequently Asked Questions About Explore 3

What is the difference between Cricut Explore Air 2 and Cricut Explore 3?
They represent technological advancements in terms of speed, cut length, and compatibility with Smart Materials.

Is the installation procedure the same as it was for the previous generation?
No, to activate the Cricut Explore 3 device, visit Cricut.com/setup.

Does it matter how you attach the power cord to your Cricut Explore 3 machine?
Yes, as the Cricut Explore 3 features a 90-degree connector to prevent Smart Materials from coming into contact with the power cord when material extends from the back of the machine. Extending the feed cable is recommended to ensure material movement is not hindered.

Can I use the cable from my previous machine with the Cricut Explore 3?

No, because the power cord connector and receptacle on the Cricut Explore 3 differ from previous models.

How should the Smart Materials be loaded into the machine to be aligned?

Smart Materials should align with the material guidelines on the left. Gently bring the material up to the rollers while pushing the Load button.

Can you use hot melt vinyl or other vinyl brands without a mat?

No, it's recommended to use a cutting mat when using other vinyl or hot melt vinyl brands. Cricut Smart Materials have been rigorously tested for matless cutting on Cricut Explore 3 machines.

For those new to Smart Materials, what are they?

Smart Materials are materials that can be cut without a cutting mat. You can start cutting by loading the material into the Cricut Explore 3. They come in various types, including Smart Vinyl, Smart Iron-On, and Smart Paper Stickers.

Do Smart Materials need to be measured and cut before loading?

No, Smart Materials are loaded into the machine without prior measuring or cutting. For Smart Vinyl or Smart Iron-On, it's recommended to leave the material attached to the rest of the roll while cutting.

How do you know if there are enough Smart Materials for your project?

The Cricut Explore 3 measures the Smart Materials loaded for each project before cutting them. If more material is needed, Design Space will prompt you to load the necessary length.

Is buying a Cricut roll holder necessary if you intend to use rolls?

No, the Cricut Explore 3 is designed to work seamlessly with Smart Materials rolls up to 22.8 meters (75 feet) in length. While not mandatory, the Cricut roll holder is a helpful accessory for longer rolls, ensuring precise and clean cuts by keeping the material straight.

What type of motor does the Explore 3 have?

Explore 3 machines use a combination of servo and stepper motors.

How can I apply vinyl in long lengths?

You can easily apply long lengths of vinyl to your project's surface by following the provided instructions.

What equipment do I need to get started?

The necessary tools vary depending on your project.

Why does it take a while from when the pause button is pressed until the machine stops?

When you press the pause button, the computer retains a small piece of information from the active project to know what to do next. There's a slight delay while pausing as the computer processes the pause.

Here's What You Need to Know About the Warranty

To facilitate and expedite the warranty process, you'll need the customer's information and equipment serial number, along with specifying the model. Registering your warranty is crucial to reduce response times, and these machines come with a 1-year warranty directly from Lideart Innovación S de RL de CV. It's important to note that the warranty does not cover wear and tear on parts such as blades or Teflon.

Important: Using non-Cricut brand mats and repositionable adhesive voids the equipment's warranty.

In the event of a Cricut Explore 3 plotter failure, it's necessary to report it to the technical support department. Technical Support may offer guidance over the phone and, if necessary, request the shipment of the Cricut Explore 3 equipment to Chihuahua. Repair costs and parts are covered by the Cricut Explore 3 equipment manufacturer. Please note that the warranty does not include shipping costs for the Cricut Explore 3 plotter.

Warranties should be registered using the appropriate form before proceeding with any repairs.

Comparison Between Cricut Maker 3 and Cricut Maker

If you're contemplating which cutting plotter to purchase, torn between upgrading to the latest model with the Cricut Maker 3 or sticking with the tried-and-true Cricut Maker, here's a summary of what has changed and what remains the same to help you make your decision.

The price difference between the previous and current versions can be significant, but prices can vary.

Smart Materials: The New Materials You Can Use

As is widely known, Smart Materials

initially launched as a product line exclusively for Cricut Joy, a small cutting plotter. However, with this new version of their machines, you can now use Smart Materials with the Cricut Maker 3 and Cricut Explore 3.

Smart Materials are materials you can load directly into your plotter without needing a cutting mat because they have a specially designed reservoir. This feature saves you a considerable amount of time, as Cricut's data suggests that its machines work twice as fast with these materials.

With your plotter's assistance, you can cut individual designs or repetitive shapes (such as stars, hearts, or confetti) up to 6 meters on the Cricut Joy or 3.6 meters on the Cricut Maker 3 and Cricut Explore 3. This marks a significant difference compared to the maximum length permitted by previous plotter models, which was determined by the size of the cutting mat.

Working with Smart Materials is effortless because they come ready to load directly into your machine. As you load the material, the machine will measure it and ensure it's sufficient for your design project.

Note: It's important to know that you can only use Smart Materials with your cutting plotter if they are at least 10.15 cm long (4.13 in). If you have smaller pieces, you should use a cutting mat as you would with regular materials.

Now that you're familiar with the new Cricut Explore 3, you can choose the one that suits your project needs best. The advice is to opt for one of the new Cricut cutting plotters if you want to work faster and take advantage of the benefits of Smart Materials, which, as we've seen, represent the brand's future direction.

If you're not concerned about having the latest version and wish to enjoy exceptional features, you can consider the Cricut Maker champagne or Cricut Maker rose. These are excellent choices due to their exceptional quality-price ratio and few differences from the new model.

CHA PTER 2

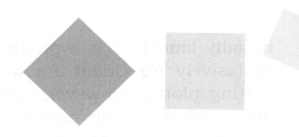

UNBOXING CRICUT EXPLORE AIR 3

"Shoot for the moon. You'll make it," is the motto of the Cricut Explore 3, which now comes with improved speed, additional features, and much more. In this chapter, you will learn in detail what you will find in the Cricut Explore 3 box.

The new Explore 3 machine now works with six tools, which are sold separately. You can slice, score, and even embellish your items with them. It can cut various materials, such as cardstock, vinyl, HTV (heat transfer vinyl), and even cardstock.

This piece of equipment has dimensions of Height: 15.01 cm (5.91 in), Length: 56.31 cm (22.17 in), Width: 17.80 cm (7.01 in), making it ideal for placement in both small and large spaces. It's a relatively easy machine to transport.

What Will You Find in the Cricut Explore Machine?

If you're wondering what you'll find in the box when you open it, rest assured that you'll discover:

- Cricut Explore 3 machine
- Premium fine tip blade + blade housing (pre-installed in the B clamp).
- Accessory adapter (pre-installed in clamp A)
- Quick Start Guide
- Safety document
- Warranty document
- USB cable
- Power adapter and power cord
- Test cutting material
- Bonus materials

Many features add value to this equipment. One interesting feature of the Explore 3 is the added shelf designed to make it easier to use tablets and mobile devices with the machine. This feature was present in previous models, and it's great to see it added to the Explore family.

If you've ever wanted to cut a small design with your scraps, you should know that it's now easy to determine whether you have enough material for the project. There's a small black sensor on the machine where the material passes through, registering the size of the materials, which will let you know if it's too small.

When you open your box, you may also notice that this machine comes with a Cricut smart plate. Cricut smart vinyl and Cricut smart adhesive paper are available and ready to use without needing an adhesive mat.

Another notable detail in the new Cricut roll holder is that it keeps any rolled material properly aligned for amazing and precise cuts. Additionally, it features a built-in trimmer that allows you to cut one straight edge at a time.

One of the Explore series' seven possibilities is the primary cutting tool. With it, you can cut cloth, mark fold lines on cardboard, write with pens, and transfer foil to other items. The Explore 3 allows for the simultaneous holding of two tools, making it feasible to swap between them without removing anything from the machine.

When compared to the riot of colors you'll find in any craft store, the range of possibilities on Cricut's website was beginning to get limited when it was launched. Offering smart material versions of everything is a significant ambition and an advantage for Cricut, given that paper, plates, and vinyl are the most popular products to use with their machines.

CHAPTER 3

THE MAIN DIFFERENCES WITH CRICUT EXPLORE AIR 2

In this chapter, you will discover the key distinctions between the Cricut Explore Air 3 and its predecessor, the Cricut Explore Air 2, a machine that has been the talk of the town since its launch. This has left many wondering about the benefits of the new version.

Differences With Cricut Explore Air 2

While the Explore 3 may not be the most advanced Cricut machine, it comes at a lower cost compared to the Maker-style cutting plotter machines, offering excellent value for money.

The Cricut Explore 3 has undergone significant changes compared to its previous version, evident from its redesigned appearance. Here are all the new features of the Cricut Explore 3:

- You can use Smart Materials with it.
- It can cut up to 3.6 meters (11.8 ft) at a time using Smart Materials.
- It can cut up to twice as fast as Smart Materials.
- The Cricut roll holder can support rolls of Smart Materials.
- It replaces the roulette wheel and buttons with a simple 4-button control panel.
- It offers larger storage for your tools.

As you can see, many of these changes are common to the evolution of the Cricut Maker 3 and are related to the use of Smart Materials.

The New Design of the Cricut Explore 3

Shared features with its predecessor, the Cricut Explore Air 2, include:

- It can cut more than 100 materials, including cardboard and vinyl.
- It offers six tools to expand its functionalities for cutting and marking.
- It features a double carriage to work with two tools simultaneously.
- You can connect to it via Bluetooth

and USB.

The Cricut Explore 3 is positioned as an intermediate option within the Cricut family, combining versatility and professionalism, like all cutting plotters in this range. It's a perfect choice to enhance the professional appearance of your crafts at a lower cost than the Cricut Maker.

Cricut Explore 3 vs. Cricut Explore Air 2

The Cricut Explore 3 is celebrated as Cricut's favorite plotter due to its versatility and convenience. It is designed as a straightforward cutting plotter, suitable for cutting thin materials like textile vinyl, adhesive vinyl, paper, or cardboard.

When comparing the new Cricut Explore 3 to the previous version, some differences are evident, while others are more subtle.

The primary and most apparent difference with the Cricut Explore 3 is the disappearance of the dial on the machine. With this change, like the Maker, you must now select the material from Cricut Design Space. This change offers more options to find the best fit.

Also, with the latest updates, where you can create your material, you need to have it in the "Custom" option to use it.

Another noticeable change is the new style of buttons on the machine. The new Explore no longer has protruding buttons; they are now flat.

Additionally, the "C" of Cricut has been changed to a "play" button, providing a more intuitive touch for starting cutting with the machine.

What You Find in the Cricut Explore 3 That Explore 2 Doesn't Have
Inside the machine, you will find a small plate that allows you to place Smart Materials straight in the machine, preventing them from entering at awkward angles.

Another visible change is in the machine's finish. Instead of the previous mint green with a glossy finish, the new Explore 3 has a matte finish.

Lastly, the machine's full name on the front has been removed, leaving only the brand name visible.

CHAPTER 4

IS CRICUT EXPLORE 3 THE RIGHT CHOICE FOR YOU? LET'S EVALUATE IT TOGETHER

If you are uncertain about purchasing this machine due to concerns about security, then in this chapter, you will discover several aspects and data that will help you make a decision.

The Noise of Cricut Explore 3

Perhaps this has been the main reason causing many to hesitate. While the Cricut is not a silent machine, it produces a somewhat loud and unusual sound that can be annoying at times. However, some believe it's a matter of getting used to it.

The Use of Vectors (SVG)

SVG files come in a flexible vector format that is easy to resize without compromising the quality of the design. It is the ideal choice for multi-layered files. You can use SVG files without incurring any extra costs. There are numerous websites where you can obtain designs at affordable prices and design them within the Cricut Design Space program.

It does not depend on your computer to work

One noteworthy feature is the ability to control the machine from your mobile phone or iPad. For example, if you find yourself far away from your Cricut but need to work on a project, you can comfortably do so from your mobile device. When you return to where your machine is located, you'll only need to press the GO button without the need to connect or transfer files to a PC. Additionally, creating stickers with personalized names is much easier with an iPad. Similarly, with a laptop, you don't need to have it nearby; Bluetooth technology allows you to stay connected, enabling you to operate the machine from a remote location and give it commands for cutting files.

Intelligent Adjustment Wheel

The most recent machine versions no longer include an adjustment wheel, as everything can be easily configured from the program.

Easy to Use

This machine is remarkably straightforward to use, suitable even for individuals who have never ventured into creative projects before. Its design is user-friendly. You place your mat and press the GO button. The software arranges the shapes on each mat, distinguishing between items to print or cut and assigning colors to each design. The most challenging decision is determining which material to use for each shape.

More Accurate Cuts on More Detailed Designs

Another reason why many opt for Cricut is its ability to make smaller, more precise cuts.

Machine Design

The design of the Cricut is visually appealing, as evident at first glance due to the wide variety of colors and designs available. While one shouldn't judge a machine solely by its appearance, there's no denying that aesthetics matter, especially when it will be a part of your workspace all day. Imagine having the machine in your favorite color.

Marker Adapter

The Cricut's marker cartridge can be used with different markers, not limited to the brand's markers, as they have a traditional design, unlike Silhouette's markers which tend to be small and chubby.

The Software Guides You When Cutting

In Cricut's Design Space, projects are practically a breeze. For elaborate designs, the system guides you on where to place materials during cutting. It also advises when to start drawing or create a folding line, and suggests which blade or accessory to use based on your chosen material.

More Reasons to Choose This Machine

Certainly, your creative mind is teeming with project ideas that are now possible with this machine. Here are some project ideas you might not have known were achievable with this machine:

- **Personalized mugs**: The first thing many make with the Cricut Explore Air 3 is custom mugs for hot beverages. Many choose to do this project first because they have several blank mugs and want to try a single-color design that they can also practice using vinyl on a curved surface.

- **Can coolers**: You can find blank can coolers online and craft a perfect gift or party favor. They can be personalized and are very easy to make.

- **Stickers** : Car window stickers or decals are everywhere. You can make them from anything you want, such as Calvin and Hobbs images, cartoon monikers, or sports logos. The best part is that the app teaches you through tutorials how to make stickers.

- **Coloring party ideas**: One of the reasons I wanted a Cricut machine was so that my kids' birthday parties would have 10s of decorations. The design of a color party is so simple and eye-catching at the same time. I appreciate the strong colors and direct concept of this proposal.

- **First birthday party ideas** : The most significant events in my family are first birthday celebrations and weddings. The year's occasion demands handcrafted, bespoke décor to make everyone speak about it.

- **Address labels**: You can create perfectly handwritten envelopes if you know all about Cricut pens. I like to use this feature, especially for birthday or thank-you cards.

- **Easter cupcake embellishments**: Any holiday may be altered for this fantastic project. You only need candy sticks or toothpicks and a Cricut Explore Air 3. You can make any image into a cupcake topper is fantastic.

- **Easter craft ideas**: If there's one event many enjoy, it's easy Easter celebrations for beginners. You can have over 500 Easter crafts and designs at your fingertips.

- **Printable Santa Claus letters**: My children and I practice writing letters to Santa every year. It's so much fun to observe how their Christmas desires shift yearly, and you can get a sense of what they want by reading the letters. Another thing I love is that they come with a free printable template.

- **Paper flower wreath**: Lindsay from Artsy Fartsy Mama is the creator of this lovely project. I adore the detailed instructions on cutting and assembling the paper flowers to make a beautiful wreath.

- **3D Paper flower magnets**: Similar in concept to the earlier project, although on a much smaller scale, these 3D paper flower magnets are incredibly attractive, and mounting the flowers on magnets to increase their adaptability strikes me as a brilliant idea. You know what? These 3D paper flowers would look cool as thumbtacks for a corkboard.

- **Photo magnets**: It is one of the next projects you must try making. It's lovely that you can use Cricut to cut and print sheets of magnets. Photo magnets are perfect for gift giving, making business cards, or even to use on a to-do list.

- **Easter coloring cards**: If you're having a big family gathering, chances are there will be kids, and there will probably be youngsters during a large family gathering, so this activity is a terrific way to utilize your Cricut Explore Air 3 to create coloring pages for the small visitors.

- **Valentine's coloring cards**: This design builds on the party themes and is for Valentine's Day. You can use crayons, markers, or colored pencils to decorate the cards.

- **Wooden tray**: Printing ordinary vinyl or heat transfer vinyl on wood is one of my favorite uses for the Cricut Explore Air 3. Giving something old, like a wooden tray, a new life is lovely.

CHAPTER 5

PROS AND CONS

Before making a purchase, it's important to understand the benefits and drawbacks of a Cricut Explore Air 3 machine. In this chapter, you will gain a detailed understanding of the pros and cons of these machines.

The Pros of the Cricut Explore Air 3 Machine

1. *Extraordinary Design*: One standout feature of this machine is its exceptional design. It introduces both convenience and aesthetics for creators. Gone are the protruding buttons; they are now flush with the surface

2. *Versatile Material Cutting*: Among its most outstanding features is its ability to cut more than 100 materials. It works seamlessly with smart materials, bringing innovation to your projects.

3. *Multiple Tools*: It offers six available tools designed to expand its functionalities, including cutting, marking, and more.

4. *User-Friendly Software*: Cricut Design Space, the software used with this machine, is available for free via the app. You can find it on the App Store, Google Play, and it's compatible with iOS, Mac, Windows, and Google platforms.

5. *Mobile Flexibility*: You can take photos from anywhere, edit them according to your needs, and create designs using the Cricut Design Space software on your phone, tablet, or laptop.

6. *Dual Carriage*: It integrates a dual carriage, allowing you to work with two tools simultaneously.

7. *Connectivity Options*: You can connect it via Bluetooth and USB. The Cricut Explore Air 3 is positioned as a middle-ground option within the Cricut family, offering versatility and professionalism akin to other cutting plotters in this range,

all at a more affordable price point than the Cricut Maker.

8. **_Improved Program Modification_**: It's never been easier to make modifications within the program. However, it's worth noting that Cricut's instructions in its materials can sometimes be inaccurate.

9. **_Flexibility and Mobility_**: The ability to design from anywhere is a significant advantage. Cricut has made remarkable strides in this regard.

10. **_No Cartridge Space_**: The space for cartridges, which had become outdated, is no longer present.

11. **_Extensive Typefaces and Shapes_**: You can expand your design options with hundreds of typefaces, shapes, and design concepts through the Cricut Access subscription service.

Cons of the Cricut Explore Air 3

Here are the drawbacks of the Cricut Explore Air 3

1. **_Costs_**: The Premium membership can only be purchased annually for a minimum of $120, without a monthly payment option. In contrast, the Standard subscription does offer monthly payments but is more economical when purchased annually, at a similar price to the Premium. Many users hesitate to commit to these costs unless they regularly work with the machine.

2. **Connectivity**: Some users have reported instability with the Bluetooth connection, which is a common issue with Bluetooth technology in general. It's advisable to stick with the reliable USB cable, unless your computer has an AMD Ryzen chip, in which case Cricut recommends using Bluetooth exclusively.

3. **Unidentified Materials**: Even when using genuine Cricut materials, several possibilities don't have the Smart Materials logo on the back. The Explore 3 may require significant adjustments to work properly with certain materials, similar to the challenges faced by Explore One users when cutting materials like glossy vinyl

4. **Basic Design Space Software**: The Design Space software, while functional as a controller for the machine, is relatively basic and may not be suitable for designing

intricate or high-quality items. It primarily serves as a commercial platform for Cricut, showcasing potential additional purchases and subscription-based options.

5. ***Accessory Purchase Requirement***: To unlock the machine's full potential and perform certain creative tasks, additional accessories are necessary. Additionally, you'll need specific Cricut pens for drawing or writing, which can contribute to increased costs beyond the initial investment.

TABLE OF CONTENTS

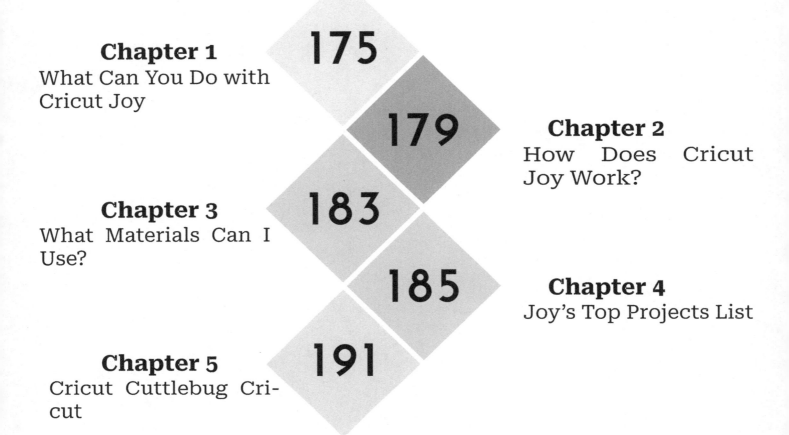

Chapter 1
What Can You Do with Cricut Joy — 175

Chapter 2
How Does Cricut Joy Work? — 179

Chapter 3
What Materials Can I Use? — 183

Chapter 4
Joy's Top Projects List — 185

Chapter 5
Cricut Cuttlebug Cricut — 191

BOOK 7 - CRICUT JOY

CHAPTER 1

WHAT ARE SOME USES FOR CRICUT JOY?

Cricut stands among the elite manufacturers, crafting top-tier plotters tailored for the artistry of handcrafting. If you're now the proud owner of a Cricut Joy, the ensuing nuggets of information are tailored for you.

Here's The Magic You Can Unleash With Your Cricut Joy

This nimble machine empowers you to cut and draw akin to other plotters, with a unique twist—you can do so up to a maximum width of 11 cm (4.3 in). Unlike its counterparts, it boasts a single carriage, where both the blade and markers find their home. Depending on your creative whim, switch between cutting or drawing by merely swapping the accessory. One notable feature is its specially designed mat for cardmaking.

Now, crafting folded cards is a breeze—the machine delicately cuts only the top layer, allowing you to slide in textured cardboard beneath.

And yes, the long-anticipated feature of mat-free cutting is here. With Cricut Joy, unleash cuts up to 10 cm wide and 1 meter long. For vinyl cuts, go ahead and extend that up to a staggering 6 meters.

What Materials Are Used on the Cricut Joy?

Embark on projects with common materials of moderate thickness—textile vinyl, adhesive vinyl, cardboard, paper, and adhesive paper. A word to the wise, veering towards thicker materials might spell peril for the machine, as it's not designed for such.

Understanding the essence and capabilities of this machine is pivotal to avoid any surprises down the creative lane.

At a first glance, you'll notice it lacks buttons—a Bluetooth connection is your gateway. Whether via mobile or tablet, the Design Space app is your conduit to creativity.

175

PC users, ensure you have Bluetooth; else, it's a no-go. The simplicity of this cutting plotter makes it a darling for last-minute, petite projects.

Why The Cricut Joy is a Gem?

Even for those with a larger cutting plotter, the allure of Cricut Joy is irresistible. It's a time-saver, whisper-quiet, and a portable companion for your creative quests. Essentially, it's a priceless addition for the creatively inclined, either as a first-time acquisition or a companion to larger machines.

Your Cricut Joy Package:

- Cricut Joy Machine
- Blade with a Blade Holder
- 0.4 mm Black Felt Tip Pen
- One 11.4 x 16.5 cm (4 x 6.5 in.) Regular Adhesive Mat
- Welcome Book
- Power Adapter
- Free Trial of Cricut Access (New Subscribers Only)
- 50 Free Projects

Note: Sample materials are for a maiden voyage, and the accessories and materials are exclusively compatible with Cricut Joy, not suited for the Cricut Maker or the Cricut Explore Air 2.

This compact marvel, despite its humble size, promises a plethora of creative adventures. Its petite frame invites you to keep it handy on your counter, ready to leap into action at a moment's notice.

Key Features to Fawn Over

Curiosity piqued about what this gadget can do? The Cricut Joy is your personal cutting, writing, and drawing companion, making mundane tasks a creative joy. From sprucing up your home and workspace to lending a personal touch to virtually anything, this machine is your go-to.

Dive into projects like labels, stickers, and cards with the Cricut Joy app, discovering endless ways to organize, decorate, and personalize your world. The Cricut Joy isn't just a smart, compact cutter; it's your ticket to a world where creativity knows no bounds.

Some quick highlights:

- Customize a plethora of ideas.
- Organize with tailor-made labels.
- Craft personalized cards in a jiffy.
- Decorate products or items in 15 minutes flat.
- Cut through at least 50 different materials, including smart materials designed for Cricut Joy.
- Perfect penmanship and drawing.

- Compact, portable, and ever-ready for creative action.

Utilizing the Cricut Joy

Create unique and functional items in a snap, from wall decals to personalized water bottle decals and beyond. Cut everyday materials with precision, making it a go-to for card crafting, vinyl decals, textile transfers, and various other projects. Plus, you can cut materials you already have at home, like paper and cardboard.

Its flawless writing and drawing capabilities make it ideal for penning a personal note, crafting an invitation, or labeling nearly anything.
Craft personalized cards in minutes, whip up last-minute birthday cards, thank you notes, or event invitations with pre-scored cards.

Reasons to Embrace the Cricut Joy

Here's a list of compelling reasons to consider bringing home a Cricut Joy:

Portable Creativity: If you already own a machine from the Cricut family like the Explore Air or Maker, and use it frequently, you've likely wished to take your creativity on the go.

The Cricut Joy is your travel-friendly companion. It's designed to be your secondary machine—the one you carry to the living room for a quick cut or take along on trips.

It's also a perfect companion for trade shows to whip up a personalized T-shirt on the spot, a scrapbooking workshop to create those missing decorations, or to the site where you plan to install a vinyl mural.

Despite its petite size, it's far from lacking in capability—in fact, it's quite the opposite!

No laptop needed—you can execute perfect cuts from your phone or tablet.

Quiet Operations: Known for their noise, cutting plotters aren't exactly stealthy. However, the Cricut Joy, despite its small stature, operates at half the volume.

The designers at Cricut have diligently worked to make it much quieter, eliminating those annoying noises common to many cutters. So, whether you're working late into the night or during a child's naptime, the Cricut Joy is a considerate choice. When a quieter time arises, you can switch to the larger machines for projects beyond the Joy's scope, but until then, this little machine keeps you crafting.

Maximize Your Space: When in the throes of a project, workspaces can quickly resemble a chaotic scene, and clearing space for the Explore or Maker might feel like a chore.

With the Joy, a small cleared space on your table suffices for a quick cut—it's a minimalist's dream come true.

It's estimated that 90% of your projects may fit within the Joy's cutting width. Cricut has taken great strides to ensure this machine aligns with users' demands and needs.

Exploring the Capabilities of the Cricut Joy Machine

Transitioning to a new system can pose challenges initially, especially when accustomed to a particular set of operating features.

However, the curiosity surrounding the jobs this innovative machine can handle is palpable. It's beneficial to have both machines, as it allows for a practical evaluation to determine if the Cricut Joy could potentially replace your existing machine someday.

Cricut enthusiasts often remain loyal to the brand. If you've tested and loved the Cricut Joy, even if you still have a preference for your old machine, you can continue using both without a hitch.

Seeking a Convenient Alternative: Some find it a hassle to use their Cricut machines, especially without a dedicated space.

The Joy addresses some of the inconveniences posed by other versions. For instance, it requires no clear space, there's no need to power up a computer, and it operates quietly.

The Cricut Joy emerges as a convenient, less demanding alternative, making the crafting process a bit more joyful.

CHAPTER 2

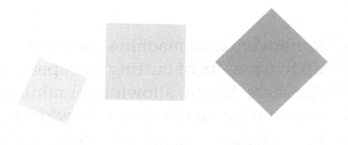

HOW DOES CRICUT JOY WORK?

In this chapter, you will learn about the workings of the Cricut Joy Mini Cutting Plotter, a perfect machine for home crafts and creative personalization projects.

With its ideal size, this innovative and stylish plotter becomes an incredibly versatile and indispensable machine for those who enjoy creating projects such as stickers or gifts. Simply put, this Cricut machine can accomplish many tasks for you, and we're here to delve into its capabilities.

If you have had or currently own a Maker, it's worth noting that the Cricut Joy continues the tradition of quality, but in a portable version with fewer features—it can cut and draw, but lacks an optical reader for Print & Cut functionality.

The Mini Plotter Cricut Joy is introduced as a fantastic smart crafting companion that is fun and easy to use for the inexperienced user wanting to customize practical everyday items such as cards, textiles, labels, jars, cups, bottles, folders, and boxes. It instills confidence in undertaking simple, everyday, yet original projects.

The Perfect Equipment for Your Crafts

If you already have it in your hands, you will undoubtedly notice its compact size—it fits comfortably in the palm of your hand, making it easily transportable and convenient to place anywhere. It operates at a good speed, delivering quality to every project, big or small.

Its maximum cutting width is precisely 11.4 cm (4.48 in), but it can cut up to 1.20 meters (3.93 ft) at a time using Cricut's Smart Cut materials that do not require a mat.

Moreover, this machine can achieve up to 6 meters of cutting by repeating the same design, allowing for minimal material waste thanks to the wide and revolutionary range of textile vinyl and adhesives that are easily loaded onto the machine.

Cricut Joy Cutting Materials

The Cricut Joy machine can cut conventional materials such as textile and sign vinyl, cardboard, paper, thin acetates, thin synthetic leathers, and other not very thick or dense materials.

A notable advantage is that Cricut offers its Smart Cut materials, which can be cut without a mat as they have a rigid backing or liner that prevents damage to the machine.

Although not recommended by Cricut, you can create smart materials by trimming them with a guillotine to a width of 14 cm (5.5 in), ensuring the cut is perfect and clean to avoid damaging the machine. Precision is key. An interesting detail is that textile vinyl comes with a plastic backing. On lettering vinyl, which has a paper liner, over-cutting can occur if the material is not adjusted correctly.

Cricut Joy Accessories

This section is a favorite among creators. With the purchase of the Cricut Joy, you'll receive the blade along with the specific blade holder, a black marker with a 0.4 mm stroke thickness, and the conventional cutting mat with a cutting area of 11.4 x 16.5 cm (4.48 x 6.49 in).

- The Cricut Joy machine and the Cricut Joy blade holder are compatible.
- Note that the Cricut Joy blade holder is silver and white.

Additionally, it may be used with any Cricut Joy materials, including Smart Materials, Infusible Ink transfer sheets, insert cards, vinyl, heat transfer vinyl, paper, cardstock, cardboard, and many more. It can also be used with regular DIY materials.

Important: The blades are sharp, so exercise extreme caution. Only adults should handle them.

It's crucial to note that the blades and markers are specific to the Joy, so those from other machines are not interchangeable.

Moreover, you can purchase the long cutting mats, standard adhesive, and low-adhesion adhesive mats, each with a cutting area of 11.4 x 30.5 cm (4.48 x 12 in). A special mat for cards is also available for purchase if desired.

Regarding mat usage, Smart Materials are available in various types, including Smart Vinyl, Smart Iron-On, Smart Label Writable Paper, and Smart Label Writable Vinyl.

These DIY Smart Materials do not require a cutting mat, so you can feed the material directly into your Cricut Joy.

Connectivity and Software

Given that the Cricut Joy machine lacks USB ports, connectivity is achieved exclusively via Bluetooth. It operates with the Cricut Design Space software, which has a desktop version, eliminating the need for an internet connection to use your Joy. Furthermore, you can operate the plotter from your phone or tablet using the free app available in the app store of your electronic device.

Cricut Joy Mini Cutting Plotter: A Remarkable Creative Toy

The Cricut Joy Mini Cutting Plotter emerges as a remarkable toy for crafting enthusiasts and entrepreneurs seeking to add unique touches to their creations. This device enables cutting, writing, and drawing on a variety of materials to personalize objects like cell phone cases, plastic containers, glass jars, glasses, T-shirts, bodysuits, pants, slippers, and to decorate spaces.

What more can you do? Create adhesive stickers for helmets, skateboards, flashlights, wooden signs, and acrylic panels, or embellish corporate cards, greeting cards, or invitations.

This machine packs a punch with the same precision and speed as its larger counterparts, the Cricut Maker and Cricut Explore Air 2, while being easily transportable. It's ideal for infusing personality into your everyday life and crafting original items that make your loved ones feel special.

Did you know you can also create identification stickers with the Cricut Joy? It's perfect for organizing your kitchen sections, personalizing back-to-school gear, and many other uses. Its versatility also makes it a valuable tool for businesses.

Installation of the Cricut Joy

Installing the Cricut Joy is a breeze, and the steps are as follows:

1. Select the machine in the Design Space.

2. Connect the device via Bluetooth.
3. Follow the guidelines in the Design Space to create the initial cut.

As you may have observed, the Cricut Joy lacks buttons, so all operations are conducted via Bluetooth from your cell phone or computer screen.

It's undeniable that ordinary, useful endeavors have never been simpler. If you own a Maker or Air 2, the Cricut Joy expands your creative horizons with its unique features, making it the ideal companion for short projects that don't require mats or lengthy cuts.

Importantly, if you own another Cricut machine, you might consider purchasing the Cricut Joy for crafting on-the-go. Its portability is perfect for those engaging in projects at bazaars or decorating events, among many other activities. Additionally, the Cricut Joy has a carrying case available, making it a travel-friendly option.

CHAPTER 3

WHAT MATERIALS CAN I USE?

The Cricut Joy cutter is versatile in handling various basic materials for your DIY projects. In this short chapter, you will discover a list of materials compatible with the Cricut Joy. A significant benefit is that Design Space already includes the cutting parameters for these materials. This list will continue to expand as more materials are examined.

Materials You Can Use with the Cricut Joy

Here is the list of the official materials you can use with the Cricut Joy machine:

- Artboard
- Corrugated Cardboard
- Flat Cardboard
- Metallic Cardboard
- Cardboard
- Glitter Cardboard
- Insert Card, Cardstock

- Medium Thickness Cardstock, 216 g (80 lb)
- Heat Transfer Vinyl
- Everyday Heat Transfer Mosaic
- Hot Melt Adhesive Vinyl Mesh with Glitter
- Holographic Heat Transfer
- Holographic Heat Transfer Mosaic
- Holographic Heat Transfer with Glitter
- Infusible Ink Transfer Sheet
- Smart Iron-On
- Smart Iron-On, Glitter
- Smart Iron-On, Holographic
- Smart Iron-On, Embossed
- Sportflex Heat Transfer Vinyl
- Leather
- Synthetic Leather (very thin)
- Paper
- Deluxe Paper
- Deluxe Paper with Adhesive Backing
- Deluxe Paper with Metal Embossing
- Aluminum Foil, 0.36 mm
- Pearlized Paper
- Glossy Paper
- Smart Label Writable Paper
- True Brushed Paper

- Plastic
- Acetate with Embossed Metal
- Vinyl
- Foil Adhesive - Metallic Vinyl
- Chalkboard Vinyl
- Dry Erase Vinyl
- Holographic Vinyl with Glitter
- Premium Vinyl
- Premium Vinyl, Frosted Gloss
- Premium Vinyl, Frosted Grey
- Premium Vinyl, Frosted Opaque
- Premium Vinyl, Holographic
- Premium Vinyl, Holographic with 3D Texture
- Premium Vinyl, Art Deco Holographic
- Premium Vinyl, Holographic Bubbles
- Premium Vinyl, Holographic Frosted Film
- Premium Holographic Spun Holographic Film
- Premium Vinyl, Mosaic
- Premium Vinyl, Pearlized
- Premium Vinyl, Textured
- Premium Vinyl, Metallic Textured
- Premium Vinyl, True Brushed
- Smart Label Writable Vinyl
- Smart Vinyl, Holographic Embossing
- Smart Vinyl, Matte Metalized
- Smart Vinyl, Permanent
- Smart Vinyl, Temporary
- Smart Vinyl, Glossy
- Vinyl Stencil
- Plastic Chip Paper, Glossy
- Window Sticker

Identifying Smart Materials

Smart Materials are distinguished by a special backing, allowing them to be inserted into the Cricut Joy without a cutting mat.

The software will prompt you when to load your Smart Materials and indicate the amount needed. Once the material is loaded, the machine will measure it to ensure there is enough for your project.

The Cricut Joy maintains an upper margin of 2.5 cm (0.98 in) and a lower margin of 1.25 cm (0.49 in) to allow the rollers to grip and feed the material. The sensor checks that enough material is loaded for it to move through the machine smoothly.

These margins are considered by the software when calculating the Smart Materials needed for your project. To ensure you have enough Smart Materials for your design, wait until the cutting process is complete before trimming.

CHA PTER 4

JOY'S TOP PROJECTS LIST

This machine unlocks the potential to personalize bottles, mugs, cups, glasses, glass jars, and more. Hence, it's essential to familiarize and practice this list of projects you can easily execute. The beauty of it shines through once you delve into the projects! After exploring its main features, the next step is to put it to work. Here's a simple project many people enjoy, which you should try out:

Projects You Can Do on the Cricut Joy

Below is a list of projects you can tackle with the Cricut Joy. This small, lightweight machine can bring endless ideas to life, from the simplest to the most elaborate.

Please note that this chapter is not designed to guide you step-by-step through the implementation of these projects. Instead, it aims to provide a simple list of the most popular and frequently requested projects that the Cricut Joy can accomplish. While a few steps to complete each project will be provided, detailed step-by-step instructions for executing the projects will be covered in later chapters. Rest assured.

"Baby on the Way" Card
1. For this project, use the Cricut Joy card mat.
2. Click on the option that leads you to enter the design.
3. Prepare the file for production.
4. Correctly insert the card.
5. Place the marker for the text to enable writing.
6. Switch out the marker and insert the cutting blade.
7. Then remove the mat and place the colored base inside the card.
8. Finish with extra embossing details.

Baby Bodysuit with Cricut Joy + Mini Easy Press 2
1. For this project, only smart black vinyl is required.
2. Click on the option to access this design.
3. Prepare the file for production.
4. Insert the smart vinyl into the Cri-

cut Joy for cutting.

5. Remove excess material.
6. Place the iron-on over the baby bodysuit.
7. Execute iron-on with the Easy Mini Press 2.

Cricut Joy Stickers/Labels

1. The baby control stickers are perfect for monitoring the baby's activities.
2. For this project, only Smart Label material is required.
3. Next, navigate to the Cricut Design application and prepare the file for production.
4. Then, insert the smart label material into the machine.
5. Start drawing.
6. Proceed to cut.

Customize Bottles

Upload your image, trace it based on its complexity, and save it as a cut image. You'll assemble two pieces of vinyl, so upload and trace two images:

1. Insert them into your workspace.
2. Change the color of the bottom layer to enhance its visibility and align them.
3. Resize to fit within the drag blanket area.
4. With your chosen image selected, click "Make it."
5. Select the "On Mat" material loading option. You'll see the two cuts

appear separately.

6. Pick the one you want to cut first and select a material from the list. Remember, you can create and edit your materials by clicking on settings.
7. Consider selecting premium vinyl for the sign vinyl.
8. Cut the vinyl using a guillotine or scissors and place it on the drag blanket.
9. Ensure the blade is properly positioned and load the cutting mat; it will automatically insert as you bring it close to the rollers.
10. Press GO, and it will start cutting.
11. After cutting, press UNLOAD.
12. Remove the material from the mat, place the other one, and load it into the plotter.
13. Press GO, and it will cut the second vinyl.
14. Unload and peel it off the drag mat.
15. Now, discard the excess from the two vinyl pieces. Utilize peeling tools for assistance.
16. Cut a piece of vinyl carrier, peel off a portion, and adhere it over the top design with a putty knife's help.
17. Slowly lift the protractor, and the design will adhere.
18. Place it on the bottom vinyl and use the spatula to secure it properly.
19. Lift the protractor, and you have the two designs together.
20. Carefully position them on the bottle, ensuring it's centered.

21. Press firmly and remove the carrier.
22. Eliminate any air bubbles to ensure it adheres well.
23. Your personalized bottle is now ready!

Personalized Cards

In this project, which is highly popular among creatives, you can test this machine's capabilities. Additionally, you will be combining the use of a marker and blade:

1. Use the shapes panel to create a rectangle measuring 11.4 x 15.9 cm (4.48 x 6.25 in); this will serve to position the entire design.
2. Create 2 cm (0.78 in) diagonal lines and place them at equidistant corners. These will be used to insert special cardboard.
3. Upload your image, trace it, save it as a cut image, and insert it into the workspace.
4. Resize and position the image.
5. Now click the "path" dropdown above and select "draw."
6. Add text and a heart for cutting. Position everything appropriately and turn off the rectangle layer.
7. Select all layers, click "attach," then click "make it."
8. Select the card mat this time.
9. Click continue and select the material. In this case, choose medium card stock to cut regular cardstock.
10. Cut a 22.8 x 15.9 (8.97 x 6.25 in) card stock and fold it in half.
11. Open the inside of the card mat and insert the folded card.
12. Remove the protective plastic and secure the card stock so it won't move during cutting.
13. Now, you need to load the marker into the Joy. Open the tab, remove the blade, and drop the marker until it stops. Close the tab and load the mat.
14. In Design Space, press GO, and it will immediately start drawing. For a complex drawing like this, it may take a few minutes.
15. Once done, switch the marker to the cutting blade, and in the software, press GO.
16. It will start cutting immediately. When finished, carefully unload the mat and remove the card, as it will be quite stuck.
17. Then, as a final step, insert the metallic effect card you have not previously cut inside, taking advantage of the cuts in the corners.

Stamping T-Shirts with Cricut Joy and Hobby Iron

Although the cutting area of the Cricut Joy is limited, you can combine pieces of vinyl of different sizes and textures to create a larger set, as in this t-shirt that you can easily stamp using the Hobby Manual Iron.

Here's how you can make it:

1. Upload your image, trace it, and insert it into your workspace.
2. Scale it to the desired size.
3. Now duplicate the layer and click 'contour' at the bottom right.
4. Click on Hide all contours and select the parts you want to cut separately.
5. Close and repeat for the rest of the design.
6. Now go to the sync tab at the top right. Select a color for each part of the design that you will cut with a different vinyl.
7. Click "Make it." Choose "on the mat," and you will see that it has automatically organized the designs by color.
8. Choose the material. Since this is turbo vinyl, we will choose everyday iron-on.
9. Remember to activate mirror mode for textile pieces of vinyl.
10. Place the vinyl on the mat, and load it. Press the cut option.
11. When the cut is finished, unload the material.
12. Now, on the next cut, we are going to change the material to cut to glitter vinyl; we will choose holographic sparkle Iron-On.
13. Load the vinyl onto the mat and insert it into the Joy.
14. Repeat the operation for the rest of the colors.
15. Perform weeding of the vinyl with the help of weeding tools.
16. Heat the iron to 160°C (320F) and set it for 5 seconds.
17. Place the protective pad on the table.
18. Place the T-shirt on top and pre-iron for a few seconds.
19. Arrange the design and leave the first vinyl to iron.
20. Iron for 5 seconds applying pressure.
21. Remove the hot carrier. If it lifts, press for a few more seconds.
22. Repeat the operation for the rest of the pieces of vinyl.
23. Perform a final ironing of 20 seconds using protective paper and applying even pressure.

Remember: The free Cricut Design Space software is required for the Cricut machine, regardless of model. The design is created using this program, which then sends it to the cutting tool.

If you intend to cut out items like illustrations and graphics, you might wish to complement your Cricut with additional design tools like Adobe Photoshop or Adobe Illustrator.

Remember that the Cricut is not a printer; it cannot print graphics. Instead, it cuts materials like cardstock, sticky paper, vinyl, and others.

Wooden Photo Frame

Did you know that you can decorate a wooden photo frame with the help of your Cricut Joy mini-cutting plotter? You will only need materials such as:

- Acrylic paints
- A wooden word from Sweet Möma
- Sweet Möma decorative elements.

Here's how you can make it:

1. Cut some 3D flowers (design "flowers shoppe") with your Cricut Joy and shape them using tweezers. Also, cut some leaves ("flowers in spring" design).
2. Paint the frame with acrylic paint, creating a color gradient.
3. Choose a small wooden message piece, from Sweet Möma in this case, and add a touch of glitter.
4. Create a composition using the flowers and leaves, the wooden message, and some die cuts from Sweet Möma's Aire collection. If desired, glue all the elements together.
5. Add the final touches, and your project is complete!

Vinyl stickers with Cricut Joy

Here's what you'll need:

- Cricut Joy
- Design Space software
- Cricut Removable Smart Vinyl
- Cricut Regular-size Removable Vinyl with a Blue Matte Cut
- Weeding Tool
- Sticker Sheets (I was overjoyed with sticker sheets as a kid!)
- Seasonal Window Decals
- Wall Decals
- Party Decals
- Bounty Boards
- Homemade Board Games
- Envelope Stamps
- Pantry Labels

Follow these steps:

1. Click on the Images option in the left bar and search for images. I created summer-themed sheets, so I searched for terms like ice cream, summer, beach, bike, and car.
2. When selecting images, individual ones work best, like the example below. Ensure the image is fully connected to peel off in one piece.
3. Choose a single color for your mat images. All images should be of the same color to be successfully cut on the same sheet of vinyl.
4. If your sticker image has multiple layers, you have two options: you can ungroup it and remove unwanted parts by navigating to the right corner as shown below, or you can weld it together. Welding will turn it into a solid image.

To remove the black glass in my image, I ungrouped and discarded the glass.

5. If you wish to cut shapes into a single image for your stickers, overlay the image you want to cut, right-click, highlight to select, and then click SLICE in the lower right corner.

6. To arrange your images for Cricut Joy vinyl decals and ensure you have the right quantity, work on the mat sized 4.5" wide x 11" deep (or more if you have longer vinyl). This will give you a visual idea of how much more space you have.

Cutting your Cricut Joy Vinyl Stickers

1. Click in the upper right corner to preview how your stickers will be cut. Design Space will arrange them to save space and minimize waste, although it may not always be optimal.

2. You'll need to select the material before you can view the cut mat. Here, you'll see the final cut design.

3. Joy will now extend the vinyl to ensure there's enough for your cut.

4. To minimize waste, consider adding a few more images to cut. However, you'll need to manually drag the images on the mat to create room.

5. To drag an image, click on it and drag; this is an excellent way to fill negative space and conserve vinyl.

6. Continue this process until your mat is full. The boundary lines on the edge of the mat represent the cutting limit; it won't allow you to go beyond that line.

CHAPTER 5

CRICUT CUTTLEBUG CRICUT

Discover a portable and versatile crafting companion in the Cricut Cuttlebug Cutting and Embossing Machine. This device allows you to cut and emboss a variety of materials, making your creative ideas come to life.

Commonly recognized as an embossing machine, the Cricut Cuttlebug stands out for its non-electronic operation. It's compatible with several materials including leather, thin felt, thin metal, acetate, foil, thin wood, chipboard, card stock, and paper, provided the material thickness does not exceed 1/8 of an inch to prevent jamming.

Here's what's included:

- 1 x 6×8 chuck
- Instruction manual
- A2 embossing folder
- 2 B cutting plates (6×8)
- 2 metal dies
- One 6×8 embossing mat

Note: The C plate is an optional accessory not included with the machine. Although earlier versions featured it, the V2 version does not. The C-plate is only necessary if you plan to use dies from brands like Sizzix and Spellbinders.

Cricut Cuttlebug Discontinuation

Cricut continually strives to innovate and introduce products that expand creative horizons. However, this also entails making tough decisions regarding the discontinuation of existing product lines.

Limitations

The Cuttlebug has a material depth limit of 1/8", while the Cricut Explore can cut deeper with a deep cutting blade. Despite this, the Cuttlebug excels in delivering clean, crisp cuts, and professional-quality embossing on paper, card stock, and more.

Moreover, it's compatible with various brand dies, enabling you to cut a range of materials from paper and cardboard to stiffened fabric, felt, and Eva foam—ideal for scrapbooking!

Your package includes everything you need to start: 1 bottom plate, 2 spacer plates, 1 rubber base, 1 embossing folder, and a pair of metal cutters. The machine has a mouth opening of 6" (15.2 cm) and weighs 3.2 Kg (7 lb).

With the Cuttlebug Scrapbooking machine, expressing creativity becomes a breeze. This machine is your go-to ally for texturizing and cutting all kinds of materials including leather, fabric, felt, Eva foam, and cardboard. It empowers you to craft fun felt accessories, fabric appliqués, EVA photo accessories, cut-outs, and decorations for your scrapbooking albums.

The compact, easy-to-transport design of the Cuttlebug, which requires no electricity, is a notable feature. Its unique lamination technology ensures sharp cuts and professional-grade embossing. The suction cup mechanism, activated by opening its side wings, ensures a firm grip on the work table.

Operating the Cuttlebug Scrapbooking Machine:

1. Position your Cuttlebug on a smooth surface, open its side wings, and deploy its crank.
2. Place the main plate "A" on a flat surface. Assemble a sandwich with its methacrylate plates "B" or "C," alongside one of its metal cutters, embossing folder, and the material you wish to customize (cardboard, felt, Eva foam, etc.).
3. Insert the assembled sandwich into your Scrapbooking Cuttlebug machine using its rotating crank. And voila!

Comparison with Sizzix Big Shot:

Both machines share similar functions, yet the Cricut Cuttlebug scores high on portability due to its foldable design.

Compatibility with Other Brands:

The Cuttlebug machine accepts many creative cutters and embossing folders. You can also use brands like Sizzix, Nellie's, Tonic, etc., by adjusting the spacer plates to achieve the right height sandwich. However, due to ongoing product innovations, it's not guaranteed that 100% of accessories from manufacturers other than Provocraft will be compatible.

If you opt for this machine, it's advisable to research whether it shares the same functions as other Cricut machines.

TABLE OF CONTENTS

Chapter 1
Cricut HatPress

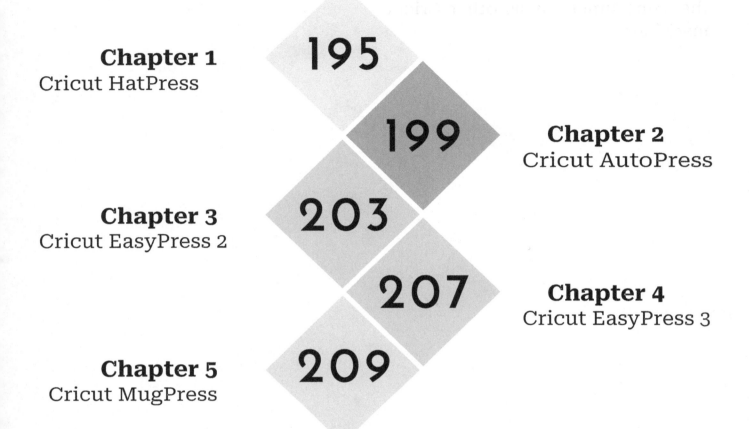

195

199

Chapter 2
Cricut AutoPress

Chapter 3
Cricut EasyPress 2

203

207

Chapter 4
Cricut EasyPress 3

Chapter 5
Cricut MugPress

209

BOOK 8 - CRICUT PRESS

CHAPTER 1

CRICUT HATPRESS

There was a time when printing on specialized materials was both expensive and cumbersome, typically requiring outsourcing to a specialized company. Fortunately, those days are behind us, thanks to a plethora of technologies now available for a wide range of hobbies and professions.

Have you ever imagined printing on caps right from the comfort of your home, without needing extensive equipment? It's now possible! With the advent of hot melt materials, Cricut's EasyPress line has emerged as one of the most notable players in this space.

Over the years, Cricut has developed practical, multi-purpose presses in various sizes to cater to a broad spectrum of users. One of their exciting new offerings is the Cricut Hat Press.

The Cricut Hat Press is designed with a handle, simple front buttons, and a power cord. It's a cutting-edge machine boasting a thermally safe cradle that dissipates heat even at maximum temperature settings. Cricut has ingeniously designed a special portable hat form to hold the hat securely while working.

Unboxing

Inside the box, you'll find:

- Cricut Hat Press.
- Cricut Hat Pressing Form: to securely hold the hat and provide a firm curved surface.
- Heat-stick design for practice projects.
- Heat-resistant tape.
- Quick start guide and user's guide.

One of the stellar features of this robust machine is its versatility. It accommodates a variety of products, ranging from fisherman's hats, grid caps, to regular hats.

The Cricut Hat Press is compatible with Cricut hot melt vinyl, Infusible Ink pens, and foils, facilitating quick, easy, and professional-quality heat transfers.

Its innovative technology pairs a curved heat plate with a flexible cap and hat press die, ensuring a smooth transfer process. The press die is compatible with a wide variety of adult caps and hats, including sun and baseball caps, providing a solid surface for curved materials. Ease of use is at the forefront of the Cricut Hat Press design. It comes with customizable thermal settings based on the material, alongside three presets, heating up to 205°C (401F) to work harmoniously with all major brands of hot melt vinyl, Infusible Ink, and sublimation products.

An additional benefit is its wireless capability. Although it comes with a box, there's no need for a wired connection; its technology syncs effortlessly with mobile devices via Bluetooth.

The Cricut Hat Press seamlessly integrates with the Cricut Heat app, transmitting settings directly to the device. Through the complimentary app available in app stores, step-by-step directions guide you from pre-preparation, ironing, all the way to removing the protective paper, making the process straightforward and enjoyable.

What Materials Can Be Used

The Cricut Hat Press is ideal for crafting baseball caps, yet its versatility extends to various hat styles including fisherman's hats, visors, certain children's hats, and more. The Cricut Heat app facilitates settings for ten different materials, encompassing cotton, nylon, mesh, and neoprene.

Cricut has introduced two new compatible blanks: the Cricut Trucker Hat and a Grey Ball Cap. These hats are compatible with hot melt vinyl and Infusible Ink. Additionally, the Cricut Hat Press can transfer various types of heat transfer vinyl (HTV), Infusible Ink, and sublimation materials.

To craft a hat with the Cricut Hat Press, you'll need the following items:

- Cricut Hat Press
- Hat press form
- Strong, heat-resistant ribbon
- A hat blank: any hat of your choice
- Heat-set vinyl
- Infusible ink transfer sheets or pens
- Mobile device to access the Cricut Heat app
- Cricut machine and tools

- StandardGrip cutting mat
- Weeding tool

Cricut blank hat material compositions include

1. Blank Cricut baseball cap, gray: 80% polyester, 20% cotton
2. Cricut blank grid cap, black mesh with white front: 100% polyester

The hat press mold features a solid core made of a special material that allows the mold to adapt to your blank hat while providing a firm pressing surface. It's engineered to remove moisture and direct heat to the project.

Successful heat transfers necessitate a solid pressing surface, and this pressing mold is specifically designed to offer a moldable yet sufficiently firm surface for projects.

What Items Can Be Made

The Cricut Hat Press comes with a pressing die and a roll of heat-resistant tape, enabling you to execute projects on both caps and hats.

Initiating a unique design in Cricut Design Space is the first step. For beginners, a free cap design setup project has been specially crafted for Cricut customizable caps, simplifying design and cutting processes. Once the design and materials are finalized, time and temperature settings are configured via the Cricut Heat app, with the rest being a straightforward step-by-step process guided by on-screen instructions.

The app transmits the time and temperature settings to the press, and upon pressing the start button, a countdown commences based on the material and customizable item in process. The machine will sound an alert upon completion; additionally, the app notifies when to remove protectors and adhesives.

How It Works

The marvels of technology have birthed functionalities that simplify device usage, and Cricut Heat is no exception. All setup and management are handled through the mobile app, available for free download from Google Play and Apple App Store, compatible with iOS or Android devices meeting the same system requirements as Design Space.

It's vital to note that the app is required to activate the Cricut Hat Press. Post activation, the device is ready for use without any further setup.

Activation also entails automatic account registration online.

Step by Step to Configure the App

On an iOS or Android mobile device, utilize the Cricut Heat app to activate the Cricut Hat Press. Once connected and powered on, precise settings can be transmitted and step-by-step directions for each project received.

Upon power-up, the Power/Temperature button will flash white, signaling activation mode. If you already possess a Cricut.com/Design Space account, it's advisable to use the same login for the Cricut Heat app.

Cricut Hat Press employs Bluetooth Lite technology to pair with your smart device and communicate with the Cricut Heat app. Manual pairing through Bluetooth settings isn't required; simply power on the machine within 7 feet of the smart device, ensuring Bluetooth is activated, and it will connect automatically.

In the Cricut Heat app, select the Configure option to initiate activation. Next, select the unit from the list of available Heat Presses and tap on Connect.

The app will display "Connecting to Hat Press" alongside the Bluetooth logo.

You'll be prompted to confirm the activation of the Cricut Hat Press and the email address for registering the unit will be displayed. After reviewing the Cricut Terms of Use and Privacy Policy, check the box next to them, and click Activate.

CHAPTER 2

CRICUT AUTOPRESS

The Cricut Autopress is a game-changer for at-home T-shirt and garment design creation. This commercial-grade heat press enables easy, professional design crafting right from your home.

Technologically akin to the EasyPress 3, the Cricut Autopress, although smaller, delivers consistent results thanks to a heat plate that distributes heat evenly. It's designed to the standards of a commercial-grade hot plate, making it a formidable tool for creating customized T-shirts, bags, beddings, and other items with hot melt vinyl and materials like Cricut's proprietary Infusible Ink.

Sporting a modern "clamshell" design, the Autopress is crafted to save space and comfortably fit on a standard desk or crafting table. It measures 15 x 12 inches (38 x 30 cm) and weighs 53 pounds (24.13 kg)—a necessary heft to ensure stability.

Despite its somewhat large and heavy stature, the Autopress embodies elegance with its sleek curves and simple design, aligning with the aesthetic of its Cricut siblings. This shiny, curved gadget exudes a classy and understated appeal wherever placed. A notable design feature is the four-point hinge, which facilitates an upward opening, while the lid straightens and descends vertically onto the ceramic firing plate when lowered. This feature, coupled with its ability to accommodate varying material thicknesses, enhances its ease of use. The tool autonomously adjusts its pressure according to the material in use, requiring minimal effort.

With the Cricut Autopress, reaching high temperatures is a matter of seconds, and the clamped lid alongside the heat plate transfers a pattern onto each garment in approximately 30 to 40 seconds. This efficiency enables the creation of hundreds of designs in mere minutes!

Unboxing

Upon unboxing the Autopress, you'll find:

- A white envelope containing a warranty information card with a redirect to the website for machine access and activation.
- Smart vinyl sample sheet.
- Superior packaging parts.
- USB power cord.
- Plastic sleeve with sample material: This includes a holographic smart hot melt vinyl sheet, smart removable vinyl sheet, transfer paper sheet, and smart adhesive paper sheet.
- A fine tip blade already installed on the machine in clamp B.
- Attachments for the power cord and USB cable.

What Materials Can Be Used

The Cricut Autopress is engineered to work with a variety of heat-transfer materials such as:

- Infusible Ink and sublimation materials.
- Heat Transfer Vinyl (HTV).
- Screen print transfers.

Additionally, the following are also utilized:

- Cricut Thermal Guide: Contains recommended time, temperature settings, stacking, and pressing instructions for diverse projects.
- Cricut Press Mat (included with the Cricut Autopress).
- Cricut smart cutting machine for design cutting.
- Design Space software accessible on a mobile device or computer.
- Profiling tool.
- Scissors.
- Pressure cushion (optional).
- Heat transfer vinyl (HTV) protection sheet/Teflon sheet (optional).

For those printing designs at home, sublimation inks should be used with a sublimation printer.

Other essential materials include:

- Lint roller
- Heat-resistant tape
- Lint paper (included with Infusible Ink Transfer Sheets)
- Cardstock (80 lb, white)
- Outlining tool
- Tweezers

The Cricut Autopress bridges the gap between commercial and at-home design creation, making professional garment designing an accessible venture for all.

What Can You Create?

With a simple two-finger action to turn on the press, let the machine take over from there. The motors activate and autonomously apply pressure depending on the material thickness, showcasing one of the market's easiest-to-close heat presses.

Distinct from other presses, the Cricut Autopress employs a hinge system that moves the heat platen vertically before it closes onto the material. It auto-adjusts to materials up to 2" thick, eliminating the need for manual pressure setting adjustments. Once the timer hits zero, the machine opens up, raising your pressure set. As you push down, a motor automatically activates to measure the material thickness, ensuring perfect pressure.

The Cricut Autopress automatically opens post-pressing, a feature designed for handling large batches or orders. While it's working, you can prep and align your next press with an additional mat, epitomizing efficiency when tasked with producing a stack of bags or a large T-shirt order.

For designs too large for the 12" x 10" EasyPress, the Cricut Autopress, with its 15" x 12" heat platen, is ideal for crafting T-shirts and other sized clothing.

How It Works

With a click, the Autopress lid securely shuts. Once the Autopress control is triggered, the preset temperature settings warm the plate to the desired temperature for your material.

For substantial jobs, set the timeframe and let the machine do the rest—the presets are programmable. The hot plate also facilitates easy material removal.

Manage your creations wirelessly in the Autopress via Cricut Design Space. The Control Pod can handle any preset, and a timer that displays the temperature can also be manually adjusted and saved using the knobs.

While the Cricut Autopress is operating, it can't be opened until the automatic cooling is complete; the machine's top is air-cooled for safe touching, unlike other heat press machines.

Configuring the Cricut Autopress requires following a few steps. Included with your purchase is a card with a website address for activating and setting up the machine. A computer with a USB port is necessary for connecting to the machine for activation and registration before operation.

Plug the cable into the control box's back. The heat press can be switched from Fahrenheit to Celsius on the back of this control panel. Next, connect the power cable to the press: one end to the back of the Autopress and the other to an electrical outlet.

On the Cricut Design Space card, navigate to the website and select the new product configuration. The program, upon clicking on Heat Press and Design Space, will guide you through the process.

Once Design Space recognizes the control module, accept the terms of use and click Activate. The machine preparation will commence, and the controller will start counting down. Once the control module update concludes, your interaction with Design Space ends.

Cricut AutoPress Buttons

Featured on the side are a power button and a lock/unlock button. If turned on when locked or closed, the machine will display a lock icon and will not heat up.

For Autopress to warm up, it must be unlocked and opened. Upon turning on the press, you'll hear a fan motor activate. This internal fan ensures the entire hot plate heats uniformly. Based on the temperature setting, heating up will take about 8 minutes.

The left area of the control capsule indicates the temperature, and the right one represents the time. Rotate them to adjust the settings up or down. The maximum temperature is 400°F, and the maximum time is 600 seconds or 10 minutes. This press is suitable for HTV, Infusible Ink, and even sublimation.

The Cricut AutoPress doesn't work with the new Cricut Heat app, necessitating manual time and temperature setting adjustments. Settings can be found in the Cricut Heat Guide or with the materials you are using.

The buttons at the top are for presetting. Initially, they come with a programmed setting, but pressing each button allows you to switch to a preset. It will flash and beep, indicating that the preset has been adjusted to your preference.

CHAPTER 3

CRICUT EASYPRESS 2

The Easy Press range of machines from Cricut is ideal as they blend the efficiency of an iron with the speed of a heat press, delivering swift, reliable heat transfer results that endure through several washes.

The Four EasyPress Models

The Cricut EasyPress was followed by the Cricut EasyPress 2, a line of products available in three sizes to accommodate a variety of heat transfer projects: 6 in. x 7 in. The Cricut EasyPress 2 achieves a higher temperature and heats up quicker than the original model.

A year later, the Cricut EasyPress Mini was introduced, which is perfect for heat transfer on unconventional objects such as shoes, hats, and stuffed animals, as well as tight, hard-to-reach areas like pockets and sleeves. The precision tip navigates around seams, buttons, and zippers. The Cricut EasyPress Mini can be used independently.

The Cricut EasyPress 3, compatible with the Cricut Heat app, connects to a mobile device via Bluetooth and features an advanced ceramic-coated heating plate, an easy-to-hold comfort handle, and an automatic shut-off feature.

What Materials Can Be Used

Stamping shirts with the Cricut EasyPress is a primary reason many begin using Cricut machines. While it may seem daunting, you'll be astonished at how effortlessly projects can be crafted on these machines.

Iron-on vinyl is the ideal material, with the most commonly used tools being the Cricut Maker, Cricut EasyPress (or an iron), the cutting mat, and a computer.

Before stamping shirts with Cricut EasyPress or embarking on any project of this kind, the design is the starting point. In the Cricut Design Space, click "Text" to select the font and type the message.

You can upload custom typography, adjust letter spacing, color, and much more. Additionally, you may add other elements such as icons or drawings.

Once the design is finalized, click "Make it" to view the grid and activate the "Mirror" feature necessary for this material. Click "Continue" and now select the type of material. For this stamping project, I chose "Everyday Iron-On," and the blade is the "Fine-Point Blade."

Place the vellum on the mat, shiny side down. Insert the mat into the Cricut and press to start cutting.

What Objects Can Be Made

Typically, vinyl and similar materials specify the temperature and duration for heat application. You can confirm this with Cricut's Heat Guide, a highly versatile page filled with tips and clear instructions from Cricut to aid users in their projects.

Next, select the material. I'm choosing "Express Iron-On." Under "Base Material," select "100% cotton," which corresponds to the shirts to be printed. Check the box for "Cricut EasyPress Mat" or "Towel."

The page will display all the printing instructions.

Ensure to apply firm pressure, repeat the process on the other side of the shirt, and remove only when it has cooled.

Place the Cricut EasyPress Mat and lay the shirt on it. Once the iron reaches the correct temperature, preheat the shirt with it. Then position the design and apply the iron for 15 seconds with firm pressure, flip the shirt over, and repeat. Once cooled, remove the plastic, and your shirt is ready.

How It Works

Three basic temperature settings are needed to complete any heat transfer project, including permanent Infusible Ink. Click the button once to turn it on and lower the temperature. It heats up when the lights are orange, and the temperature is reached when the lights turn green.

Setting the Temperature

Cricut EasyPress 3
Press the temperature button, then adjust the setting using the plus (+) and minus (-) buttons. To convert between Fahrenheit and Celsius, press and hold the temperature button until the display changes from °F to °C.

Next, adjust the time using the plus (+) and minus (-) buttons. Indicator light significance: It's warming up when the light is orange. The temperature is reached when the indicator turns green.

Press the Go button to initiate the countdown and start the timer.

Cricut EasyPress and Cricut EasyPress 2

For accurate time and temperature settings for a specific heat transfer vinyl project using the original Cricut EasyPress or Cricut EasyPress 2, please refer to the Cricut Thermal Guide.

Heat Transfer Vinyl

First, ensure that your design fits within the Cricut EasyPress Mini's recommended maximum design sizes for use with heat transfer vinyl (4" wide x 3.5" long or 1.7" wide x 5.25" long).

Prepare a solid, flat, heat-resistant surface at waist height and cover it with an EasyPress mat for flat base materials.

For hollow or well-shaped items like shoes and hats, use a mold or a towel folded inside to provide a firm pressing surface.

1. Set the timer to the suggested duration.
2. Preheat the base material by passing the Cricut EasyPress Mini over the application area for the specified time.
3. Position the design ensuring that the glossy side of the transparent protective film is facing up.
4. Apply heat to both sides.
5. Once the countdown reaches zero, move the Cricut EasyPress Mini consistently across the design.
6. Cover the entire design, including the corners and center, allowing the heat plate to extend about 0.5" (13 mm) past every design edge.
7. Turn the base material over and heat the back of the design according to the instructions.
8. Consult the Cricut Thermal Guide to determine the appropriate peel temperature; before removing the protective film, check whether the peel temperature should be warm or cool.

Instructions for Infusible Ink

1. Find a level, solid, heat-resistant surface at waist height.
2. Avoid delicate ironing boards.
3. Set the temperature and timer.
4. Start the timer, then adjust it using the +/- buttons.
5. Cricut Heat may transmit the set-

tings to the Cricut EasyPress directly.

6. Ensure that the shiny side of the clear carrier foil, which holds the design, is facing up.

7. Apply heat to both sides.

8. After placing the Cricut EasyPress on the base material, press the Go button to start the timer.

9. Hold the Cricut EasyPress in place and apply the recommended pressure.

CHAPTER 4

CRICUT EASYPRESS 3

The Cricut EasyPress 3 delivers professional-quality heat transfers courtesy of the dry, uniform heat from its ceramic coating. Unlike traditional irons which produce uneven heat and inaccurate temperatures, leading to unreliable and lower-quality heat transfers over time, the EasyPress 3 melds the convenience and comfort of an iron with the accuracy and speed of an industrial heat press.

Once connected via Bluetooth, follow the step-by-step instructions on the screen to set the time and temperature for the heat transfer project. With just a click, the settings are transmitted. The Cricut Heat app also informs you about the materials needed to complete the project, how to layer materials before pressing, and when to remove protective films. Conveniently, the app automatically saves your last three settings, eliminating the need to re-enter them.

The EasyPress 3 is available in two sizes: Medium 22.86 cm x 22.86 cm (9 x 9 in); and Large 30.48 cm x 25.40 cm (12 x 10 in).

Before deciding, consider the size of the projects you wish to create. The medium EasyPress is suitable for personalizing children's clothing and small decorative items like cushions, napkins, and coasters. The large model is more fitting for personalizing projects such as bags, blankets, or adult clothing.

Main Differences Between EasyPress 2 and EasyPress 3

The EasyPress line aims to alleviate the struggles associated with printing on special materials, offering a novel platform for users to unleash their creativity. But how does it fare against its predecessor?

Cricut EasyPress 2: Available in three sizes, the Cricut EasyPress 2 has a maximum temperature of 400°F.

It features buttons to adjust the time and temperature, along with a button to initiate or halt the process. It excels in applying hot melt vinyl as its heat plate is flat and smooth, ensuring perfectly even heat distribution across the entire surface.

- Heat plate included
- 3 different sizes
- Time duration adjustable up to 40 seconds
- Temperature up to 400 °F
- Quick heating
- Automatic shut-off after a set time for safety

Cricut EasyPress 3: Like the EasyPress 2, the EasyPress 3 is also available in three sizes and boasts a maximum temperature of 400°F. However, the button icons have been slightly redesigned. The standout feature of this machine is its Bluetooth capability, allowing for connectivity with the Cricut Heat app (available for Android and Apple) to pair with EasyPress 3.

- Heat plate included
- 3 different sizes
- Ability to change the time duration up to 40 seconds
- Ability to change the temperature up to 400 °F
- Fast heating
- Automatic shut-off after a set time for safety

- Bluetooth capabilities
- Connectivity to the Cricut Heat app, guiding you through all the steps in the correct order

CHA PTER 5

CRICUT MUGPRESS

The Cricut Mug Press is a heat-emitting sublimation iron designed for easy creation of personalized mugs. It's a comprehensive tool, aimed at simple handling. The Mug Press is intended for home use, not industrial, although it's very durable, enabling you to create a multitude of personalized mugs. Remember, it's not designed for bulk production.

It's essential to note that the Mug Press only accommodates specific sublimation mugs, not just any mug you have on hand. Photo designs aren't an option as photos can't be transferred to the mug; instead, one must utilize sublimation materials.

Unboxing

The box's exterior showcases the sleek design of the Cricut mug press, boasting the potential of creating professional-quality mugs in minutes.

On the top, images of eye-catching mugs stir excitement for the creations awaiting us.

Upon opening the box, a small package is revealed, initially seeming irrelevant, but is crucial as it contains the fundamental elements needed to set up the mug press. This is a step we cannot skip, ensuring it's carried out precisely is imperative.

Also enclosed is a small green folder with the URL for configuration instructions and a warranty folder. Post-activation, the product will be registered to the Cricut account. A Windows/Mac-compatible computer with a USB type A port is required.

At the bottom, nestled next to the power cable, is the meticulously packaged mug press. The included USB cable is necessary for activating the cup press, which will update the product firmware and register the cup press during the setup process.

What Materials Can Be Used

While Cricut EasyPress 3 is limited to mugs, the Cricut Mug Press won't stifle your creativity. Instead, it unveils a plethora of creative possibilities. However, understanding how to personalize mugs with this machine and knowing the required materials is crucial.

Sublimation mugs: It's vital to use polyurethane-coated sublimation mugs, like Cricut's brand of mugs, which are fully compatible with Infusible Ink. These mugs are dishwasher and microwave safe, offering smooth white walls. They come in varying capacities—acceptable by the Mug Press ranging from 11 to 16 oz (350 to 470 ml) with a diameter of 82 to 86 mm (3.2 to 3.4 inches). The design dimensions for the smaller mug are a maximum of 22.2 cm x 9.6 cm (8.74 x 3.77 in), and for the larger mug, 22.2 cm x 10.8 cm (8.74 x 4.25 in).

Infusible Ink: Infusible Ink, designed by Cricut, showcases an innovative heat transfer system allowing the design to fully meld into the mug for sublimation, achieving a flawless finish. Typically, an Infusible Ink transfer sheet is employed to cut the desired design for mug decoration. These sheets come in a myriad of colors and inspiring patterns.

You may opt for Infusible Ink markers for a freehand design. These markers contain specific ink for sublimation and can be installed in the Cricut machine to autonomously draw the selected design.

Cutting Plotter: To transfer designs by sublimation to the mugs using Infusible Ink sheets, prior cutting of the design with a cutting plotter is necessary. These devices precisely cut out your preferred design. Fortunately, any cutting plotter can be used, including Cricut machines like the Cricut Maker 3, the Cricut Explore 3, or the compact Cricut Joy, which is perfectly sized for customizing mugs with ease.

Heat-resistant adhesive tape: This tape ensures the design remains stationary and is accurately positioned on the mug. Place the tape around the edges of the transfer sheet to secure the design.

What Can We Create

Upon fulfilling all on-screen instructions to configure the mug, a simple button press sets you on your creative journey. Before beginning, it's highly recommended to place the mug press on a heat-resistant surface.

One advantage of the mug press is its lightweight design and compact size, making storage a breeze. As has been clarified, this line of machines solely facilitates the creation and printing of designs on mugs, hence materials are limited to those offered by Cricut.

Navigating to the "Projects" menu of the official Cricut app and typing "Mugs" in the search bar reveals various mug projects compatible with Infusible Ink. A blank template option is also available, alongside the Cricut Access subscription to add images and create your design. Text designs are also applicable.

Selecting the blank template option unveils a drop-down menu featuring mugs of varying sizes and border styles.

How It Works

Create the design: You can either purchase or create designs in the Cricut Design Space on the Cricut Infusible Ink transfer sheet. It's recommended to review the design before cutting it with your plotter to save materials in case of any errors. Remove any remaining Infusible Ink that doesn't need to be transferred. There's no need for a hook; simply roll up the Infusible Ink sheet, and the cut lines will begin to separate.

Place the design on the mug: Carefully position the design prepared for sublimation, securing it in place with tape. Always ensure the design faces the mug with the protector on the outside. A helpful tip is to place the mug on a desk, with the handle facing you, and tape the base first to achieve perfect positioning.

Heat the machine: Turn on the Cricut Mug Press to preheat it until the green LED lights up and the machine emits an alert sound, signaling it's ready. At this point, insert the mug and press the lever to secure it inside the machine. The transfer process will commence, with small white lights indicating the progress.

Remove your product: This line of Cricut machines features a helpful built-in alert sound; when you hear the machine's beep, it indicates readiness, and the mug should be carefully removed and allowed to cool for about 15 minutes. Then, remove the Infusible Ink protector and the adhesive tape, completing the process.

Step-by-Step Activation of Your Mug Press

1. Connect your computer to the Cricut Mug Press using the USB cable.
2. Navigate to com/setup on your Mac or Windows computer.
3. Click "Open" if Cricut Design Space is already installed, or click "Download" to install it on your device. Locate the downloaded file and run it.
4. Log in with your Cricut ID and password. If you don't have a Cricut account, you'll need to create one to continue with the setup.
5. Next, navigate to the Cricut welcome page and select "Heat Press > Cricut Mug Press."
6. Follow the on-screen instructions to connect the machine until activation is complete.
7. At the end of the installation process, click "Start" to begin enjoying your Mug Press.

Please note that designs cannot be transferred to the inside of the mug, the base, or the handle. The Cricut Mug Press is recognized for its advanced technology and safety features, enabling exploration of all creative options without concerns. It automatically shuts off after 13 minutes of inactivity and includes a protective casing to prevent heat damage to the table or any surface it comes into contact with. Moreover, while the mug becomes very hot, the handle remains cool, preventing burns when removing it.

TABLE OF CONTENTS

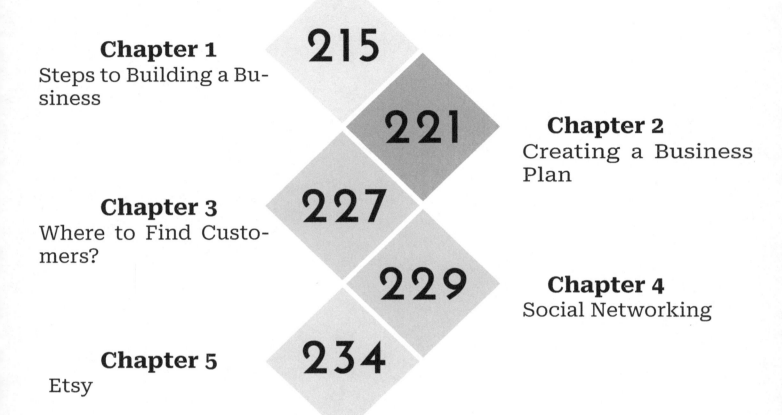

Chapter 1
Steps to Building a Business

215

221

Chapter 2
Creating a Business Plan

Chapter 3
Where to Find Customers?

227

229

Chapter 4
Social Networking

Chapter 5
Etsy

234

BOOK 9

BUSINESS OPPORTUNITIES

WITH CRICUT

CHAPTER 1

STEPS TO BUILDING A BUSINESS

Have you ever wondered if you can make money with your Cricut? In this chapter, you'll discover that by working smart and paying attention to the products, you can indeed earn legitimate money by starting your own business selling products made with your Cricut.

Before attempting to monetize your Cricut skills, it's essential to ask yourself certain questions to ensure this path aligns with your desires and expectations.

These questions will help gauge what starting a Cricut business entails for you:

1. Are you pursuing this solely because friends praise your projects?
2. Is your goal to financially support your family?
3. Are you looking for a way to earn some extra money?
4. Are you prepared to handle challenging customers?
5. Do you aspire to transform your hobby into a serious endeavor?
6. Are you willing to learn about marketing, both online and offline?
7. Do you have the necessary time and space to initiate a small business?
8. Do you enjoy crafting with your Cricut enough to do it repetitively?

Your suitability for this venture can be assessed based on various political, social, economic, and personal factors. To kickstart your business, follow these steps:

Define Your Reasons

If your primary objective is to generate income, pursuing a conventional career might be a better option. Identify what motivates you to establish a business.

Evaluate Yourself

Ascertain whether you have the required skills or if you're willing to acquire them.

Select an Idea

Your mind can achieve whatever it believes.

Draft a Business Plan

Detail your business concept, market strategies, objectives, investments, profitability projections, etc., on paper.

1. Assemble your team: Select individuals who share your enthusiasm.
2. Seek financing: Obtain financial support from individuals or organizations.
3. Dive in: Learning occurs through hands-on experience and the trial-and-error method.
4. Promote and advertise: Spread the word about your offerings using technology, word-of-mouth, and your website.
5. Gain insight and refine: Understand your clients, vendors, true costs, turnaround times, etc., and continually fine-tune your business operations.

As a final piece of advice, "Think big." Once you start seeing results, the objective should be to find ways to progress and set new milestones.

Create Your Logo

Remember, a logo is the embodiment of your corporate brand identity. As a marketing strategy, it should be well-designed to inspire confidence and present a serious and committed business demeanor to your clients.
It should be conceived from an internal analysis of your business, highlighting and emphasizing the values you wish to project.

How to design a good logo?
Your logo should reflect an integral part of your brand, ensuring coherence between the visual-material and intangible-emotional aspects of your business.

Here's what you should analyze:

1. About your brand: What are your core values? What is your history, and how has it influenced the creation of your business? What message do you wish to send to the world? What's the significance behind your company's name?
2. About your competition: What are their strengths and weaknesses? What messages are they sending to the market? Can you discern what sets you apart from them?
3. About your ideal customer: Who is your target audience? What is their age range and purchasing power?

These three points form the foundation of any business execution decision; without them, you lack a brand image, corporate identity, content marketing strategy, advertising, info-products, or any direction for your business to grow.

If investing in a professional designer for a custom logo isn't feasible, consider using a logo creator tool like Adobe Spark, which offers pre-designed logos. This can be a temporary solution until you have the necessary funds to invest in professional design services.

Creating your logo: Identify good references and ideas while maintaining originality. Establish a physical or digital inspiration board to organize your ideas regarding colors, textures, and images. This board should convey the values you wish to communicate through your brand.

Creation: The fundamental elements to consider when designing a logo include typography, color, and an emblem or symbol, should you choose to use one.

Classification of logos
- Logotype: A typographic logo consisting solely of letters. Many well-known logos, like those of Google or Canon, are simple, employing just one font and color.
- Imagotype: Comprises letters and an image. Brands like Lacoste and Spotify utilize imagotypes.
- Isotype: A symbol-only logo. Classic examples include Apple and Nike.
- Isologotype: Combines typography and a symbol in a manner that they cannot be separated. Starbucks and Burger King are notable examples.

Characteristics of a good logo
- Simple: Easy to understand without requiring visual effort. Avoid cluttering your logo with too many elements as it may hinder readability for your audience.
- Timeless: Avoid following fleeting trends; otherwise, your logo may quickly become outdated.
- Versatile or flexible: Easily adaptable to various mediums your brand may require, and simple to reproduce.
- Harmonious: Balanced with no excesses or shortages.
- Coherent: Effectively communicates your brand's message.
- Memorable: Easily recognizable and memorable for the audience.

Need a Free Logo?

Here's a stellar tip for you. Looking to create an eye-catching, stunning logo but lack the budget for a graphic designer and the technical skills to craft one yourself? Fret not. Here's a trick that will not only save you time and money but also provide you with a professional-looking logo.

It's a breeze! Simply visit the following site and whip up your logo in minutes with the help of artificial intelligence:

https://looka.com/

Follow the steps and behold the fantastic result!

Create Your Brand

Beyond captivating imagery and quality products, a successful brand should offer unique value to its users, be it an experience, a level of social status, product durability, or similar benefits.

In this regard, providing quality and unique value fosters trust in customers, enhancing the likelihood of growth and sales as each satisfied customer becomes a potential brand ambassador.

Relevance is achieved when your customers and users take an interest in what you do because they identify with your brand. This level of connection is crucial as it allows for more effective message transmission, contributing to your business's success and growth.

The steps to create a relevant brand are:

- Research your environment to define your target audience.
- Identify the market position of your company and your products.
- Create your company's brand identity.
- Integrate your brand across all business channels.
- Strengthen and promote your brand.
- Research your environment to define your target audience (this point is repeated, consider removing or merging with the previous mention).

Thorough understanding of the economic and social landscape where your brand will operate is crucial. Conduct a market study to obtain in-depth knowledge of your environment.

Some guiding questions might include:

1. What are the characteristics of the individuals you're targeting?
2. What are their habits, motivations, and interests?
3. What needs do they have that your products can fulfill?
4. What strategies have proven successful for your competitors? Where have they failed?
5. What opportunities are present?

The responses to these questions will assist in constructing profiles that define your ideal customer, their interests, the factors influencing their decisions, and the most effective communication methods. This user profile, known as a buyer persona, should be created for each type of customer you aim to reach.

Identify the Market Position of Your Company and Your Products

Armed with market research and buyer persona insights, it's time to evaluate your offerings against reality.

Understanding your potential customers as well as your products or services is vital. It provides a clear perspective on the ease or challenges you may face in persuading them based on the unique attributes that distinguish your products from competitors.

Create Your Company's Brand Identity

Brand identity is the essence that renders your brand appealing, distinct, and, above all, relevant. It comprises four complementary components:
- Name
- Image
- Culture
- Personality

Create Your Social Account

Social networks are integral to business operations. To develop an effective social media plan, consider the following:

1. **Pay to Play:** Although registration on social networks is free, maximizing their reach often requires a solid social marketing plan and investment in advertising. Choose channels where you can generate brand-aligned content.

2. **Create a Community**: Your followers are there to learn about your company's updates, express their opinions, and be heard.

3. **Offer Added Value**: Provide discounts, event invitations, exclusive news, and other valuable content to your followers.

4. **Engage Opinion Leaders**: Every market has opinion leaders on social networks. Engage them in conversation and inform them about your products or services as it could foster beneficial relationships down the line.

5. **Respond to Your Followers:** If a user takes the time to write to you, respond. Whether it's a question, opinion, or complaint, engaging with your followers is crucial to maintain their connection with your company.

6. **Don't Overly Focus on Sales**: Offer relatable content that doesn't solely push sales, but enhances your brand's relationship with the audience.

7. **Engage in Conversations with Other Brands:** One of the major advantages of social networks is the ability to connect with both customers and other brands. Engage in conversations that could relate to or complement your actions.

8. **Monitor Metrics:** All social media activities can and should be monitored. Utilize this data to formulate better strategies.

9. **Remember the Human Aspect**: People on social networks expect to interact with a human, not a robot. Ensuring a human touch in your responses and interactions will make your social media platforms more user-friendly, effective, and functional, consequently increasing your audience and reach.

CHAPTER 2

CREATING A BUSINESS PLAN

Organizing Your Ideas and Resources is the First Step! This chapter serves as a guide to efficiently organize your ideas and resources, which is the initial step in your business journey. Having a structured guide for your company operations enhances the likelihood of profitability as it clarifies the value proposition and ensures that finances, processes, and actions are well-organized and focused for the long term.

A business plan is a crucial document that outlines the objectives and viability of a company. It encompasses detailed information about the business identity, operations, costs, and growth potential, facilitating the definition of strategies and goals to attain tangible economic benefits.

This document is pivotal for attracting investors or securing financing, as it showcases the legitimacy and potential of your business to various institutions and audiences.

Calculating Your Business Costs

When embarking on a business venture, there's a common tendency to overestimate revenues and underestimate expenses initially. Such misjudgments can be detrimental to your business. Ensuring accurate financial projections is key to maintaining a healthy financial outlook for your business.

Conduct a Preliminary Market Study: A thorough understanding of the sector, target audience, market dynamics, and competition prepares you for unforeseen circumstances and minimizes surprises.

Budget for Each Stage: Allocate financial resources for each project stage. For instance, set a specific budget for goals you aim to achieve in 6 or 12 months. This approach, aligned with the "minimum waste" philosophy, aims to mitigate economic risks before launching your product or service.

Consider Various Scenarios: Before setting a price for your product, assess the competition's pricing. Ideally, envisage three scenarios: optimistic, pessimistic, and realistic. Have a contingency plan for each scenario. For instance, determine three different pricing strategies for each circumstance.

Calculating Business Revenue

To project your expenses for the first year, consider the sales volume and product or service pricing, among other factors:

Secure Additional Financing for the First Year: Anticipate lower initial revenues and plan for additional financing to bridge the income gap during this period.

Determine Total Product Demand: Utilizing market research, ascertain the actual demand for your product and the market share you aim to capture, considering the competition.

When making revenue projections, evaluate the following aspects as guiding factors:

Target Audience: Identify your target audience, their spending capacity, and segment them by demographics like age and gender.

Competition: Assess the market share you can acquire from competitors and the unique value proposition your company offers.

Suppliers: Familiarize yourself with major market players to compare prices, as your product's price and profit margin will depend on your suppliers' costs.

Pricing Strategy: Adjust pricing based on the exclusivity of your product. Typically, exclusive and unique products command higher prices.

Seasonality: Acknowledge the seasonal highs and lows inherent to your business and plan accordingly.

Profits: Determine your earnings by subtracting the product cost from the selling price. Although profits may be minimal or nonexistent in the first year, establishing a profitable pricing structure is essential for long-term success.

Calculating Expenses

The "expenses" category in your accounting plan encompasses all costs associated with generating revenue.

Here are some key factors to consider:

Tax Costs: Include corporate taxes, VAT, fees, etc., along with costs for property rights, software licenses, and legal compliance.

Logistics and Suppliers: These costs can impact your revenue as they are part of the process that can escalate product costs beyond your control. Account for all costs related to this segment of production, including delays, complaints, returns, and exchanges.

Customer Acquisition Cost: Encompasses marketing and communication expenses.

Financing Costs: If relying on external financing, include installment and interest costs.

Investments: These are inevitable and include costs for materials, office rent, computers, patents, etc.

Operational Costs: Determine the geographic scope of your operations and the costs associated with maintaining a presence in that area, whether through stores or shipments.

IT Updating Costs: Account for expenses related to IT equipment updates and R&D that add value to your product or service over time.

Cost of Own Labor: Include the entrepreneur's labor as an expense, starting with a baseline hourly rate and projecting how this rate might increase as the company grows.

Labor Costs: Estimate the overall cost of your employees during the first year based on the needs of each project phase. You won't need a full team initially; prioritize hiring based on project requirements.

Supply Costs: Cover expenses for utilities like electricity, water, gasoline, and communication devices.

Tips for Calculating Income and Expenses

To achieve a realistic balance between income and costs, consider halving your profit projections and doubling your cost estimates. Maintain separate accounts for company finances and VAT to ensure accurate financial management. Adjust expenses according to the level of activity, and consider hiring financial expertise if necessary.

Reducing Costs: Cost reduction is vital for enhancing business profits and sustaining productivity and profitability.

Maximizing Resource Utilization: Optimize the use of available resources to improve profitability and productivity.

Enhancing Business Flexibility: Adapt to external and internal constraints to foster a less stressful work and operational environment.

Fostering a Cost-Efficient Culture: Establish a culture of cost minimization and expense management to ensure financial health.

Before resorting to drastic measures like personnel layoffs or supplier changes, consider effective cost reduction strategies:

- ***Business Process Reengineering (BPR):*** Radically redesign production processes to optimize results, focusing on performance, costs, services, quality, and speed.

- ***Corporate Expense Management:*** Utilize expense management tools to control lodging and travel costs, automate expense processes, and prevent accounting errors.

- ***Supplier Evaluation:*** Consider changing or renegotiating terms with suppliers to achieve better pricing and cost-saving advantages.

- ***Energy-Saving Measures***: Seek alternatives to minimize electricity, fuel, and energy costs, and adopt eco-friendly practices to attract environmentally-conscious customers.

- ***Customer Loyalty Programs***: Implement pricing strategies and loyalty programs to retain customers, and consider outsourcing certain services to reduce operational costs.

- ***Inventory Management***: Focus on "star" products with high demand and evaluate whether to eliminate or optimize the disposal of low-demand products.

- ***Technology Integration***: Embrace technologies that enhance internet connectivity, social networking, and communication to achieve significant savings in the short and long term, with professional guidance.

By addressing these aspects, you'll be better equipped to manage your business finances, reduce costs, and enhance profitability.

How to Calculate the Right Price

The cost of sales primarily consists of variable costs that fluctuate based on production levels. It represents the monetary investment made in the manufacture and acquisition of an item at a specific time for sale.

Cost of sales is a crucial aspect of accounting and financial management. It informs decisions regarding pricing, product mix, production levels, and more.

Types of Cost of Sales

The expenses to include when calculating the cost of sales are those directly related to the production of your products. These include labor, raw materials, manufacturing overhead, packaging costs, storage costs, and the cost of goods.

Expenses that should not be included in the cost of sales are marketing or customer acquisition costs, salesperson commissions, and other general business expenses.

Determining Cost of Sales: Key Formulas

Cost of Sales = Beginning Inventory + Purchases - Ending Inventory

Example: If your beginning inventory is $25,000, purchases are $20,000, and ending inventory is $15,000, the formula would be:

Cost of Sales = $25,000 + $20,000 - $15,000 = $30,000

At the end of your accounting year, it's essential to account for inventory to ascertain your cost of sales accurately. The inventory quantity represents the investments made to market your goods. This includes the costs of raw materials and associated supplies, compensation to workers directly involved in manufacturing, transportation charges, and service costs incurred throughout the production process.

Cost of Sales Formula for Manufacturers

Cost per Unit Manufactured = Total Manufacturing Costs / Total Number of Units Produced

To determine the cost of sales, you need to know the total manufacturing costs and the number of units produced. Divide the total manufacturing costs by the units produced to calculate the cost per unit.

Cost of Sales Formula for Intermediaries

Total Cost of Sales = Cost of Goods Sold + Marketing and Advertising Expenses + Commission Paid to the

Intermediary

The cost of sales formula for intermediaries calculates the total cost of selling goods or services through an intermediary.

It includes the cost of goods sold, marketing and advertising expenses, and commissions paid to the intermediary.

CHA PTER 3

WHERE TO FIND CUSTO-MERS?

Considering the venture of acquiring customers? It's essential to devise a strategy to captivate them and explore the avenues where they can be found. In this chapter, by following the outlined steps and recommendations, you'll navigate through this process:

Efficient conversion of new consumers into sales is the primary aim of attracting them, and certain tactics are indispensable for achieving this goal.

Starting With Family and Friends

Numerous instances showcase groups of friends embarking on entrepreneurial journeys, navigating through the inherent challenges and complexities, and eventually attaining success.

It's crucial to well-define the working agreements when the venture involves a group of friends. Understand what matters to them and what they aim to preserve. A harmonization of expectations is vital.

Online Presence

Your task is to craft an irresistible offer that could sway even the most skeptical. Ensure to include the following information:

- Name of the product and/or service
- Benefits
- Testimonials
- Urgency and scarcity
- Bonuses
- Payment options
- Guarantee
- Target audience

Prior to studying your target audience, acquaint yourself with the following:

- What motivates them?
- What problems do they face?

- Who are their influences?
- Which magazines, websites, and/or blogs do they frequent?
- What could possibly deter them or hold them back?

To grasp these aspects, it's imperative to conduct thorough internal and external research. Bear in mind, a lack of clarity on what you're selling and to whom, could undermine any marketing strategy you deploy. Dedicate ample time to this phase.

The Hook

In modern selling, the traffic you generate should initially be directed not to the sales page, but to a squeeze page. This landing page aims solely at obtaining potential customers' information, offering them a piece of free content, known as a hook, in return.

Landing Page and Squeeze Page
As mentioned, the traffic should first land on a squeeze page and then a sales landing page; each with a distinct structure and promise based on your objective.

Customer Recommendations

This method is often one of the first resorts when promoting a product.

A recommendation from a satisfied user can significantly influence others. Hence, never overlook this strategy that has aided numerous businesses in the past.

CHAPTER 4

SOCIAL NETWORKING

In this chapter, you will acquire the necessary recommendations to enhance your business through social networks. We will explore the most popular platforms, which are undoubtedly excellent channels to achieve your goals.

Facebook

This popular platform remains a viable channel for entrepreneurs, although its functionality has evolved over time. It's crucial to adhere to fundamental steps that yield consistent results:

Share and Create Valuable Content
Your social media posts should contain relevant material that resonates with your audience and encourages them to share with their peers. This approach lays the foundation for referral marketing.

Consider your audience's perspective when posting, providing material related to your brand that also encourages discussion, reflection, and most importantly, sharing with others.

Types of valuable content:

- Photographs (recent, nostalgic, emotional, etc.)
- Drawings, illustrations, and graphics (that inform, illustrate concepts or evoke empathy)
- Videos (tutorials, documentaries, testimonials, explanatory, humorous, etc.)
- Information about the origin of the brand or product
- Videos or images showcasing the "making of" your brand or product
- Screencasts, podcasts, and interviews
- Audio and music files
- Challenges, polls, riddles, quizzes
- Tips, formulas, and recipes to achieve a goal
- Guides, templates, practical and useful information, etc.

To guide people to these resources, consider publishing additional in-depth material in a manual or catalog linked to your blog or website. Regardless of the format, the goal is to elicit engagement and feedback from your audience.

Engage Beyond Your Wall

Interacting on other Fan Pages is tactically intriguing. Participate on pages related to or within your industry by sharing your insights and adding value. Engage with the pages and their followers. If possible, post one or two insightful comments. In other words, make your presence known. By engaging on other Fan Pages, you'll attract new followers and establish your identity. Moreover, it provides an opportunity to network with other businesses.

Maximize Segmentation

Segmentation allows you to direct your content to specific groups within your followers, making the content appear tailored for them. This not only enhances its effectiveness but allows slight modifications to the same post for different audience segments.

Facebook offers segmentation variables like age, emotional status, language, hobbies, level of education, and geographic location, enabling you to tailor content to the audience you aim to engage or educate.

After publishing segmented content, you may hide previous posts to ensure only the desired content is visible on your wall, presenting your audience with tailored posts and avoiding monotony.

Manage Timing and Post on Past Dates

This strategy allows you to add relevant information to your business timeline as needed. The posts will augment your brand's Time Line retroactively, as they are arranged chronologically based on the date and time you provide.

Even if your Fan Page is newly created, this tactic helps establish your brand on Facebook, creating an impression of long-term activity.

Schedule Future Posts

You can also schedule posts for the future, with a maximum spacing of six months and fifteen minutes. The content can be prepared and disseminated at your chosen times.

By considering time differences across countries or continents, your community will view the content at the most convenient times. Scheduling posts is crucial for providing content at the right times, especially if your brand has an international presence or if a specific post needs to go live at a particular time when you can't do it manually.

Remember, by adhering to the correct schedule and segmenting your audience, your posts will reach your audience at the perfect moment to foster engagement.

Instagram

Social networks are valuable tools for enhancing business visibility globally. To reach your goals, it's essential to set objectives aligned with your social media marketing plan and maximize your impact across networks.

Why Use Instagram?

Recent global reports have revealed that nearly 60% of the world's population uses the internet, and over half of them engage with social media platforms. Among these platforms, Instagram boasts 1 billion users, ranking as the fourth most-used social network worldwide.

Notably, 50% of Instagram users follow at least one commercial brand, presenting a significant opportunity for companies to expand their reach via this platform.

Tips to Increase Followers and Engagement

- *Instagram Stories:* Stories, displayed for 24 hours on the platform, are a visual format tailored to the device's screen. Utilize various resources like GIFs, emoticons, and music to animate your photos or videos and boost your visibility on the platform.

- *Content:* Users often respond more favorably to visual stimuli than textual information. Instagram provides a plethora of tools to foster creativity and enhance your profile's appeal for your business.

- **The Role of Influencers:** With established audiences, influencers can aid in rapidly expanding your following due to their credibility and reach on Instagram. They act as intermediaries, promoting your products or services in a relatable manner to their followers, making your messages resonate without seeming overly salesy.

- **Call to Action (CTA)**: Publish engaging content that invites participation and ensures your followers receive feedback. Utilize Instagram's interactive features like surveys, questionnaires, and countdowns to foster a direct relationship with your followers.

- **Paid Advertising:** Primarily aimed at attracting new followers, you can create ads from your posts or design content for advertising via Stories. Set a budget aligned with your goals and monitor your ads' performance.

- **Hashtags:** Research suggests that utilizing between 3 and 5 hashtags is optimal for this platform. Regarded as the keywords of social networks, hashtags are instrumental in categorizing your content, making it discoverable and interactive for new users.

Pinterest

Though not a conventional social network, Pinterest is often compared to other platforms due to its popularity for sharing content. Users can share photos, infographics, videos, and more, creating collections of intriguing content like books, clothing, courses, etc., all stored on a virtual cork-board-style platform.

How Does Pinterest Work?

You can opt for a personal or a business account via Pinterest Business. With a business account, you can edit your profile by clicking on the "..." icon on the screen's right side and navigating to "settings."

Pinterest Environment

Once your profile is set up, you can link your social networks to Pinterest, keeping in touch with contacts and sharing boards or content. The platform's top bar houses the search engine and options to explore Pinterest, create your own "Pin," send direct messages, and receive notifications about recent posts, trends, and news.

TikTok

TikTok has revolutionized social media, particularly among young individuals aged 13 to 24. With over 800 million active users monthly, it's an engaging platform for businesses to connect with audiences in a unique and entertaining manner.

How Does TikTok Work?

TikTok allows users to upload short video clips (up to 15 seconds), enhancing them with music, sound clips, effects, hashtags, filters, or stickers. Users can also string together multiple videos as long as the total length doesn't exceed 60 seconds. The platform is renowned for its playback and choreography videos, challenges, and comedic content. TikTok's home section showcases trending videos, and the "trends" button facilitates hashtag searches for topics of interest. During live broadcasts, TikTokers can send virtual gifts to creators, which can be converted into diamonds or real money, starting from $100 in diamonds.

CHAPTER 5

ETSY

Selling on Etsy should be one of your top choices if you create unique, original, and creative Cricut pieces. This chapter provides a detailed guide on selling your products on this platform.

Why Etsy? Etsy is the premier marketplace specializing in handmade items and vintage products, making it one of the most sought-after e-commerce platforms.

What is Etsy?

Etsy is an e-commerce web platform or marketplace where individuals can sell and purchase products. The platform primarily focuses on handicrafts, handmade products, and antiques, catering to sellers of specific products. People worldwide use Etsy as an international online marketplace to create, promote, purchase, and collect unique items.

Etsy boasts over five million active sellers who choose the platform for its global reach, allowing them to connect with customers worldwide. Additionally, the platform offers various visibility options, helping creators or sellers find buyers for their works and vice versa. Many choose Etsy as it provides an opportunity to earn money from the comfort of their homes, requiring only a designated area for crafting their products.

Etsy Numbers

There's no need to spend weeks studying other stores. Here, the key is to have favorable numbers like:
- The number of products for good SEO.
- The number of products for a coherent catalog and a store that sells, ensuring your catalog is well optimized.

Registering on Etsy is Easy

If you have a clear idea of what you

will sell, start by creating your account on the platform. The registration steps are as follows:

- Go to Etsy.com
- Select the "Sign in" option or press the person icon from your smartphone.
- Enter your email and press continue; the platform will then ask for your name and password.
- Alternatively, when entering your email, you can choose to continue with Google, Facebook, or Apple for direct access.
- If you followed step 3, check your email for a confirmation message from the official Etsy email: regi-stration@etsy.com.

Study Your Competitors

An effective way to compete with similar stores is to study them. Explore stores selling similar products and observe how they market themselves. If they have substantial sales, check their social media to see their promotional strategies on platforms like Twitter and Facebook.

How to Open Your Store?

Open your Etsy store in 5 steps:

1 - Sign Up on Etsy:

The first step is to create a user account to open your Etsy store. If you are new to Etsy, create an account, but if you have shopped on Etsy before, you can skip this step.

In the "Sign up" box, fill in your personal information, choose a username and password for Etsy, and click "Register."

Note: By doing so, you agree to the site's conditions and policies. It's advisable to use a unique password for Etsy, different from other sites. Consider using a password manager like LastPass for managing multiple passwords. You can also sign up via Facebook or Google to save some time. However, your account won't be valid until you confirm it via the email sent by Etsy titled "Confirm your Etsy account."

2 - Create Your Store and Choose Your Preferences

Once your user account is active, create your store to start selling on Etsy. Follow the prompts to select the default language, location, and currency for your store.

The selection doesn't restrict your store's visibility in other countries; Etsy automatically translates the store for global visibility.

Also, specify your level of involvement, whether selling full-time or part-time, and click "Save and continue" to proceed.

3 - Name Your Store
If you have been in the craft business for a while, you may already have a business name. Ensure it's unique on Etsy, adhering to Etsy's naming guidelines of using 4 to 20 characters, without numbers, accents, or spaces. Once the name is accepted, click "Save and continue" to move to the next step.

4- How to Publish and Sell Your Products
When you click on the "Add a listing" box, you will be directed to a page with four sections:

1. Add photo
2. Listing details
3. Inventory and prices
4. Shipping

It's crucial to carefully complete each section. Take your time, as this step is pivotal in setting up your Etsy store.

Add Photo - Firstly, upload a high-quality photo of the product you intend to list. Upon clicking "Add photo," a window will appear, allowing you to select a photo from your folders.

To streamline this task, consider having a dedicated folder for your products, with subfolders for each item, housing various angle shots.

If you wish to adjust the thumbnail image that will be displayed in your store, click on "Adjust thumbnail."
A window will appear, enabling you to zoom in and save the image accordingly.

Listing Details - Fill out all the requested information about the product you're selling: its name, who manufactured it, and the type of product it is.

Follow the gray text instructions provided for each field. Fill in the data accordingly or select the relevant options. Some fields are mandatory, while others are optional.

Pay special attention to the name and description fields. The keywords you use are crucial as they help your listing appear in search results when potential buyers look for such items.

Inventory and Prices - Specify your product's price and available quantity. You also have the option to add identification numbers for your product for your own tracking purposes—these won't be visible to buyers.

Lastly, if your product comes in different sizes or colors, add these variants.

Shipping - Provide realistic shipping details: origin, estimated delivery time, and shipping costs from different countries, among other options. If shipping costs are similar for various products, create a shipping profile to reuse these details without having to re-enter them. Name and save your shipping profile for future use.

5 - Preview
Once you've filled out all the necessary information, click "Preview" to see how the finished listing will look. If any changes are needed, continue editing.

If it looks good, save it.

Now you have two options:

- Continue adding more listings to your store: Repeat the steps you've followed to create your first listing for other products you wish to sell.

- Save and proceed to the next phase to set up your payment receiving methods.

TABLE OF CONTENTS

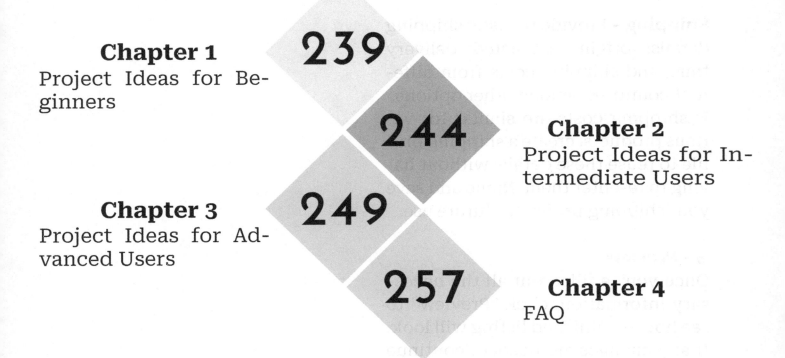

Chapter 1
Project Ideas for Beginners

239

244
Chapter 2
Project Ideas for Intermediate Users

Chapter 3
Project Ideas for Advanced Users

249

257
Chapter 4
FAQ

BOOK 10

CRICUT PROJECT IDEAS

FROM BEGINNER TO PRO

CHAPTER 1

PROJECT IDEAS FOR BEGINNERS

If you are delving into this book, it implies you are brainstorming project ideas or aiming to develop a project that will yield profits upon sale. This chapter unveils how to mold those ideas into tangible forms and highlights a series of guidelines to adhere to before and during each project's execution.

If you revel in customizing your creations but are a novice in the Cricut realm, or still feel a need to grasp the vast array of accessories and materials this brand avails, embarking on a project will dispel your uncertainties. Hence, this chapter categorizes projects based on your level of expertise.

It's prudent to consider what captivates you and what appeals to others when scouting for ideas, as this often poses a challenge in the design journey. The most stellar ideas aren't always the easiest, but rather those that ignite your enthusiasm.

Fancy designing cake toppers or inventive packaging for food gifts due to your culinary inclination? Rather than fixating on Cricut's top-selling projects and overindulging in trend chasing, ponder on the projects and products you'd cherish utilizing.

What Products Can You Create with a Cricut?

Given that Cricut is a preferred apparatus for crafting DIY and craft ventures, aspire to broaden your horizons. Commonly, it's employed to cut various paper and vinyl types.

Moreover, it serves as a scoring tool, crafting precise creases for items like cards. Some models can even slice through thicker materials.

The answers to such inquiries are vast and open-ended. Truthfully, a Cricut can birth a plethora of items. T-shirts and birthday cards are merely the tip of the iceberg, with your creativity being the only boundary.

On a brighter note, you can embellish your business cards with gold foil using your Cricut. It also has the knack to transform your original artwork into die-cut stickers, or fabricate gift bags, card stock photo frames, and die-cut postcards. The options are seemingly endless, which is the essence of selling your creations. There's a plethora of Cricut projects for neophytes, including easily marketable Cricut crafts.

The Cricut EasyPress 3, available in three distinct sizes, can reach a peak temperature of 400 °F. It has revamped button icons from EasyPress 2 for a slightly altered appearance. Bear in mind, *the Cricut isn't a printer*—it doesn't print graphics. Instead, it excels at cutting materials like cardstock, adhesive paper, and vinyl.

Is Selling Cricut-Crafted Items Legal?

Affirmatively, albeit with certain restrictions such as the imperative to peruse Cricut's Angel Policy, which delineates the commercial use stipulations.

Cricut's angel policy is susceptible to amendments and additions at any juncture. Always reference the policy for the most precise, comprehensive, and up-to-date information.

For instance, YandiDesigns proposes a project idea utilizing their Shaly Cute display font, permitting users to churn out up to 10,000 commercial products annually—a fairly generous quota for many small enterprises, artists, and crafters.

If your endeavors burgeon into large-scale production, it might be prudent to invest in industrial products or manufacturers.

Restrictions to Heed Before Embarking on a Cricut Project

Prior to initiating a Cricut project, acquaint yourself with certain restrictions. For instance, while content from the Walt Disney Company is accessible to Cricut users, they are prohibited from selling any items crafted from this content.

Bear in mind, this prohibition encompasses distribution as well. For instance, crafting Disney T-shirts and distributing them at charitable events is against the terms of service and copyright limitations.

These restrictions solely pertain to commercial, not personal, use.

In essence, items crafted using a Cricut machine can only be sold if specific laws are adhered to. Familiarize yourself with these restrictions to ensure compliance.

What Are Cricut Maker Projects, and How Do Cricut Machines Differ?

It's imperative to note that various Cricut models come with distinct advantages before diving into a project concept. Cricut categorizes the Cricut Maker as "Pro Level," which is noteworthy when contemplating a project. Acquaint yourself with the functionalities and operation of your equipment to make informed decisions.

In the Maker's case, this machine can manipulate more materials and a broader spectrum of accessories. For example, it can handle fine woodworking and fabric—it's essentially a powerhouse.

So, if you're eyeing Cricut Maker projects for larger tasks, your options have expanded. Create doll outfits, fabric flower bouquets, or coasters. The Maker model also boasts a more robust scoring system and enhanced durability, simplifying tasks like paper folding.

When selecting projects to sell, consider the materials that mesh well with your Cricut model. The Cricut Explore Air is a commendable model with a plethora of options, albeit it's incompatible with wood.

Keen on exploring the capabilities of various Cricut models? Visit the Cricut website (cricut.com) for the official comparison. Thereafter, you can determine which machine suits you best or learn more about your existing equipment's capabilities.

The design realm is laden with exhilarating ideas; the key is possessing pivotal information for your business ventures, personal commercials, and other tips.

Some Ideal Cricut Projects for Beginners

Absolutely! There are myriad beginner-friendly projects to delve into. However, remember, like any endeavor, a learning curve is inevitable.

Exerting excessive effort on crafting something "easy" might rob you of the opportunity to toil on creating something truly remarkable. Here are some simple alternatives, with the aim of enhancing them by adding a personal touch.

Here are some beginner-friendly ideas to experiment with:

1 - Create a Personalized Journal

Purchase a few basic Kraft journals, then use your Cricut to cut out inspirational phrases and shapes from cardstock or other types of paper. These can be adhered with glue or adhesive paper.

Materials Needed:
- Blank journals
- Inkjet printable adhesive vinyl or regular adhesive vinyl

Accessories Needed:
- Self-adhesive protective film
- Spatula for applying sign vinyl

Difficulty Level: Beginner

2 - Car Decals with Cricut

Car decals are a fun and popular vinyl project for the Cricut; you'll need to design your project, cut it out, and prepare it for your customers. You can create car decals using a Cricut for sale or distribution by following this advice:

Use outdoor vinyl whenever possible. This makes it waterproof and UV resistant, which are desirable traits for material applied to a car.

Choose a color that stands out! White is a common choice as it contrasts well with a car's back window, though the choice may vary based on where you plan to apply it.

Vinyl weeding can be challenging. Weeding is the process of removing excess vinyl from your cut design that isn't needed. You might want to use an X-Acto knife, tweezers, or a weeding tool, which looks like a pen with a curved, pointed tip, to help you remove the excess vinyl.

Materials Needed:
- Outdoor vinyl

Accessories Needed:
- Weeding tool (which looks like a pen with a curved, pointed tip)
- A pair of tweezers
- X-Acto knife

Difficulty Level: Beginner

3 - Cricut's Fun Christmas Ideas

The possibilities for Cricut crafts and Christmas ideas are virtually endless. From unique home decor to festive apparel, there are hardly any limits.

Some starting points could include creating greeting cards, among many others.

Materials Needed:
- Easy-release glossy transfer sheets for creating any design of your choice

Accessories Needed:
- Cricut Maker or Explore machine

Difficulty Level: Beginner

Greeting cards can be a fantastic project to share and sell, whether you want to add beautiful die cuts or are looking for a tool to mark your cards effortlessly.

Cute Valentine's Day Cricut Ideas to Sell

Valentine's Day is a fantastic occasion to get creative and design unique gifts. Consider the types of items you desire and how you can add your distinctive touch;

one suggestion is to create couples' outfits. This idea and many more are made possible by Cricut machines.

Materials Needed:
- T-shirt vinyl
- T-shirts

Accessories Needed:
- T-shirt alignment ruler: 18.0 in wide x 5.0 in high x 0.2 in; a quick, inexpensive, and easy way to try t-shirt alignment tools in various sizes.
- Shirt guide ruler, a t-shirt design tool for aligning your design with your t-shirt.
- Shirt guide tool: helps you achieve left, center, or right alignments and save time centering your designs.
- T-shirt vinyl alignment ruler.
- Sublimation ruler for T-shirts.

Difficulty Level: Beginner

This revised text provides clearer instructions and corrects some terminologies, ensuring a professional and polished presentation for your readers.

CHA PTER 2

PROJECT IDEAS FOR FOR IN-TERMEDIATE USERS

If you are at this level or aspire to be, you likely have a Cricut Explore or Maker machine and may still use them for crafting. In this chapter, you will discover numerous creations you can craft with these machines, aiming to reach an intermediate level. Take note, and embellish the details as you explore these exciting ideas.

These are the projects you've been waiting for to enhance your skills.

Dive into these designs that take creativity up a notch; you're surely going to enjoy:

Watercolor Decals

Create vibrant labels, stickers, or decals in various sizes and shapes with printable vinyl, leveraging Cricut's print-and-cut capability, like watercolor flower decals.

It's fun to give a fresh look to your old appliances; how about adding a witty phrase to your coffee maker?

Materials Needed:
- Sticker Paper

Accessories:
- Design Space or alternative design software
- Cricut Maker printer
- Computer, tablet, or cell phone

Difficulty Level: Intermediate

Wooden Tray

Printing or applying vinyl to wood with the Cricut Explore Air 2 is one of my favorite applications. I love breathing new life into something old, like the wooden tray in this tutorial.

Materials Required:
- 2.0 mm cardboard
- Balsa wood

Accessories Required:
- Knife blade
- Cricut purple mat
- Cricut Maker machine

Difficulty Level: Intermediate

Picture Magnets

We're 100% sure this is one of those projects all Cricut users will want to try. This idea is a must-try as you can cut and print sheets of magnets with your Cricut Maker. Photo magnets are perfect for gift giving, experimenting, creating business cards, or even using on a to-do list.

Materials Required:
- Magnet paper
- Paper for printing stickers

Accessories Required:
- Black blade

Difficulty Level: Intermediate

Ideas We Shouldn't Discard

Ideas, as you know, are endless, so here are more projects you might want to execute:

Felt Flowers
I've created paper flowers before, but these felt flowers are even better. Did you know that your machine can cut felt? You should try this project now! Making cards with 3D felt flowers is a unique concept I adore. The flowers give homemade cards a special touch.

Engraved Wine Glasses
Creating personalized wine glasses as a wedding gift for the bride and groom is an excellent idea. Engraving is very easy, and the result looks professional. They can be done on any glass surface, such as glasses, plates, bowls, or trays that can even be put in the oven.

Imagine your loved one's reaction when you give them a baking pan engraved with their name. You can create your engravings using the many free fonts and crafts on Creative Fabrica.

Personalized Necklaces
Leather, like the kind used to create these unique name necklaces, is another material the machine can cut. It requires a casing and a deep-cut blade, an additional tool you can purchase for the Cricut Explore.

Birthday Gift Bag

Why spend money on a gift bag that will end up in the trash when you can create a personalized gift bag that can be reused (and is much prettier too)? With very little money, you can acquire the materials to craft this special bag for your gift.

Soy Candles

This guide will show you how to apply heat-transfer vinyl to glass jars to personalize candles, which make the ideal gift. It's an easy task with a fantastic outcome.

Glitter Tumbler

Insulated tumblers make great gifts and are completely customizable.

Money Tree

This is a great idea for a wedding gift or for that individual you never know what to get — because who doesn't like money? Build and design this unique gift.

Personalized Mugs

The first project many often tackle with their Cricut Explore is creating personalized mugs for hot chocolate or other beverages. If you have several blank mugs and want to try a single-color design, you might also want to practice using vinyl on a curved surface.

Can Coolers

By purchasing blank can coolers online, you can create the perfect gift or party favor. They are really simple to construct and easy to customize.

Car Window Decals

Car window stickers or decals are ubiquitous. You can make them from anything, like Calvin and Hobbes images, cartoons, or sports logos.

The Orange Party

The design of this party is simple yet eye-catching, with its bright colors and straightforward theme.

Summer First Birthday Party Ideas

In my family, the most significant events are first birthday celebrations and weddings. These occasions demand handcrafted, bespoke decor to create a memorable experience.

Address Labels

With Cricut pens, you can create perfectly handwritten envelopes. My favorite projects are those for birthday or thank you cards.

Easter Cupcake Decorating Ornaments

This fantastic project can be adapted for any holiday. All you need are candy sticks or toothpicks and a Cricut Explore Air 2. Any image can be used as a cupcake topper.

T-Shirts with Heat Transfer Vinyl

Printable vinyls are very versatile and easy to use.

Printable Santa Claus Letters

Writing letters to Santa is a tradition that children and their parents cherish. You can get a sense of what kids want for Christmas by reading the letters, and it's interesting to observe how their desires change each year. Additionally, you can use a free printable template.

3D Paper Flower Magnets

These 3D paper flower magnets are adorable, and attaching them to magnets to make them more versatile seems like a great idea. Did you know? 3D paper flowers also look great as thumbtacks for a corkboard. You can find more great 3D projects here.

Print and Cut Agenda Stickers

These planner stickers are my favorite because you can personalize them for your family, lifestyle, special events or appointments, and so much more!

Easter Coloring Cards

If you are having a large family gathering, there will most likely be kids, and this activity is a terrific way to create coloring cards for the little visitors with your Cricut Explore Air 2.

Coloring Cards

Although this design is originally intended for Valentine's Day, it's also suitable for Halloween. You can innovate and color the cards with crayons, markers, or colored pencils. It is a fun gift for both children and adults.

Cushion Covers

Also, create your cushion cover with a personalized font. It is an easy project with a single layer of vinyl with hardly any waste, perfect for beginners and intermediates using heat transfer vinyl (HTV).

As you consider the Cricut crafts to create, consider these more entertaining ideas that you may build upon:

Wedding Place Tags or Markers

Numerous options are available. Beautiful paper flowers and layered sheets are just some amazing materials for weddings and other formal parties.

Faux Fur Accessories

Faux fur can be cut on many Cricut cutters. Use it to cut out sweet shapes like hearts, stars, or even flowers to make a lovely personalized headband. Transform your cutouts into key chains, earrings, and other accessories.

If you feel you are at an advanced level and your machine is ready to work, consider creating personalized confetti for birthdays, graduations, or even in someone's favorite colors. Experiment with different shapes, colors, and designs to make it more environmentally friendly. You can even recycle or use recycled paper.

T-shirts, Sweatshirts, and Clothing:
You can get quite creative with clothing. If you have a particular hobby, consider creating T-shirts that reflect that interest.

CHA PTER 3

PROJECT IDEAS FOR FOR ADVANCED USERS

This chapter commences the advanced level with project ideas tailored for experienced users. Understandably, after progressing through beginner and intermediate levels, you're eager to advance and demonstrate your enhanced capabilities. Below, you'll find some ideas and pertinent information on what you can now accomplish.

Projects You Can Create at an Advanced Level

Here are four project ideas along with the required materials, tools, and accessories:

Christmas Balls

If you've reached this stage, you're undoubtedly committed to this project.

Materials needed:
- Acetate (or thick cardboard if preferred; white is recommended).

- Holographic adhesive vinyl

Accessories needed:
- Peeler and scraper
- Adhesive protractor
- Purple and green mat

Difficulty level: Advanced

Initially, you'll need the file with two neutral balls where you can insert two words of your choice, and another file with the proper names.

Simply right-click the images to save them to your computer, and then upload them to Design Space.

With a few simple clicks, your ball design will be ready, whether you choose to use the blank base with your favorite typography or one of the pre-designed options by Nerea.

Now that your design is ready, what next?

Now comes the thrilling part—cutting! Place the acetate on the purple mat and cut it using the deep-cut blade. As for the holographic vinyl, place it on the green mat and cut it using the standard blade that comes with our machine.

After cutting, peel the carrier off the adhesive vinyl. With the aid of a peeler and scraper, this task is completed in no time!

Now, adhere the vinyl to the acetate. We recommend placing the adhesive side face down on the table and then positioning the acetate on top. It's much simpler this way!

Portal Wreath

Elevate your home's aesthetic with this creative idea. Opt for a wreath that you can hang on the main door, transforming your home into a winter Christmas paradise. This is the season when such ideas truly shine.

Accessories:
- Rotating Maker Blade
- Extra-deep cutting blade
- Adhesive Cricut Joy Mat Ref 2007964
- Green and red textured cardboard

Remember, you have the freedom to design the shapes you wish to incorporate into your wreath.

If design isn't your forte, utilize images from Cricut Design Space. Once you've decided on the elements for your wreath, prepare the mat, place the cardstock on it, and proceed to cut them using the cutting plotter.

Note: Ensure the cardstock is properly positioned on the mat before commencing the cutting. Remember, this project allows for as much creativity as you desire. Let your imagination soar as you bring your unique wreath to life.

Christmas Tree Skirt

Ever felt like your Christmas tree looks a bit bare? Here's a stellar idea to ensure that never happens again. Simply design what you want to be showcased on your project, get it printed and cut, and you're good to go. Utilize masking tape to adhere the vinyl to it, making it ready to be transferred to the surface where you intend to stick it.

Accessories:
- Cutting blade (type dependent on the machine you're using)

Materials:
- Gold vinyl
- Masking tape

Difficulty Level: Advanced

Gift Ornaments

Tired of the usual superhero wrapping paper or repetitive labels on your gifts every year? Once you venture into designing your own tags, there's no going back. Send your designs to your cutting plotter, and voila! The innovation in your designs will undoubtedly add that special touch.

Materials:
- Cricut glitter cardboard (color of your choice)
- Cricut textured white cardstock
- Cricut 1mm markers
- Cricut green mat

Accessories:
- Pink mat

Stickers for Christmas, Valentine's Day, and More

The joy of decorating folders, cell phone cases, and laptops with personalized stickers is unparalleled. Here's a brief on the materials you'll need for this project.

Materials:
- White printable adhesive vinyl
- Holographic vinyl

Accessories:
- Green/blue mat

Kickstart the process by conceptualizing the shape and design, either through creating illustrations in your preferred program or using images from Cricut Design Space. If you're designing them yourself, work with two layers: one for printing and cutting the stickers, and another for the sticker sheet background details that you don't want cut out. Don't forget to set up the washi sheet cutting. For an extra flair, cut out some sticker elements in holographic vinyl and adhere them to your sticker sheet for a more refined finish.

Advanced Level Projects

Now that you're well-versed with the cuts you can make and the materials at your disposal, here are some project ideas:

Fabric Cuts
A hallmark feature of the Maker is its brand-new Rotary Blade, designed to cut almost any fabric with its unique sliding and rolling motion powered by a robust 4-kilogram (8.8 lb) motor. This is a game-changer for Cricut users who previously had to resort to specialized fabric cutters as desktop cutting machines struggled with thicker textiles.

The Maker revolutionizes this, acting as an all-in-one device. It also comes with a fabric cutting mat, allowing you to cut hundreds of fabrics without any backing.

Sewing Patterns

The access to a vast array of sewing patterns is another feather in the Maker's cap. With hundreds of patterns to choose from, including some from Simplicity and Riley Blake Designs, select your desired pattern, and let the Maker cut it out for you. A washable fabric marker is provided to indicate where the pattern parts should align, making your sewing projects a breeze.

Balsa Wood Cuts

With a remarkable blade force of 4 kg (8.8 lb), cutting through materials up to 2.4 mm thick is a breeze. This means that thick fabrics, which were a challenge for previous version machines, are now easily manageable.

Personalized Cards

The machine's strength and precision make cutting paper and cards quicker and easier, elevating your handmade cards to a new level.

Puzzles and Jigsaw Puzzles

Thanks to the Knife Blade, the Cricut Maker can now cut through thicker materials than ever before. What's the first project you're excited to tackle?

Christmas Tree Ornaments

The spinning blade, renowned for its ability to cut through any fabric, is ideal for crafting Christmas decor. Browse the sewing pattern collection for Christmas-themed patterns, cut them out of felt or any other fabric of your choice, then stitch each one separately.

Quilts

The collaboration between Riley Blake Designs and Cricut has brought a variety of quilt designs to the sewing pattern collection. Utilize the Maker to precisely cut your quilt pieces before assembling them.

Felt Dolls and Plushies

One of the Simplicity designs featured in the sewing pattern collection is the "felt doll and clothes" pattern. Several youngsters we know would cherish a handmade doll to add to their collection. It's as simple as selecting the pattern, cutting, and sewing!

Vinyl Decals and Vinyl Stickers

Cutting vinyl decals and stickers with the Cricut Maker is our favorite pastime. Create your design in Cricut Design Space, command the machine to start cutting, then weed and transfer the design to your chosen surface.

Baby Clothing

The Cricut Maker's cutting surface measures 12 by 24 inches, which, while not suitable for adult apparel patterns, is ample for cutting baby apparel patterns.

Fabric Appliqués

Available for purchase is the fabric blade attachment which enables you to cut more intricate fabric designs like appliqués. Unlike the spinning blade, the bonded fabric blade requires a backing attached to the fabric for efficient cutting.

Typefaces

The Cricut Maker's adaptive tooling method is a key selling feature. This function ensures you remain engaged with your Maker. Essentially, it's a tooling system compatible with all of the Explore family's tools and blades as well as any future tools and blades produced by Cricut.

Jewelry Making

If you enjoy dabbling in jewelry making and craft cutting, consider merging the two. The Cricut Maker's strength enables it to cut thicker materials ideal for elaborate jewelry designs. While it may not cut gold, silver, or diamonds, you can surely craft a lovely pair of leather earrings.

Wedding or Birthday Invitations

Savvy creators know how to cut costs by crafting invitations for birthdays or wedding celebrations. The Cricut Maker is perfect for creating beautiful invites as it allows you to cut intricate designs from paper and repurpose that calligraphy pen.

Party and Restaurant Menus

Your crafting journey doesn't stop at pre-wedding projects; you can also use your Maker to enhance the big day. While the possibilities are vast, you could start by creating menus, place cards, and favor tags. Employ a cohesive design across all your table settings to maintain a prominent theme.

Create Coloring Books

Coloring books are hugely popular, and now you can create your own. It's yet another exciting venture. All you need is paper, a card, and a detailed design. Instruct the Maker to use the Fine Tip Pen tool to craft your original coloring book.

Coasters

Coasters are among the items you'll be eager to create with your new Maker. The material choices are vast: leather, felt, metallic sheets, and everything in between. The sewing library also boasts excellent designs you may want to try.

Fabric Key Chains

The sewing pattern collection features simple designs for fabric key chains. Once again, the Cricut makes it easy: just cut out the pattern and sew it.

Custom Headbands

With Cricut unveiling a device capable of cutting thick leather, crafting elaborate headbands and hair accessories with a steampunk theme is now possible.

Trimmed Christmas Trees

During the holidays, a genuine Christmas tree is a common desire. However, if space is a constraint, crafting your own interconnecting wooden tree is a fantastic project this year. With the Cricut Maker's ability to cut heavy materials like wood, who needs lasers?

Cake Toppers

Remember when Cricut released the "Cake" cutter for shaping materials like fondant and gum paste? While the Maker isn't specifically a cake machine like the Cake, it excels in crafting tiny, beautiful paper crafts to adorn your cakes.

Fridge Magnets

Both the Cricut Explore and Maker machines can cut magnetic material, a delight for those who love collecting magnets and adding a personal touch to their refrigerators.

Decorative Stickers

Whether you desire a motivational quote on your windows or a charming design on your car's back window, simply insert the window cling into the machine and start crafting your intricate design.

Scrapbooking Embellishments

Enhance your scrapbooking projects with embellishments created using your Maker. Although Cricut machines have always excelled at cutting intricate designs, the new ultra-sensitive blades take precision to a whole new level.

Custom EVA Cutting

Craft foam has reportedly been cut with Cricut machines in the past, but the results were often unsatisfactory. However, the Maker's 4 kg (8.8 lb) of force cuts through craft foam like butter, surpassing the performance of Explore machines.

Boxes, 3D Figures, and Flowers

The Maker excels in all the traditional paper crafts we cherish, including crafting 3D shapes, boxes, and tackling any sewing patterns thrown its way. The supplied scoring stylus is a major contributor to this versatility.

Templates of All Kinds

If your goal with the Maker is to create items that will facilitate the crafting of other beautiful items, you're in luck. It's the ideal stencil maker, especially now that thicker materials like wood can be used to create stencils.

Removable Tattoos

If you're contemplating a tattoo but hesitant about the lifelong commitment, fear not. Emboss your design on tattoo paper, a sheet covered in transfer film that can be applied to your skin.

Washi Tape

Washi tape is a scrapbooker's cherished accessory, but purchasing it at craft stores can get pricey. Why not make your own? Thanks to the Cricut Maker's capabilities, you can print and cut your designs on washi sheets.

Addressed Envelopes

Once done with homemade wedding invitations, move on to the envelopes. No need to exert manual effort when you have the Maker. It features a fine-point pen and a calligraphy pen, enabling you to automatically address the envelopes with the elegant font of your choice.

Glassware Stickers

Experiments with vinyl cutting often include crafting designs for glassware, especially effective for themed events.

Home Decorations

The Maker is undoubtedly fantastic for crafting standard home decorations, a capability shared with most desktop craft cutting machines. Create stunning signs for your cabinets, adorable cutouts for your living room, or 3D wall decorations with the Cricut Maker.

Cushion Transfers

Adding a personal touch to a plain pillow or cushion is as simple as imprinting one of your unique designs. Many will utilize the heat transfer vinyl of their new Maker machine. For cushions, flocked iron-on vinyl is recommended due to its appealing textured feel.

Gift Tags

Gift tagging can be an annoying expense that quickly adds up, especially during the holiday season. However, with a Cricut, you can create your adhesive tags, so you never have to purchase them again. Just add cardstock.

Purses and Bags

Thanks to the extensive collection of sewing designs, crafting various handbags, full-size purses, and even tote bags is possible with the Maker. If planning to work with thick leather, purchasing the necessary blade is advisable.

Pincushions

The sewing pattern collection features at least eight unique pincushion patterns that may inspire you to take up hand sewing again.

Dog Clothing

At this advanced level with the Cricut, crafting fascinating items for small or toy dogs is a possibility. Currently, it's limited to accessories, notably dog hats. Though it's well-known that most dogs won't tolerate such items for more than a few seconds, if your furry friend enjoys participating in photo shoots, this could work for you.

Socks

Although it's summer at the time of writing, fall and winter are just around the corner. Utilize the Cricut Maker to cut out some cozy wool sock patterns, ensuring your toes aren't left in the cold. It appears that this project will include some sewing as well!

Christmas Stocking Patterns

The sewing pattern collection features a particularly fantastic Christmas stocking pattern to try out in December. You can craft your item out of durable leather.

Wall Art

Wall art is another viable option worth exploring. With the Cricut, crafting something beautiful and flawless is easily achievable due to its high precision.

FREQUENTLY ASKED QUESTIONS

Here are some commonly asked questions by users

Can You Upload Your Own Images?

- Yes, you can! Cricut Design Space allows you to turn your uploaded images into cut-out shapes. Here's how to do it:
- Launch Cricut Design Space and start a new project.
- Click on the Upload button and choose the image file you wish to upload.
- Select the image type, and use the eraser tools to remove the background (this step applies only to raster images like jpg and png).
- Finally, name your image, provide tags for easier searching, and click Upload to complete the process.

These steps can be followed on the Cricut Design Space app whether you're using a computer, laptop, or mobile device (such as an iPhone or iPad).

Can You Upload Your Own Fonts?

Have you ever wanted to use your own fonts in Cricut Design Space? Well, uploading fonts is much simpler than you might think. Here are the steps:

- Save a copy of the font you intend to use.
- Unzip the font file's folder. Double-click each font file to open it and follow your computer's instructions to install the font.
- Once the font has been installed, launch Cricut Design Space.
- Create a new text box and a new project on your canvas.
- Click on the font drop-down option in the top toolbar to change the font.

Is the Design Space Software the Same for Cricut Maker and Cricut Explore?

Yes, the Design Space software is the same for all Cricut cutting machines. Visit design.cricut.com to download the app and log in. Design Space will adjust the available options such as tooling, material cutting settings, and loading options based on the machine you are using.

Do Cricut Maker Machines Require an Internet Connection?

Not necessarily. You can create and send projects to your machine without an internet connection by installing the Design Space software on your PC or iOS mobile device. However, to use some features and functions like syncing content and uploading photos, an internet connection and login are required.

Note: Offline functionality is not supported on Android mobile devices in Design Space.

What are Smart Materials?

Smart Materials are specialized materials designed for use without a mat. Once you load the material, your Cricut Maker 3 machine is ready to go. They come in various types including sticky cardboard, iron-on, and vinyl.

Can I Use Other Brands of Vinyl or Heat Transfer Vinyl Without a Mat?

No. It's recommended to always use a mat with other brands of vinyl or heat transfer vinyl. Cricut Smart Materials have been thoroughly tested for matless cutting on Cricut Maker 3 machines.

What is the Purpose of the USB Port on the Side of My Cricut Maker?

The USB port serves as a charging port for your tablet or other mobile device.

Will I Lose My Cartridges, Projects, or Uploaded Images if I Switch to Cricut Maker 3?

No, you won't. Your projects, cartridges (image sets), and uploaded images are all tied to your Cricut account ID. To retain your content, activate your new machine using the same Cricut ID.

How do Cricut Maker Machines Determine Which Blade I Have Loaded?

After completing a cut, Cricut Maker machines rotate the carriage to the right (a process known as "homing") and then scan the blade to identify which blade is loaded.

Can I Use the Cable from a Previous Machine with Cricut Explore 3?

No, you can't. The power cord connector and receptacle on the Cricut Explore 3 are different from previous models.

Do Cricut Maker machines require an internet connection?

Not necessarily. With the Design Space app installed on your computer or iOS mobile device, you can design and send projects to your machine without an internet connection. However, for certain features such as synchronizing content and uploading images, an internet connection and login are required. Note: The Offline feature is currently not available for Design Space on Android mobile devices.

What are the differences between Cricut EasyPress 3 and Cricut EasyPress 2?

The Cricut EasyPress 3 retains all the beloved features of the Cricut EasyPress 2, including even heating, a safe-touch plastic exterior, and precise controls for time and temperature. Additionally, the Cricut EasyPress 3 is equipped with built-in Bluetooth® technology to connect to the Cricut Heat app. This handy app allows you to select the transfer material, base material, and pressing surface, and then send time and temperature settings directly to the press with a simple touch.

Should I use the Cricut EasyPress 3 with the app?

It's necessary to use the Cricut Heat mobile app to activate the Cricut EasyPress 3. Once activation is complete, you can use the Cricut EasyPress 3 with or without the app.

TABLE OF CONTENTS

Step-by-step project for Beginners Users

261

267

Step-by-step project for Intermediate Users

Step-by-step project for Advanced Users

273

275

Step-by-step project for San Valentine Day

Step-by-step project for 4 July

279

283

Step-by-step project for Christmas

CRICUT PROJECT

STEP-BY-STEP PROJECTS

FRIDGE MAGNETS

DIFFICULTY
●●

REALIZATION TIME

🕐 **15 Minutes**

Procedure

MATERIALS

- Printable magnetic sheets

ACCESSORIES

- Cricut Maker or Cricut Explore, Deep blade

1. Click on "**New Project**" to begin.
2. In the left sidebar, click on the "**Shapes**" button and insert a circle and a heart.
3. Click on the "**Images**" button in the left sidebar. Select two images of your choice.
4. In the sidebar, click on the "**Upload**" button to import a photo from your PC.

⬆
Upload

5. Resize the photo so that it is slightly larger than the heart. Then, position the heart over the photo at the desired height.
6. Select the heart (or the shape you chose) and the photo together by pressing the **SHIFT key** on your keyboard. Then click on the "**Slice**" button located at the bottom of the Layers panel.
7. You'll notice excess layers at this point. Delete them, keeping only the heart with the photo.
8. For the second magnet, resize the circle(or the shape you chose) to the desired size, place your chosen image in the center, and then select both layers (circle and image). Now click the "**Weld**" button.
9. Lastly, to create the final type of magnet, utilize the offset feature. Select the second image you chose and click the "**Offset**" button found

in the toolbar at the top. You can adjust the offset by moving the slider from the center to the left or to the right. Note: Starting from the center is advisable as moving the slider all the way to the left will create an internal offset instead of an external one.

10. Now select the offset layer and the image layer together by holding down the **SHIFT key** on the keyboard along with the mouse button.

11. At this point, the magnets are ready to be printed and cut.

12. Click the "**MAKE IT**" button and, immediately after, click the "**Send to Printer**" button. Select the printer connected to the PC which you intend to use for printing the magnetic sheet.

13. Insert the newly printed magnetic sheet into the green mat and select "**Magnetic Sheet**" as the material type.

14. When finished, eject the mat by clicking on the button with the two arrows.

15. Your magnets are now ready to be placed on the refrigerator. They make great gifts for birthdays, christenings, party favors, Mother's Day, Christmas, and more!

BOTTLE FAVORS

DIFFICULTY

REALIZATION TIME

🕐 **15 Minutes**

Procedure

1. Click on "**New Project**" to begin.
2. In the left sidebar, click on the "**Shapes**" button and insert a rectangle, sizing it to 3.23 centimeters in width by 4 centimeters in height.
3. Click on the "**Images**" button in the left sidebar. Select an image of your choice, and consider adding text and a frame as well.
4. Select all elements and click on the "**Weld**" button located at the bottom of the layers panel to merge the layers.
5. Click on the "**MAKE IT**" button, and immediately thereafter, click on the "S**end to Printer**" button. Select the printer connected to your PC that you intend to use for printing on the printable vinyl.
6. Insert the sheet you just printed into the green mat and select either "**Printable Vinyl**" or "**Medium Cardstock**" as the material type.
7. Once the cutting is complete, eject the mat by clicking on the button with the two arrows.
8. Carefully remove the label you just cut out and place it centered on the clear part of the bottle.
9. Fill the small bottle with Smarties or other candies of your choice.
10. For a decorative touch, consider adding a bow with a bead or rhinestone in the center.

MATERIALS

- Cricut printable vinyl
- Mini bottles

ACCESSORIES

- Cricut Joy, Cricut Maker, or Cricut Explore
- Fine point blade

These adorable little bottles serve not only as wedding favors but also as delightful party favors for various occasions.

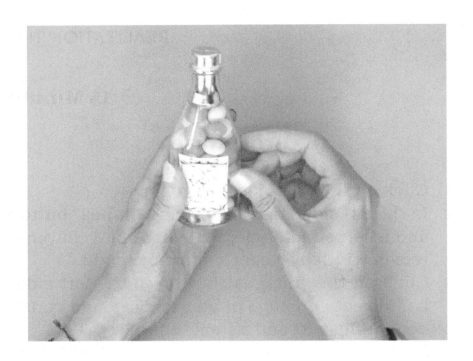

INSERT CARD TEMPLATE

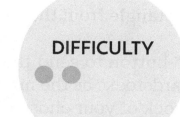

DIFFICULTY

● ●

REALIZATION TIME

🕐 **10 Minutes**

Procedure

1. Begin by clicking on "**New Project**"
2. In the left sidebar, click on the "**Shapes**" button and enter a rectangle sized 20 centimeters in width by 13 centimeters in height.
3. Once more from the "**Shapes**" button, click on the first line at the top (labeled "**Crease Line**") and insert it in the center of the rectangle. Utilize the buttons on the top toolbar to achieve precise alignment.
4. In the left sidebar, click on the "**Images**" button. In the search box, enter the phrase "**Card Curved Corner Cuts**" or the corresponding image code: **#M139D52E1**.
5. Insert the image on the right side of the rectangle (divided by the crease line) and center it perfectly.
6. Now, add an image of your choice that you wish to carve into the main side of the card. Optionally, you may add little hearts or stars around it to enhance the card's aesthetic.
7. Additionally, select a font of your choice by clicking on the "**Text**" button in the left sidebar. All fonts are accessible from the drop-down menu in the top bar.
8. In the "**Layers**" panel, select the writing layer and click at the top of the operations drop-down menu to select "**Pen.**"

MATERIALS

- 270 gram cardstock

ACCESSORIES

- Cricut Maker, or Cricut Explore
- Fine point blade
- Creasing stylus or creasing wheel 02

9. Now, select everything using the appropriate button found on the top tool-bar, and click the "Group" button.

10. Separately, add another rectangle from the "Shapes" button, sized 8.85 x 11.7 centimeters.

11. Lastly, click the "Make It" button to send the project to your Cricut cutting machine. Select "Heavy Cardstock" as the material type.

12. Insert the 270-gram cardstock of your chosen color into the green mat.

13. If you have the creasing stylus, add it to the marker slot. Otherwise, insert the creasing wheel into the blade slot as directed by Cricut Design Space.

14. When prompted, insert the marker(s).

15. Upon completion, unload the mat by clicking the button with the two arrows.

16. Now, place another piece of cardstock, around 250/270 grams in weight, in a color that contrasts with the previous one.

17. After cutting, execute a crease at the crease lines and insert the newly cut rectangle inside the holes made by the machine.

18. Et voila! Your card is ready. You can create as many as you like in the size you prefer, without the necessity of using pre-cut cards.

PERSONALIZED CHOCOLATE BARS

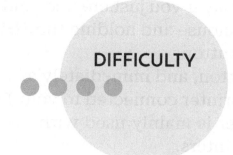

DIFFICULTY

●●○○○

REALIZATION TIME

🕐 **20 Minutes**

Procedure

MATERIALS

- 120-gram photo paper or 115-gram glossy coated paper (for laser printers)

ACCESSORIES

- Cricut Maker, or Cricut Explore
- Fine point blade
- Creasing wheel 01 or creasing stylus

1. Begin by clicking on "**New Project**"
2. In the left sidebar, click on the "**Shapes**" button and select a square. Unlock the proportions using the lock icon found in the toolbar at the top, enabling you to transform it into a rectangle. Set the dimensions to 13 centimeters (***width***) by 13.3 centimeters (***height***). The dimensions might vary depending on the brand of the candy bar you use.
3. Select the resulting rectangle, and from the operations menu, select "**Print then Cut**". Next to it, in the color selector, choose "**Pattern**." Select the pattern you prefer or upload one from your PC by clicking the "**Upload**" button, followed by "**Upload Pattern**."
4. Now insert the crease lines starting from the right: the first at 1 centimeter, the second at about 4 centimeters, the third at 1 centimeter, the fourth at 4 centimeters, and the fifth again at 1 centimeter.
5. Click on the "**Images**" button and enter keywords in the search box: "***princess***" and "***birthday princess***."
6. Return to the design area by clicking the "**Canvas**" button.
7. Place the images between the second and third crease lines starting from the left. If needed, add the name of the birthday girl by clicking on the "**Text**" button.

8. Select all layers except the crease lines and click the "**Group**" button.

9. Now select the printable layer you just created, and together with all the crease lines (by clicking the mouse and holding the **SHIFT** button on your keyboard), click the "**Group**" button.

10. Click the "**MAKE IT**" button, and immediately after, click the "**Send to Printer**" button. Select the printer connected to your PC for printing on photo or coated paper. The former is mainly used with inkjet printers, and the latter exclusively with laser printers.

11. Place the sheet of paper you just printed on the green mat and select "**Medium Cardstock**" as the material type. Insert the creasing stylus or creasing wheel 01 when prompted by Cricut Design Space.

12. When finished, unload the mat by clicking the button with the two arrows.

13. Now wrap the chocolate bar with the newly printed paper, making creases at the crease lines.

14. Glue the longer side together using a simple glue stick.

15. Join the top and bottom sides together. You can seal with glue or use a mini sealer.

16. Finish it off with zigzag scissors.

These kinds of wrappers are popular at parties and can be paired with party gadgets or mini favors for the little ones.

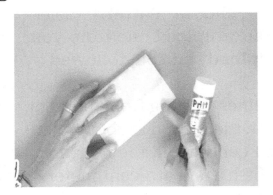
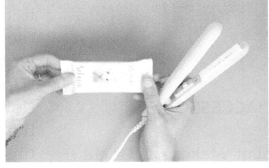

TRIANGLE PARTY CANDY

DIFFICULTY

● ● ○ ● ●

REALIZATION TIME

🕐 **20 Minutes**

Procedure

MATERIALS

- 120-gram photo paper

ACCESSORIES

- Cricut Maker, or Cricut Explore
- Fine point blade

1. Start by clicking on "**New Project**."
2. In the left sidebar, click on the "**Shapes**" button and insert a rectangle measuring 9.5 centimeters x 21 centimeters. Rotate it to a vertical orientation.
3. Navigate to the operations menu and click on the "Print" button, then "Cut." Adjacent to it, you'll find a color selector; click on it and then click on "**Pattern**."
4. Choose your preferred pattern to create a background for your triangle. Remember, by clicking on the "**Edit Pattern**" button, you can either enlarge or shrink the selected pattern. Moreover, you can import a pattern from your PC to Cricut Design Space using the "**Upload**" button found in the left sidebar. Ensure that the patterns are square, not rectangular.
5. To add an image, click on the "Images" button found in the left sidebar.
6. Position the selected image about 7 centimeters from the top edge and 5 centimeters from the side edge.
7. Now select all elements and click the "**Group**" button.
8. Click the "Make It" button and, immediately after, click the "**Send to Printer**" button. Select the printer connected to your PC for printing on photo paper.

9. Insert the newly printed sheet of photo paper into the green mat and select "**Medium Cardstock**" as the material type.
10. Once done, unload the mat by clicking on the button with the two arrows.
11. Take the resulting rectangle and roll it up from the long side, ensuring an overlap of about 2 centimeters.
12. Using a glue stick, adhere the sides together securely.
13. Now, join the top very well by adhering the two sides together, again using the glue stick.
14. Insert candies or treats inside.
15. Now close on the opposite side to form a triangle.
16. Finish it off using zigzag scissors.

These triangle candy holders are super cute and are perfect for both your parties and Halloween night. Consider adding a mini card inside for a personalized touch.

BABY BOTTLE SHAPED BIRTH ANNOUNCEMENT CARD

DIFFICULTY

● ● ● ○

REALIZATION TIME

🕐 **25 Minutes**

Procedure

MATERIALS

- 270-gram cardstock of various colors

ACCESSORIES

- Cricut Maker, Cricut Joy or Cricut Explore
- Fine point blade

1. Begin by clicking on "**New Project.**"
2. In the left sidebar, click on the "**Images**" button. In the search box, type "**Baby Bottle**" or enter the code **#M3B694EC5** and select the image.
3. Without returning to the canvas, enter "**Elephant**" or code **#M47B51476** in the search box.
4. Now return to the design area by clicking on the "**Canvas**" button.
5. From the layers panel, select "**Baby Bottle**" and click on the "**Silhouette**" button. Here, deselect the second and third layers, leaving only the base outline checked. Close the window by clicking the "**X**" at the top. You will now have only the bottle silhouette without the decorative stripes.
6. Select the resulting layer and click the "**Offset**" button. Move the slider to the left to create an internal offset. This will serve as a border.
7. Position the little elephant downward to visualize the final placement once the card is assembled.
8. Click the "**Shapes**" button to insert a scalloped circle shape.
9. Within the scalloped shape, insert a circle. Inside the circle, add text by clicking the "**Text**" button. You could insert the name of the baby, for instance.
10. Place the group of shapes above the little elephant.

11. For additional decoration, replicate the steps you followed for the scalloped circle, but use a small rectangle instead. Insert a suitable inscription for this type of card within the rectangle. For example: "All the greats were once children, but few remember."
12. Now select the rectangle along with the text and click the "**Group**" button. Do the same with the circle and the text containing the baby's name.
13. Optionally, add a paper bow by clicking on the "**Images**" button and entering "**Paper Bow**" or the code **#M11B526** as the search term.
14. Click the "**MAKE IT**" button and, immediately after, click the "**Send to Printer**" button. Select the printer connected to your PC for printing on the 270-gram cardstock.
15. Place the newly printed sheet on the green mat and select "**Heavy Cardstock**" as the material type.
16. Once done, unload the mat by clicking the button with the two arrows.
17. Now send all the other parts you see in the mat preview to cutting, using the same setting for all the cards of various colors.
18. Upon completion, unload the mat by clicking the button with the two arrows.
19. Gather all the cut and printed parts for assembly. Start with the base template, and on top of it, glue the inner offset using a reliable glue stick.
20. Continue with the little elephant, followed by the circle with the name on top, then the rectangle with the phrase. For added depth, adhere these elements with double-sided tape. Lastly, glue on the bow. To create the bow, fold the main template in half, adhere it with hot glue, and finish it off with the center part, also glued with hot glue.
21. Decorate with beads or rhinestones, and optionally, embellish the elephant's eyes with plastic eyes.

Despite its originality, this project is fairly simple to execute and is suitable for births, christenings, and birthdays.

SINGLE-PORTION CONFETTI

DIFFICULTY

●●●●●●

REALIZATION TIME

🕐 **30 Minutes**

Procedure

1. Begin by clicking on "**New Project.**"
2. In the left sidebar, click on the "**Shapes**" button and select a square. Unlock the proportions using the padlock icon found in the toolbar at the top to transform it into a rectangle. Adjust the dimensions to 10 centimeters (width) by 8 centimeters (height). *Note*: The dimensions may need adjustments based on the single-portion confections used.
3. Select the resulting rectangle and, from the operations menu, choose "**Print Then Cut**." Adjacent to it, in the color selector, choose "**Pattern**." Pick the pattern you prefer, or upload your own pattern from your PC by clicking on the "**Upload**" button and then "**Upload Pattern**."
4. Click on the "**Images**" button and enter "elephant name frame" in the search box.
5. Return to the design area by clicking on the "**Canvas**" button.
6. Position the newly imported image horizontally in the center of the rectangle and slightly lower vertically.
7. Click the "**Text**" button and insert text inside the frame with the little elephant.
8. Select all layers and click on the "**Group**" button.
9. Click on the "**Shapes**" button again and add a square. Adjust it into a rectangle with dimen-

MATERIALS

- 120-gram photo paper or 115-gram glossy coated paper (for laser printers)

ACCESSORIES

- Cricut Maker, or Cricut Explore
- Fine point blade
- Creasing Wheel 01 or Creasing Stylus
- Perforation Tip

sions of 9 centimeters wide by 0.5 centimeters high.

10. From the "**Shapes**" panel, now add the shape called "**Pennant**" and join it to the rectangle.

11. Click the "**Combine and Merge**" button to unite them into a single shape. Select the group/layer obtained and click in the operations drop-down menu. Choose "**Perforate**."

12. Now select the previously obtained printable layer, and along with the perforated layer, click the mouse and the "**SHIFT**" button on your keyboard. Once done, click the "**Group**" button.

13. Click the "Make It" button and, immediately after, click the "**Send to Printer**" button. Select the printer connected to your PC, set to print on photo or coated paper. ***Note***: Photo paper is mainly for inkjet printers, while coated paper is exclusively for laser printers.

14. Place the newly printed sheet on the green mat and select "**Medium Cardstock**" as the material type. Insert the Creasing Stylus or Creasing Wheel 01 when prompted by Cricut Design Space. Do the same with the Perforation Cutting Tip.

15. Once done, unload the mat by clicking the button with the two arrows.

16. Wrap the single-portion confection, initially gluing along the long side with a glue stick.

17. Utilizing a mini-sealer (***available on Amazon***), join the top two sides and the bottom two sides. The mini-sealer will slightly loosen a small part of the single-portion package, attaching the two paper flaps seamlessly without the need for additional glue. ***Note***: This aspect might vary depending on the brand of sugared almonds used.

18. The sugared almonds are now ready and can be accessed by simply pulling the tab created with your Cricut cutting machine. This product is highly professional in appearance and is exceptionally well-received for christenings.

COUPLE T-SHIRT

DIFFICULTY

REALIZATION TIME

🕐 **15 Minutes**

Procedure

1. Click on "**New Project**."
2. Click the "**Images**" button and enter "**Index Finger**" as keywords in the search bar. Choose your preferred image; for this example, I'll use the image with the code #**M211AD806**.
3. Upon inserting your image into the canvas, click the "**Contour**" button and deselect the two parts that form the heart. Close the contour window to save changes.
4. Rotate the image so that the finger is positioned upright, as if indicating something.
5. Navigate to the left sidebar and click the "**Text**" button. Create two text boxes; type "**HE'S**" in the first box, and "**MINE**" in the second. For the first box, use the font "**That's The Ticket**," and for the second, use "**That's The Ticket Sans**."
6. Duplicate the graphic and change the text to "**SHE'S MINE**."
7. Select the finger image under "**She's Mine**," click the "**Flip**" button (*top toolbar*), and then choose "**Flip Horizontally**." Ensure the fingers are facing inward.
8. Resize the lettering to match the t-shirt size, then select the word "**she's mine**" along with the image, and click the "**Group**" button.
9. Repeat the same grouping process with the "he's

MATERIALS

- Iron-on
- T-Shirt

ACCESSORIES

- Cricut Maker, Cricut Joy or Cricut Explore
- Fine point blade

mine" inscription.

10. If you're using a Cricut Joy, remember that you can cut up to 1.2 meters in length with Smart Iron-Ons, but the graphic width should not exceed 11 centimeters.

11. Click the "**MAKE IT**" button to send everything to cut.

12. If using a classic iron-on, select "**Everyday Iron-On**" from the materials list.

13. Place your material on the green mat, ensuring the shiny side is facing down, and the matte side is up.

14. After cutting, click the mat's "**Unload**" button and carefully peel off the iron-on.

15. Using a heat press, transfer the lettering to one t-shirt and then the other. If using Cricut's Everyday Iron-On, set the temperature to 155 degrees and press for 30 seconds, allowing it to cool before peeling off the liner. If using a different brand or product, refer to the manufacturer's instructions for the correct heat and time settings.

16. This fun and easy-to-make t-shirt is a great gift idea for young couples or anyone who appreciates quirky, yet practical gifts.

KEYCHAIN HIM/HER

DIFFICULTY

● ● ● ● ●

REALIZATION TIME

🕐 **40 Minutes**

MATERIALS

- Basswood
- Permanent Vinyl
- Transfer Tape

ACCESSORIES

- Cricut Maker
- Knife Blade

Procedure

1. Click on "**New Project**."
2. Click on the "**Images**" button and enter "**puzzle**" as the keyword. Although several types will appear, it's recommended to use the image with the code #**M514AC**.
3. Resize the image to approximately 14.7 x 8 centimeters.
4. Duplicate the image.
5. In one of the two images, click on the "**Contour**" button located in the bottom section of the layers panel. Click the "**Hide All Contours**" button and close it.
6. Repeat the same process with the other puzzle image in the design area, but in the opposite direction: select only the top contour, leaving all the curves unchecked. Now, you should only see the center line of the puzzle. Duplicate this line to place it in the other shape obtained.
7. Now, from the "**Shapes**" button, select a heart and resize it to about 3 centimeters. Position it in the center of your puzzle, on the left piece. Once done, duplicate the heart.
8. Select the left piece of the puzzle along with the heart you centered. Then, click the "**Slice**" button. Delete all unnecessary layers, leaving only the piece with the hole you created.
9. Click on the "**Select All**" button, followed by the "**Group**" button.

10. Take the other pair of puzzle pieces and click the "**Images**" button. For this example, use the word "*love*" with the code **#M34D8A**. However, you can insert custom text if preferred.

11. Center the text with respect to the two puzzle pieces. Click on the "**Shapes**" button and insert a square. Position it perfectly aligned with the cut line of the two pieces. Select the square and the word "*love*," then click the "**Slice**" button.

12. To achieve a more precise cut on the inscription, duplicate the center line of the puzzle piece. When finished, select the inscription, select the center cut, and click the "**Group**" button.

13. Separately, also select the other two center-cut puzzle pieces and click the "**Group**" button.

14. Click the "**MAKE IT**" button to access the mat preview and proceed with the cut by selecting "**Basswood**" as the material type.

15. Place the material on the purple mat, securing it well with painter's tape.

16. The machine will perform several passes. Unload the mat only after verifying that the wood has been cut correctly. If necessary, press the machine start button to perform one more pass.

17. Once the cutting is complete, click the button with the two arrows to unload the mat.

18. Now proceed with the vinyl cutting using the green mat.

19. First, transfer the permanent vinyl onto the small heart cut from the basswood using transfer tape.

20. Glue the small heart onto the wooden puzzle piece using vinyl glue.

21. Carefully transfer the word "**love**" onto the two basswood puzzle pieces.

22. Drill two holes in all the puzzle pieces using a mini drill with a wood drill bit. A Dremel or similar tool can also be used.

23. Add key rings to finalize the project.

24. Presented are two examples of his/her keychains that can be gifted or sold for Valentine's Day. Always remember to accompany your gift with a personalized box or sachet for a special touch.

4TH JULY APERITIF FLAG

DIFFICULTY

REALIZATION TIME

🕐 **5 Minutes**

Procedure

1. Click on "**New Project**."
2. Click on the "**Images**" button and enter "***American Flag***" or "***USA FLAG***" as keywords. In the sidebar on the left, open the "**Art Type**" menu and select the "**Print then Cut**" option. For this project, I chose the image with the code #**MD1BD299**.
3. Insert the chosen image into the canvas using the appropriate button.
4. Click on the "**Shapes**" button and select the first triangle you see.
5. Resize the triangle so that it is about 2.5 centimeters high.
6. Select the triangle, and while holding down the "**Shift**" key on your keyboard, select the flag. Then click on the "**Slice**" button.
7. Delete all the unnecessary layers, leaving the colored triangle with the American flag.
8. Duplicate the resulting triangle and click on the "**Flip**" button, then select "**Horizontally**."
9. Bring the two triangles close together, ensuring a minimum overlap, and align them perfectly at the top using the alignment buttons.
10. Select the two triangles using the "**Shift**" key on your keyboard and click on the "**Merge Layers**" button.
11. Send everything to cut by clicking on the "**Create**" button.

MATERIALS

- Printable vinyl or lightweight printable cardstock

ACCESSORIES

- Cricut Maker or Cricut Explore
- Fine point blade

12. In "**Preview Mats**," click the "**Continue**" button and then click "**Send to Printer**." Enter the number of copies you want to print and select the printer connected to your PC. You can use printable vinyl or lightweight cardstock.
13. Place the newly printed sheet on the machine's green mat and perform the cutting.
14. Assembly is straightforward at this point: if you used printable vinyl, wrap it around a simple toothpick, ensuring the two sides of the flag match. Use it to decorate your appetizers.

WATER BOTTLE WITH COOZIE

DIFFICULTY

● ●

REALIZATION TIME

🕐 **5 Minutes**

Procedure

1. Click on "**New Project**" to start.
2. Click on the "**Images**" button and enter "**4 JULY**" as keywords. Cricut Design Space offers a variety of images to choose from. For this project, I chose the image with the code #**M49802638**.
3. Insert the selected image into the canvas using the appropriate button.
4. Resize the image to about 7.5 inches wide. If your water bottle has a capacity larger than 500ml or is wider, adjust the graphic size to fit your coozie.
5. Now it's time to cut the design: click the "**Create**" button to proceed.
6. In the preview mats, click the "**Continue**" button, then select the "**Everyday Iron-On**" material.
7. Place the thermovinyl sheet on the machine's green mat and initiate the cutting process.
8. Ensure that the shiny side of the thermovinyl sheet is in contact with the mat, while the matte side faces upward.
9. Unload the mat by using the button with arrows or, in the case of the Cricut Joy, use the button in the app.
10. Carefully peel the thermovinyl and transfer it onto the coozie using Cricut's mini press, set to the second notch.
11. If necessary, place baking paper (or butcher paper) on top, especially when the press moves

MATERIALS

- Iron-on

ACCESSORIES

- Cricut Maker, Cricut Joy or Cricut Explore
- Fine point blade

over areas of the coozie where there is no iron-on liner.

12. Your customized water bottle coozie is now ready to be flaunted, making it a great accessory for a Fourth of July picnic on the lawns.

CUSTOMIZED CHRISTMAS MUG

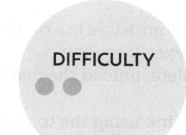

REALIZATION TIME

🕐 **15 Minutes**

MATERIALS

- Infusible Ink Buffalo
- Mug

ACCESSORIES

- Cricut Maker, Cricut Joy or Cricut Explore
- Fine point blade
- Cricut Mug Press

Procedure

1. Begin by clicking on "**New Project**."
2. Click the "**Images**" button and in the sidebar on the left, select the "**Type**" group. Then set the flag to "**Small Projects for Mug Press**." In the search box, enter the word "**design**."
3. Select "Small Circle Frame Mug Project" or enter the code #**M1469AD2D**.
4. Return to the design area by clicking on the "**Canvas**" button.
5. In the layers panel, select the design you just entered and click the "**Outline**" button found at the bottom of the layers panel. Click the "**Hide All Templates**" button so that only the template remains.
6. Next to the operations menu, use the color picker to set the template's white background.
7. Delete the second layer in the layers panel (the one with the circles).
8. Go back to the image archive and in the side toolbar, click on the "**Layers**" group and select the single item. In the search box, enter "**Merry Christmas Mug Press Wrap**" or the code #**M4B806F69**.
9. Place the newly imported image in the center of the design on your canvas. It's advisable to resize it slightly to ensure the cut-out does not come too close to the mug handle.

10. Click the "**Create**" button to access the mat preview, then click the "**Continue**" button.
11. Place your chosen sheet of infusible ink on the green mat and select "**Infusible Ink**" as the material type.
12. Once the cutting is complete, unload the mat by clicking the button with the two arrows.
13. Peel the sheet of infusible ink using the tool provided.
14. Wrap the mug with the peeled sheet, securing it tightly with a small amount of heat-resistant tape. Cover it with a sheet of butcher paper, securing that as well with heat-resistant tape.
15. Ensure the graphic is placed so that it doesn't come too close to the handle, to avoid blurring at the edges during heat transfer.
16. Place the mug in the mug press once the green light is on, and wait about 7 minutes before removing the mug.
17. When the press beeps, remove the mug and place it on a heat transfer mat or a heat-resistant surface (e.g., marble). Using special gloves, remove the sheet of infusible ink and voila—your Christmas mug is ready to use!
18. Remember, infusible inks are sublimation inks and are perfectly safe for food use.

Present your mug with a beautiful Christmas bow or in a specially made box for a festive touch.

MONEY-HOLDING GINGERBREAD

REALIZATION TIME

🕐 **20 Minutes**

DIFFICULTY ● ● ●

Procedure

1. Navigate to the layers panel and within the group named "**GINGERBREAD,**" double-click the text layer where the words "**Stefy**" are displayed. Replace "**Stefy**" with the name of the gift recipient.
2. Click the "**Create**" button to access the mat preview. Ensure all mats are correctly arranged, then click the "**Continue**" button.
3. Place the color of cardstock specified by Cricut Design Space on the green mat and initiate the cutting process.
4. Once cutting is complete, unload the mat by clicking the button featuring two arrows.
5. Adhere the red-colored base layer to the brown-colored layer of the gingerbread man using a glue stick, ensuring not to glue the two flaps on the arms.
6. Continue by affixing the white decorative strips, eyes, mouth, and bow tie.
7. Finish up with the Santa hat and, if desired, embellish with a rhinestone.
8. In the video example, I also added some holographic star-shaped elements to Santa's hat.
9. Lastly, thread a string through the small hole at the top, allowing you to hang it on a Christmas tree.

MATERIALS

- 270-gram cards of various colors

ACCESSORIES

- Cricut Maker, Cricut Joy or Cricut Explore
- Fine point blade

10. Now your Gingerbread Man is ready — you can insert a bill within the arm flaps.

The resulting gingerbread figure is, in my opinion, incredibly charming. It's a classic gift idea presented in a particularly unique manner, likely to be cherished by both young and old recipients.

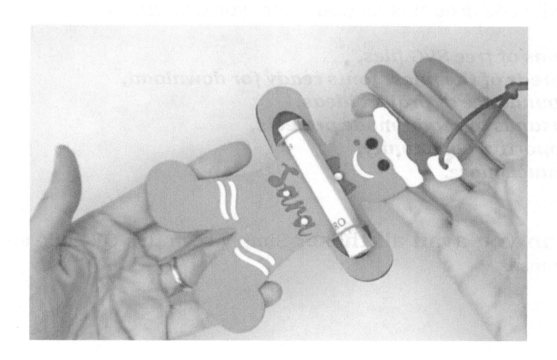

Take Your Gift

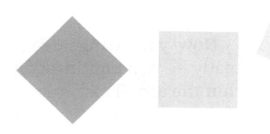

Dear reader

It's time to express my gratitude. Thank you for selecting my book amidst the hundreds of books and guides on this topic. The least I can do now is to reciprocate your trust with a plethora of bonuses crafted just for you.

That's why I devised this section where you can access:

- *Millions of free SVG files,*
- *Hundreds of the finest fonts ready for download,*
- *An abundance of project ideas,*
- *Thousands of ready-made projects,*
- *A supportive community,*
- *And much more.*

How can you avail all these? Simply scan this QR code and claim your bonuses

Take Your Gift

CONCLUSION

Dear reader

As we come to the final chapter of our comprehensive exploration, I trust that the pages preceding this have shed light on numerous facets of the Cricut universe, satisfying the curiosity that initially led you here. Together, we have traversed the intricacies of various Cricut machines, each with its unique set of capabilities, to assist you in identifying the one that resonates with your creative instincts. Our journey extended into the realm of accessories, tools meticulously designed to refine your craftsmanship, propelling it towards a professional standard. Moreover, we delved into the vast spectrum of materials that this remarkable machine can adeptly handle, each material being a fresh canvas awaiting your creative touch.

The subsequent part of our journey illuminated the potential avenues to morph our creative passions into viable streams of revenue. In this digital epoch, platforms like social media and online marketplaces like Etsy serve as bustling venues where creativity meets commerce. The insights shared on devising a sales strategy and conceptualizing a business plan aimed to provide a solid foundation for those aspiring to transform their Cricut crafting journey into a profitable venture.

The beauty of the Cricut domain is its boundlessness, where the only limitations are the ones imposed by our own imagination and creativity. With the information and guidelines provided in this guide, you now possess a resourceful companion to aid you as you embark on your own crafting endeavors. The projects elucidated within these pages serve as your initial stepping stones, from where you are encouraged to leap forward into the ocean of creativity that lies ahead. Fear not the unknown, for every master was once a beginner. It's the crucible of hands-on experience and exploration that will hone your skills, gradually morphing your initial attempts into masterful creations.

CONCLUSION

Visualize the joy and appreciation on the faces of your friends and family when you present them with personalized items, each crafted with love and a touch of creativity. The satisfaction derived from such personal exchanges of crafted items is immeasurable and serves as a fuel to continue exploring, learning, and creating.Now with the basics at your fingertips, the path ahead is one of exploration and continuous learning. Use this guide as a reference, a companion in those moments of doubt, and a source of inspiration when in search of new ideas. The projects delineated here are but a fraction of what's possible. The horizon is vast, and the possibilities, endless. The Cricut machine, with its precision and versatility, is your companion in this artistic journey, ready to translate your imaginative thoughts into tangible creations.

The concluding note of this guide is not an end, but rather a new beginning, a nudge encouraging you to explore the uncharted, to create, and to share. The world of Cricut is a community of like-minded individuals, where ideas flow freely, and creativity is the common language. I appreciate your companionship through the pages of this guide and look forward to hearing about the remarkable projects that you will undoubtedly create in the near future. As you now step into the wider world of Cricut crafting, may each project bring you joy, satisfaction, and a sense of accomplishment.

Warm wishes on your crafting journey ahead.

Made in the USA
Monee, IL
18 December 2024

74215233R00162